T0358544

Routledge Revivals

Organizations in the Network Age

The follow-up to the acclaimed *Organizations in the Computer Age* this book, originally published in 1996, reveals that since computers had become increasingly linked in networks which span the world, information could be transmitted instantaneously to all parts of the organization. It describes the experiences of six organizations and draws lessons which apply very widely.

The issues raised include the impact on employment levels and organizational structure; the effects of network technology and organization structure and control; the extent of management choice and the role of change agents.

This book shows that the introduction of computer networks raises new challenges concerning how the process of change is managed. The lessons from these cases could be widely applied in other organizations undertaking similar large-scale investments in new technology at the time.

Organizations in the
Network Age

David Boddy and Nicky Gunson

First published in 1996
by Routledge

This edition first published in 2022 by Routledge
2 Park Square, Milton Park, Abingdon, Oxon, OX14 4RN

and by Routledge
605 Third Avenue, New York, NY 10017

Routledge is an imprint of the Taylor & Francis Group, an informa business

Publisher's Note
The publisher has gone to great lengths to ensure the quality of this reprint but points out that some imperfections in the original copies may be apparent.

Disclaimer
The publisher has made every effort to trace copyright holders and welcomes correspondence from those they have been unable to contact.

ISBN: 978-1-032-19730-2 (hbk)
ISBN: 978-1-003-26061-5 (ebk)
ISBN: 978-1-032-19737-1 (pbk)

Book DOI 10.4324/9781003260615

ORGANIZATIONS IN THE NETWORK AGE

David Boddy and Nicky Gunson

London and New York

First published 1996
by Routledge
11 New Fetter Lane, London EC4P 4EE

Simultaneously published in the USA and Canada
by Routledge
29 West 35th Street, New York, NY 10001

Typeset in Garamond by Intype, London.
Printed and bound in Great Britain by
TJ Press (Padstow) Ltd, Padstow, Cornwall

British Library Cataloguing in Publication Data
A catalogue record for this book is available from the British Library

Library of Congress Cataloguing in Publication Data
A catalogue record for this book has been requested

ISBN 0–415–05325–0 (hbk)
ISBN 0–415–13223–1 (pbk)

CONTENTS

CONTENTS

PREFACE

The power of computing systems is now linked with that of the telecommunications system, enabling information to move with unprecedented speed and accuracy. Many predictions have been made about the effects of the networked computer systems which can now be created – but detailed accounts of the experience in practice are hard to find.

This book is an attempt to provide such an account. It outlines how managers in six major organizations implemented computer networks to help them run the business. We show what their original intentions were, how these changed in the light of experience and of new circumstances, and what the results of the investments of time and money have been. Particular attention is paid to the lessons which other managers may find useful in handling similar projects – which will become more frequent, and more challenging.

ACKNOWLEDGEMENTS

Many people have contributed to the long-term research on which this book is based, and we are grateful to all of them for their help and support. We particularly thank Nancy Anderson, Eric Brassington, Bob Heasman, Robert Watson and Matt Ogston, who kindly agreed to join the project steering group. This provided a valuable forum in which ideas emerging from the case studies could be explored by the participants, and helped to keep the research programme on a realistic track.

We are also grateful to the Leverhulme Trust for their financial support for the project, without which, of course, it would not have happened, and to Nan Gray who provided secretarial support to her usual high standard.

David Boddy and Nicky Gunson

1

INTRODUCTION

This book is about the opportunities that computer networks create for organizations, and the implications for their customers, the people who work for them and for the wider public. The chief technological focus of the book is the convergence of computer and telecommunications technology which has made it possible to link together widely separated computers and to pass information between them with great reliability, accuracy and speed. This convergence allows details of yesterday's sales at hundreds of retail outlets to be analysed and ready for review at head office the following morning, together with almost instantaneous replacement from suppliers of the items sold. Engineering data can be exchanged instantaneously between design offices in different continents. Examples of the influence of this technology on everyday life range from drawing cash from automatic telling machines, to purchasing travel tickets of all kinds. This book explores in detail the experience of six organizations which have introduced network technology. It aims to identify the managerial issues that need to be resolved if the technological possibilities are to be translated into business success.

As with earlier stand-alone computer systems, it is clear that human and organizational issues need to be addressed if the business potential of convergent technology is to be realized. Many of the lessons learned from earlier systems still apply, and many users of network systems are rediscovering the consequences of depending too heavily on technology alone to solve their problems or obtain strategic advantage over their competitors. In addition, even more significant changes in organizational structure and practice are needed to support the new technology to ensure it makes its full contribution to business performance. It introduces the probability of major changes in the way organizations operate and are constructed; the organizational issues are in consequence far more complex and difficult to manage than those created by earlier systems.

1

The pace of technological change is such that it becomes more difficult to learn from either success or failure. We hope this book will help those who are responsible for such changes to learn from the experience of those systems that have already been implemented. In this first chapter we outline the technology, its applications in a business context and the main themes which the book will explore.

THE TECHNOLOGY

In the 1950s it was widely predicted that the advent of the computer would significantly change the structure and processes of many organizations. In general, few really significant changes were observable as the first phase was largely concerned with the computerization of administrative paperwork. On the whole this enabled the companies to operate their existing processes more efficiently but led to few fundamental organizational changes. More recent applications of network technology have focused on the provision of management information and are coinciding with rapid organizational change, partly fuelled by dramatic developments in hardware and software, and partly stimulated by external changes. Four major trends have contributed to these organizational changes. First, the falling cost of computer hardware and the advent of the personal computer (PC) have meant that most working people will have a computer on their desks before very long. Second, the availability of software which allows users to access and use computers without the intervention of the computer expert. Third, the increasing availability of data for managers from both internal and external databases which provides information essential to maintain competitive market position. Last, and most important, the explosive development in communications technology and the increasing convergence of telecommunications and computing which has led to the creation of Local Area Networks (LANs) and Wide Area Networks (WANs).

LANs work over a restricted area, usually of less than a hundred metres, and connect a number of intelligent devices to a communications network. LANs are a major evolutionary step in the introduction of new technology in both the office and the industrial environment. The logic behind their introduction is that in any work environment 80 per cent of the work interactions are within the immediate locality and only 20 per cent outwith. Interconnected services on a LAN allow cost savings by sharing devices like file servers which can store large volumes of information, high quality print servers and so on. The more complex the system, the more simple it seems to the user due to increasingly sophisticated human-computer interfaces. The LAN is of most value when a number of different functions are carried out with the aid of a common database and/or where a number of different devices need to interface and share resources. WANs range from many metres to a worldwide coverage and can link thousands of distant users with speech and/or data transmission techniques. WANs provide international electronic mail (e-mail), transfer of text, movement of files etc.

Since the early days of computing it has been recognized that it is difficult to realize the full potential of the technology, or the expectations of the organization (Cooper and Swanson 1979; Maish 1979; Boddy and Buchanan 1983; Gibson, 1981; Eason, 1982; Markus 1983; Necco *et al.*, 1987). Social, political and organizational problems can hamper the implementation of quite simple systems and, once implemented, these systems have sometimes resulted in inflexibility and an inability to respond to environmental changes. The implementation of network technology brings similar problems, but with the added dimensions of larger scale systems, more complex technology and consequently larger technical and political issues. Cost justification of network systems is more difficult than for stand-alone systems (Johnston and Vitale, 1988), as often the simpler systems can be justified in quantifiable operational terms. Since network systems are organization-wide, different functions may have different perceptions of costs and benefits, and during the often lengthy implementation process these perspectives on costs and benefits can radically change.

Computer networks offer organizations substantial opportunities for operational and strategic innovation and are regarded as crucial business tools by many large organizations, as 'fundamental as water, electricity and heat' (Hall and Macauley, 1987). Networks can play an important part in fundamental structural changes, the gradual elimination of layers of middle management, of individual functions and internal integration of departments. They also support external integration with suppliers and customers and external links with complementary organizations (Johnston and Vitale, 1988). These opportunities stimulate the use of network technology despite the difficulties of design and implementation and the financial risks involved.

We began this study with a preliminary survey of nineteen UK organizations from a wide range of economic sectors. In each organization we interviewed key IT managers and from these extended semi-structured interviews we were able to identify a range of key questions which were relevant to organizations introducing networks. These questions formed the focus for the six detailed case studies which were conducted over a period of six years. The questions are outlined below.

WHAT BENEFITS WOULD THE ORGANIZATIONS EXPECT?

The preliminary study showed that the objectives of introducing networks were often strategic and qualitative rather than quantitative and, as such, were difficult to express in financial terms. However few of the nineteen organizations in the preliminary survey had overtly used strategic objectives to justify the system, because operational, quantifiable benefits like cutting staff numbers, reducing stock holdings, reducing paperwork and increasing the efficiency of the accounting function were so much easier to present to financial decision-makers. Often when confronted with the impossibility of justifying the investment in terms of DCF capital appraisal techniques or other versions of investment analysis, the top level sponsor resorted to making 'a bold leap of strategic faith' (Kaplan, 1986) with a 'commitment to make the future happen' (Hayes and Garvin, 1985) whilst presenting the decision-making body with operational justifications.

The costs of network systems were equally difficult to establish. The costs of training and maintenance were particularly problematic because of the scale of the projects and the involvement of many different functions and different technologies that were often 'leading-edge' and unpredictable in themselves. The cost of management time used to coordinate the project was open-ended and often much more substantial then predicted. Working practices often changed throughout the organization, in some organizations leading to some initial user resistance, and to large training and retraining commitments.

Perspectives on costs and benefits varied within the organization; the accounts department often felt that the cost of a centralized computerized accounting system was fully justified, whereas the sales function had a different perspective. Perspectives on the objectives and cost justification of the network evolved during the time it took to implement the system, which was years in some cases. The long-term empirical research on the detailed case studies allowed us to explore this aspect more closely.

WHAT WOULD NETWORKS IMPLY FOR MANAGING THE PROCESS OF CHANGE?

A substantial literature developed on the problems and the advantages of involving users in the development and implementation of earlier stand-alone computer systems (e.g. Mumford *et al.*, 1978; Eason, 1977). Attempts to involve users in the development of quite simple systems have met with limited success. Network systems seemed likely to raise new difficulties with managing user-involvement. Centralized control of the design process is essential to maintain compatibility throughout the network, and to establish external links with customers, suppliers and complementary organizations. Yet at the same time the ultimate success or failure of the network system depends heavily on obtaining commitment and support from operational users. The system designers had to demonstrate an ability to design and develop systems that would fit local circumstances which differed in important details across the network.

It has been widely recognized that the outcome of system implementation depends heavily on the presence and status of a senior management sponsor (Curley and Gremilion, 1983; Schon, 1963; Maidique, 1980). This becomes peculiarly important for the outcome of network systems as necessarily they cross departmental boundaries, disrupt existing power distributions and necessitate an overall strategic perspective rather than a sectional or operational view. The more senior the 'sponsor' the less likely that the network project will be subject to middle management resistance and implementation problems as the 'sponsor' acts as a 'change agent' or 'missionary'. This highlighted the paradox of central control of design and development against gaining local commitment to the new system and prompted us to explore in the detailed case studies how far it was possible to give local managers autonomy and scope for varying the design of network systems in response to local conditions.

HOW MIGHT NETWORKS LEAD TO CHANGES IN STRUCTURE, CONTROL AND WORK ORGANIZATION?

Earlier studies of stand-alone computer technologies and the design of work indicated significant management choice in the way work was designed as computer systems were introduced. Often such systems led to work redesign which increased autonomy and skill, although in many cases there were examples of significant skills being lost. Does the introduction of network systems follow earlier patterns or does the process have different effects on the human aspects of organizations? What is the evidence from the cases about the design of tasks and for the way groups of staff work together?

Despite predictions to the contrary (Leavitt and Whisler, 1958) the early implementations of computer systems led to few changes in managerial decision-making patterns or organizational hierarchies. The often predicted demise of middle management and centralization of decision-making either did not happen or happened extremely slowly, although the establishment of centralized IT departments was widespread. As the technology has become far cheaper, more powerful and more reliable, speculation has continued that such structural changes following implementation would occur (Child, 1984; Rockart and Short, 1989).

From the evidence gathered in the preliminary survey, the convergence of computing and telecommunications have made the telecommunications function more visible (Dickinson, 1984). This is reflected in structural changes in the way IT is managed, a common pattern being computing and telecommunications managers at the same level of seniority reporting to an 'Information Systems' manager reporting to Board level. Another significant factor influencing the process of introducing network systems is the status of the IT function within the organization. If representatives of the IT department take part in the strategic decision-making processes of the organization, and IT is seen less as a technical function and more as a source of strategic business opportunities, then the network project has a built-in advantage. There is evidence (Bernstein 1985; Rockart, 1982) that organizations which have incorporated representatives of their IT department into their strategic planning processes generally make more successful use of IT applications.

The preliminary survey also showed that network systems could be used to produce uniform procedures and structures in organizations which had grown through merger or takeovers and could be a crucial part of the assimilation and rationalization process. In addition, networks had facilitated internal rationalization in some cases, once the establishment of a central database had reduced the need for separate functions. But the evidence also showed examples where the introduction of networks had conformed with existing structural patterns rather than establishing new and possibly more rational ones. Despite the potential of the technology very few management structures had been radically changed, partly at least because it was managers who usually controlled the development and implementation of the systems and they were unlikely to undermine their own authority structures. The priority in introducing most systems was to take advantage of an opportunity or to overcome an operating problem, rather than to effect a structural change. Any structural change seemed to largely take place as a function of 'accidental incrementalism' (Robey, 1983) rather than by conscious and rational redesign. The case studies which follow provide some empirical insight into these issues. How do network systems change the tasks of managers and the balance between central and local decision-making? Are there any changes in the allocation of tasks between departments and in the relationships between different organizations?

There has been considerable speculation about the impact of computer systems on the locus of managerial decision-making. Argyris (1970), Child

6

(1984) and Robey (1981) cite examples of the centralization of important information and decision-making and the disempowerment of local decision-makers following the introduction of computer systems. This may masquerade under the guise of greater decentralization, but may actually consist of the delegation of the more routine, less significant decisions. As 'point of capture' information can now be transmitted directly to the central planning department, there is obviously less need for the intervention of middle management and supervisory levels. Although the evidence from the preliminary survey indicated that middle management had been less affected than expected, the evidence from our detailed long-term case studies allowed us to examine the long-term effects of networks on middle management in more detail. The long-term nature of our study, and the evolution of the systems being implemented, gave us the opportunity to assess whether the long-predicted decline of middle management and significant structural change was finally occurring. Were networks having a noticeable effect on the job content and job security of middle management? In summary, were organizations actually using networks to underpin fundamental restructuring of their business?

UNEXPECTED ISSUES

These were the main questions identified from the preliminary survey but, as the long-term empirical research progressed, other issues emerged. The lengthy process of implementation meant that some issues that were important during the early stages became less so as the networks became established and then, in many cases, further enhanced. For example, it allowed us to consider whether the concepts of emergent strategies (Mintzberg, 1984, 1994) as distinct from deliberate ones, characterized the way managements related the potential of computer networks to the needs of the business. To what extent did the organizations have a deliberate corporate strategy that they were using networks to achieve, or was it an emergent strategy, evolving from the flexibility provided by the technology?

An important strategic benefit illustrated by the long-term cases was the way in which the internal discipline imposed by network systems enabled organizations to behave flexibly in relation to external market opportunities (Boynton, 1993). Integrated computer networks are likely to increase the interdependence of one part of an organization on another, and thus lead to tighter prescription over the manner and timing of data collection and entry. Does this greater discipline and apparent bureaucratization of operating processes make the business less responsive or is it, paradoxically, a route to greater responsiveness to market opportunities?

The long-term empirical research provided by the six detailed case studies allowed us to take into account the way economic circumstances and competitive position of the organization change over time and how this affects managerial decision-making (McLoughlin and Clark, 1994). The six case organizations experienced multiple and parallel changes over the period of six years of research and this provided us with the opportunity to study how these contextual changes affected decision making and how the process of change was managed. For example, the move towards privatization in the cases of the ambulance service and ScotRail, and takeovers and mergers in the cases of the travel company, Kwik-Fit and the Library Cooperative had significant impact on the way the managers concerned managed the process.

One aspect of particular interest has been to compare our current findings with those of an earlier volume describing the impact of stand-alone computer systems on six case organizations (Buchanan and Boddy, 1983). One important issue identified by this earlier study was the extent to which managerial choices fashioned the outcomes of the computer systems. Our more recent research explores whether managerial choice is being restricted by the sense of inevitability and the technological imperatives of network systems. Another issue identified in 1983 was the impact stand-alone systems had had on job design, and whether the overall impact had been to deskill workers, or to complement their skills. How do networks affect the experience of work, and in particular the scope for autonomy and individual initiative? What effects do they have on the work of supervisors and middle managers?

The 1983 book also investigated the replacement effect of stand-alone systems, looking at how far jobs in the factory and the office had been displaced by computers. The conclusion then was that significant replacement was rare and that the predictions of severe effects on employment had probably been overstated. Is that conclusion still valid in view of the availability of sophisticated computer network systems, which might threaten not only the work of operating staff but also that of managers themselves? It would have been difficult to come to even tentative conclusions about these issues had we not been able to study the impact of networks on these organizations over a moderately long period of time, but even so we suspect that the full impact of network technology has yet to be fully experienced.

SUMMARY

1 The book explores the organizational implications of large scale network systems, and draws comparisons with earlier studies of stand-alone computer systems.

2 Such earlier studies showed that implementation problems were largely due to the lack of attention given to political issues and the processes of change – issues which are likely to be at least as prominent in more complex networked systems.

3 Computer networks offer organizations the opportunity for significant strategic innovation, but leave open the question of how managers relate those possibilities to business requirements.

4 To an even greater extent than with stand-alone systems, justifying the cost of network systems can be difficult, and objectives 'fuzzy', possibly placing more reliance on investment as an act of faith.

5 The size and complexity of networks also implies new problems of implementation – e.g. conventional participative prescriptions are likely to be confronted by the fact geographical distance makes it difficult to involve users in the processes of design, development and implementation.

6 Networks can enable dramatic structural changes within organizations – but do managers introducing such systems make use of the opportunity?

7 Similarly, how do networks affect patterns of managerial control and decision-making within organizations?

8 To the extent that networks affect competitive positions, is this the result of a deliberate or an emergent strategy?

9 Networks can provide organizations with the opportunity to impose greater discipline and control on their operations – does this restrict or, paradoxically, enhance their responsiveness and their ability to react dynamically to external market opportunities.

10 The long-term nature of the research allowed us to consider the impact of contextual changes on managerial decision-making – networks were not the only innovation taking place in the case study organizations.

11 There are significant 'step-change' differences between the findings of an earlier book which looked at the effect of stand-alone computer systems on organizations in the 1980s and those of the present study which considers the impact of networks on organizations in the 1990s.

2

THE TRAVEL COMPANY
A branch automation system in a travel company

SUMMARY AND LESSONS

The travel company was a family business founded in the mid-1950s which had grown quickly to be one of the top five travel companies in the UK. In the late 1980s the administrative congestion caused by this rapid growth had forced the company to implement a branch automation network system. The successes and problems experienced by the travel company provide useful lessons for managers involved in the implementation of large-scale computer networks.

The network system was introduced to alleviate the administrative paperwork problems threatening to suffocate the company and to free branch staff to sell more holidays.

This objective was slowly achieved over a period of years. The system was based on the transmission of daily branch transaction information to head office and improved both central control of branch working practices and procedures, and also the quality of management information.

Some of the lessons learnt during this process were:

- That it was necessary for senior management to change, recognizing they were now part of a professional nationwide company rather than a provincial family-owned firm.
- That because of the experience gained with introducing this system, the company will ensure that participation in the design and implementation process will be wider and users will guide the project far more next time the company engages in change on this scale.
- Training policy will be thought out much further in advance, and more attention given to making sure that the users feel ownership of the system. It was felt particularly important to make sure that the branch managers had been involved both in the design and implementation stages and the training of their staff.

- That senior staff should also be involved in the design and implementation of the system both in the regions and the divisions and also in the functional areas at head office. Increased awareness of the potential of the system should be achieved by arranging regular technology awareness events for senior staff.
- That more time should be set aside to iron out the bugs in the system before it goes live in any branch and the pilot or initial experiment should take place in a smaller number of branches throughout the network. They should as far as possible be typical branches rather than those having particular problems due to geographical location or using their own idiosyncratic system etc.
- That technical staff should have more experience of actually working at the business at branch level before they start to design the system.
- That it is important to improve communications at all levels so that the whole company knows company strategy and the progress of the project.
- That it is essential to appoint a project manager and project team right at the start.
- That it was useful to establish a Users Forum early in the project to provide peer group support to branch managers and a feeling of ownership of the system.
- That suppliers should be carefully checked to make sure they are able to live up to promises made at the time of sale.

INTRODUCTION

This case study looks at the process of designing, developing and implementing an automated accounting and receipting system in a travel company, based on a nationwide network of PC's linked to head office mainframes. The case was particularly interesting as it illustrated the problems of introducing relatively high-level technology into a comparatively low-technology industry employing people largely unfamiliar with computer systems. It also illustrated the dramatic impact human factors can have on the planned progress of a network implementation.

BACKGROUND

This travel company was a family firm founded by the present managing director's father and current chairman. The founder had been a banker until the mid-1950s when he decided to change career. The first travel agency opened in 1956 and it became a limited company in 1958. At first the growth of the company was gradual, reaching 30 branches in the late 1970s. In the 1980s the growth of the company had accelerated, largely through acquisition of a series of smaller companies, and by the end of the decade there were nearly 300 branches, mainly in urban centres. It had become one of the biggest travel companies in the UK with growth expected to continue. One result of this rapid growth had been considerable administrative 'indigestion'.

In the late 1980s the travel company was acquired by a large bank through a phased takeover. The family became minority shareholders, holding 42 per cent of the shares. The remaining family stockholding was to pass gradually to the bank over a period of 5 years after which the company would become a wholly owned subsidiary of the bank. The bank was represented by 6 out of 11 members on the Executive Board.

The company was divided into five Divisions, three in England and two in Scotland. England North Division had five Regions, England South Division had three Regions, England Central Division had three Regions, Scotland East Division had four Regions and Scotland West Division had three Regions. There were also thirteen 'implant' offices located within large companies for their own staff's travel arrangements, with restricted public access. Of the total of nearly 300 branches, about a quarter concentrated on business travel rather than package holidays. The biggest concentrations of branches were in the larger cities in northern England and Scotland.

The company in the mid-1980s

The main business of the travel company was to sell holidays and business travel. This was achieved through a nationwide network of small branches located in city and town centre locations, approximately 170 branches in England and 130 in Scotland These branches sold an infinite variety of holiday packages by linking customers who earn into the branches with holiday packages offered by tour operators like Thomsons and Horizon, and with transport provided by airlines, coach operators and railways. The business branches made all necessary travel and accommodation arrangements for business people and provided them with itineraries. This was achieved through viewdata reservation systems provided by the tour operators and through the airline booking system called TRAVICOM. The telephone was also used for reservations and bookings. The chief characteristic of the business was variety and unpredictability. No two holidays or business itineraries were exactly the same.

Although the booking and reservation systems in the travel company branches were based on the tour operators and airlines computer networks, the invoicing and receipting systems of the travel company itself were still manual. The volume of paperwork involved in each transaction was growing rapidly and it was acknowledged within the company that it was essential to find some way to reduce the amount of paperwork and provide current, accurate management information. Branch processes involved a high degree of manual processing, and heavy reliance on the written record, which had led to many errors. Commissions on sales could not be applied centrally, and commission recognition at branch level was error-prone. The lack of diary prompts in the manual system meant that not only were some dates missed leading to cancellations and customer dissatisfaction, but also the late collection of balances was having a financial impact on the company.

Banking arrangements were complicated: e.g. there were separate banking arrangements for the two main credit card companies, and the high level of cash circulating round the system was becoming a matter of concern. It was possible that if a sum was misappropriated rather than banked the loss would remain undetected for 2 weeks. There was a lack of effective control on foreign exchange dealings. At the peak of the season, stocks of foreign currency at branches could be more than £500,000. The only stock records were compiled manually from monthly returns from branches. Sales returns were also compiled on a monthly basis, and were far too late and inaccurate to be of any use for central control of the foreign exchange exposure.

Travellers cheque sales were increasing, and seen by the company as helpful to achieving turnover targets. Thomas Cook had recently installed a PC-based travellers cheque terminal in six of the travel company's locations which could produce all the necessary sales documentation and control stock, but in the other branches the manual system of maintaining stock records and sales advice to head office, plus the accounting function were all paper-intensive.

Other areas of concern were the appearance and image of the branches, the availability of local advertising, promotions and community involvement, product development in line with customer needs, the possibility of sending mail shots from head office to branches, and locally oriented holiday sales. The company felt it would have to develop ways of motivating branch managers to achieve these requirements.

Looking at the proportion of time spent on customer contact as opposed to back office paperwork in branches in the mid-1980s it was estimated that 65 per cent of available branch time was spent on customer service (with a range of 60 per cent minimum and 70 per cent maximum). The branch managers were also asked what they felt were the main factors that reduced the time available for customer contact and they cited: the maintenance of stockbooks, continual form filling (commission claim forms, accounts documents, rail returns, head office paperwork) banking arrangements, and the ordering and controlling of stationery. Head office reporting in itself was an irritant for the branch. They had to submit daily input sheets, weekly reports containing detailed booking by principal and sales turnover by major principal, monthly foreign exchange stock returns and four-weekly rail returns. There were obvious problems involved with the compilation of accurate information for transmitting to head office. There were also sources of stress for the branches in the number of telephone calls from head office, especially from the accounts department trying to sort out queries due to inaccurate information.

From the head office point of view, the lack of information made the monitoring and forecasting of profits difficult, because sales information from branches was infrequent, historical and probably inaccurate. Profit forecasting was difficult because of the lack of a database. The rapid growth of the company over recent years meant that there was a lack of historical or comparative data, and in fact there was no track record for almost half the branches. As a result turnover calculations were controversial.

Paying principals was also a problem at head office. This was partly due to the fact that there was a processing bottleneck at the end of each month. Travellers cheque settlements were also a problem at the height of the season. Value of sales exceeded £20,000,000 in 1985 causing a very high data entry requirement. Package holidays and credit tours were the highest volume data entry requirement, over one million documents a year were being processed in this category. The lack of supporting base documentation meant that only a 'reasonable' check could be carried out at head office, no client file was held so the calculation of commission was difficult. An additional problem was the recognition of commission and VAT where the branches paid by cheque individually. Monitoring VAT on commissions had become increasingly difficult as business increased and it would have been preferable to account for VAT on each transaction.

Data security was becoming a source of anxiety. Centralized processing of information from paper input resulted in a massive volume of records kept. All records had by statute to be kept for 3 years and from 1984 VAT records had to be kept for 6 years. This caused tremendous accommodation problems, and it was difficult anyway to access information from the mass of records. In addition, centralized storage at a single point was vulnerable to loss by fire, flood etc. Management information was then only available on hard copy and there was always the risk of it falling into the hands of the competition.

The main auditing function was in the form of spot checks, annual audits and investigations due to branch default were done by the accounting function together with corrective training. This led to situations where problems were not identified early enough, so that the auditor was often confronted by a 'cold trail' and considerable time was spent manually marrying credits and debits.

Management information requirements were not being fulfilled because existing systems were developed for conventional equipment in a reactive environment. Modern methods like databases and enquiry were not being used. Further acquisitions of other companies exacerbated the problems. Since 1984, the development effort had been necessarily concentrated on coping with the growth of paperwork due to acquisitions and not on developing new systems. Much of the management information needed was already present in the system but not fully used because it was so difficult to access.

All these administrative problems were leading to increasing concern about cash collection and credit control. Tour balance collection patterns varied between branches from between 5 days early to 6.5 days late due partly to lack of standardization of diary prompt systems. Credit control was hampered by lack of up to date accounting status information. Outstanding debt stood at £7,000,000 representing 50 days' sales. If the days were reduced to 45 by a new system, that would have represented a cash injection of £1,300,000 plus a decrease in the interest paid. There could also be a minimum delay of 6 days in presenting transactions to the ledger account, which added to credit control difficulties.

The fifty business houses within the system offered all the normal travel agent services with the addition of credit facilities, ticket issues and delivery, personal contacts and client knowledge, preferential rates, personal holiday discounts, business analysis for clients and corporate hotel rates. These business houses had particular problems over and above those of the retail branches. These include the manual maintenance of stock records, the large numbers of registers kept, credit control, the lack of management information for sales support, the lack of client profiles, and the production of hand or typewritten invoices.

It was obvious that what was needed was a form of branch automation that enabled the head office computer to poll the branch computer overnight and take the daily transaction file away to the central computer system. This would enable the travel company to deal with the problems of accuracy and currency of information from the system, the amount of paperwork generated and the lack of adequate management information.

Staff attitudes to change

In advance of the implementation of the computer network accounting system, virtually all the staff at every level within the company were enthusiastic about the introduction of branch automation. They felt it was essential to solve the existing administrative problems, but also because they accepted it was inevitable and that the company could not remain competitive without computerizing their basic procedures:

> We had an open evening in the first region we are going to rollout to. All the people were invited for a little demonstration, and they went away from that saying 'Come on, give us it, give us it'. They couldn't wait to get their hands on it.

There were a few branches that felt that their own way of doing things was perfectly adequate and were reluctant to change to a new relatively untried system. Four of these branches were using another computerized system which they particularly liked and were reluctant to change. In reality it was a 'user-unfriendly' system and cost a great deal to maintain. Some other branches were parts of recently taken over chains, particularly those at a distance from head office, and were less than enthusiastic about having their existing business methods disrupted by a distant and unfamiliar head office. Some older managers, who had been running branches in their own way for a considerable time were apprehensive and in some cases hostile to the new system:

> It's a case of 'my system's working so leave it alone', they just don't want change.

Branch attitudes to the new accounting system were strongly influenced by their experience of existing computer systems. The existing systems were viewed favourably on the whole and this predisposed them favourably towards the new system:

> I personally didn't like these new systems when they first came out, but now I use them just about all the time. I'd been in the business quite a while when I started using them so I think I was a bit against change, whereas the younger staff would use them straight away… but now I haven't got any problems with the technology at all.

The attitudes of regional and divisional management also varied as did their level of knowledge about the development of the new system. Many had little knowledge of its objectives and specification and felt they would have benefited from involvement in the development and training on the system before it arrived:

> I have had a quick run through with it ... but not much more than that ... I know what it is intended to do and I know what the eventual intention is ... but the day to day operation ... I have no idea.

Some regional managers had made sure that they were involved in the process of introducing automation into their branches and had strong opinions as to how to ensure the success of the system As one Regional Manager in the west of Scotland said:

> The key to it all is the thorough and absolute training of the managers ... absolute training to get their attitudes right, so they are won over and that it is something they should want to impart to their staff.
>
> I think attitude is the biggest thing. If you can, get the managers and staff to head office for a day or two to show the equipment, to see what is going to happen on the head office side. There is still a feeling that the system is being brought in to make things easier at the head office end.

Some managers indicated that there were communications difficulties between the regional and divisional managers and head office which influenced their attitudes. They felt that head office had little conception of work in the regions and branches. A Regional Manager in the north east of Scotland said of head office:

> They quite clearly have no concept at all of what that in reality means to the clerk at the counter.

Divisional and Regional Managers did not always know the policy or the reasons behind head office policy and this made it difficult for them to enforce central policy with conviction:

> It is easier to enforce policy if you have the policy from the person who made it. Otherwise I could get the wrong end of the stick and give the branches the wrong instructions

Much of the sometimes uneasy relationship between the branch, region and head office was attributed to the level of accounting errors in the manual system and the way these were dealt with at head office level:

The manager's got one of those snooty letters and twenty-five of the twenty-eight items on it were correct on dispatch from the branch and were posting errors at head office.

This uneasy relationship was an influence on attitudes to the new system, some managers viewing it as being imposed from the centre for head office's administrative convenience. But many regional managers hoped that the new system would eliminate this source of aggravation.

The senior management at head office were either very enthusiastic about the potential improvements to the efficiency of the company offered by the network system, or else accepted it as inevitable. Some saw it as a technological initiative from the systems development department and had no conception of how the system might affect their particular area of business. Once the system had been piloted, many of the senior head office managers suddenly became aware of the potential of the system and wished that they had more input into the design at an earlier stage. .

Very few of the large numbers of clerical staff employed at head office to check branch returns for errors manually seemed to realize the implication of the new system for their job security. Many seemed to assume that they would still be employed checking the returns from the automated system:

> We had a sort of frightening incident at the beginning where I discovered one day that the precheckers were quite excited about these computer documents because it was so much easier to pre-check the machine printed figures than the handwriting! So it suddenly dawned on me that perhaps they hadn't quite appreciated that once all this information was on the computer you don't have to send it all through!

Senior managers had not discussed the implications of the implementation of the network with them and were hoping that redundancies could be achieved through natural wastage or absorbing them into new jobs as the company continued to expand.

There was a feeling expressed as an observation rather than a criticism that many of the previous computer systems developed by the IS department had been too technically oriented and not enough related to the business needs of the company:

> Too many of our systems have been developed by systems development people telling people what they think they want. That's commendable for energy and such like, but it leaves you open now and again to attack ... because you roll out the system and all of a sudden it is not what we wanted.

The systems development people retaliated that operational users *ought* to have had more input into the systems but they preferred to leave it to Systems Development and then to grumble afterwards.

Existing Technology

The main technology used by branch staff up to the mid-1980s was view-data reservation systems provided by the tour operators and also the airline booking system, BA's TRAVICOM. Most of the technology in the branches was driven by the 'principals' (the tour operators and the airlines) based on their own computer network systems and had only been available since the early 1980s. Before that, most reservations were made via the telephone. The internal invoicing and receipting systems in the branches were manual. The volume of paperwork generated by each holiday or business travel transaction was growing at such a rate that it had become essential for the company to develop a solution or sink under the weight of paper. As long ago as the early 1980s it had been recognized that branch accounting would have to be fundamentally reorganized and computerized. In the early 1980s a new manual branch accounting system was designed operating on a secure basis using sequentially numbered documents and daily input into the centre, rather than the previous weekly system. The basis of the new manual system was that paper was manually produced at the branches and sent to data capture points at head office where it was entered onto the central IBM mainframe computer system.

In 1983 as the result of a merger the company acquired a relatively new Honeywell DPS7 mainframe computer and new systems were written to support the company's systems. Towards the end of 1984, as a result of another merger, the company acquired a Data General MV4000. This was programmed to become the data capture device for the Honeywell and was on-line to the IBM mainframe computer systems at head office.

Some of the taken-over companies had their own automated accounting systems. One small company taken over in mid-1988 had a sophisticated centralized computer system:

> They had a true database accounting system at the centre ... statistics could be produced from the centre and separate accounts of turnover, tourheads ... they covered the technology gap with very impressive central systems and central control.

There were also a few branches which already had an accounting system called DPAS and were reluctant to change to a new, relatively untried, system. DPAS was particularly liked by those using it, although in reality it was a 'user-unfriendly' system and was costing the company over £18,000 a year to maintain.

Systems development staff

The travel company had a small systems development team at the beginning of the branch automation project. There were three programmers, three programmer/analysts and two staff concentrating on the training of branch staff and the implementation of the system in the branches. These staff had worked for the company in various capacities for a long time. They had considerable experience of head office business systems, but little branch level experience. They had practical experience of working with mainframe computers, and the younger staff had formal computing qualifications and experience of working with PCs. There was also a Data Processing Manager in charge of the day-to-day running of existing systems, who had wide experience of working with mainframe systems. No one had full time responsibility for the telecommunications aspect of branch automation; the company hired a telecommunications consultant to work for 2 days a week for the duration of the project.

As the project progressed this basic team was expanded gradually, partly by employing young computer professionals, five of whom were recruited straight from university with an IT-based qualification and PC experience. Others were recruited on short-term contracts. These were experienced IT people who had taken early retirement from such companies as IBM, and largely had mainframe rather than PC experience. As time went on the number of people employed to train branch staff and implement the system was increased to ten. No project manager was appointed at the start of the project to take overall charge, manly because it took some time to finally get Board approval, and this left most of the responsibility on the systems development manager and the DP manager who still had responsibility for the day-to-day running of the other IT systems.

Summary

1 The travel company was a nationwide company consisting of about 300 branches selling holidays and business travel.
2 The system implemented during the case study was an automated branch accounting system based on IBM PCs.
3 This system replaced an increasingly overloaded manual system.
4 In general staff at all levels felt that automation was inevitable and had had favourable experience of previous computer systems.

5 The technology already being used in the branches included viewdata reservation systems and an airline booking system.

6 There was a small systems development team many of whom had primarily mainframe experience.

THE BRANCH AUTOMATION NETWORK SYSTEM

The study group felt that it would be to the company's advantage to avoid lengthy in-house systems development with the limited technical and staff resources at the company's disposal. They therefore recommended that the company looked for suitable 'travel agent' packages that were available 'off the shelf'. The systems development manager and a small team then spent 6 months evaluating various packages and came to the conclusion that a package to be called here 'Holidata' (not its actual name) most nearly fulfilled the requirements laid down in the original analysis.

'Holidata' was a software package specifically designed for the requirements of the travel industry by a small independent company and to be run on IBM PCs. Holidata could be linked with TRAVICOM, the airline reservation system, as from 1985 it was opened up to non-TRAVICOM developed equipment for the first time, particularly the IBM PC. Two of the study group saw a demonstration of the package in a live environment, and subsequently it was demonstrated to the whole study group at head office.

Ostensibly Holidata was able to produce most of the requirements that had been laid down. It could link to TRAVICOM and viewdata and print tickets, itineraries and invoices. It had facilities to manage holiday bookings, ticket stocks and diary prompts. It could be extended to any number of branches and could also produce mail shots and letters. The features that Holidata could not offer were the ability to communicate directly between branch and head office, and the ability to interface with existing systems at head office. However it was hoped to solve these two problems by using the communications facility on the PC and acquiring a networked auto-dial facility, and also by acquiring an IBM38 and using it as a front-end device to the existing Honeywell equipment. This device would edit and validate the data, store it in a database and make it available and accessible to management.

The study group indicated that there were also a series of desirable enhancements to Holidata. For example, it would be desirable for the company to develop their own screen layouts and choose their own style of forms for invoices and itineraries. Also it was felt desirable to have a facility to produce a uniquely numbered receipt to be linked to a client file record, and to have local control of currency.

The study group then proceeded to draw up a design for the network system based on the Holidata system interfaced with TRAVICOM and viewdata. This involved the installation of an IBM PC and letter-quality printer in each branch.

Summary

1 The company set up a joint study Group with IBM which decided to recommend an 'off the shelf' software package designed specifically for travel companies.
2 The package chosen was able to link to the existing systems in the branches.
3 The telecommunications element had to be designed and implemented by the travel company using the telecommunications facilities of the PC.
4 The systems development also customized the paychecks in terms of screen layouts etc.

GOALS AND OBJECTIVES

There was a consensus within the travel company that the automation of branch paperwork processes was inevitable. The volume of paperwork and telephone checking was threatening to swamp the business:

My first impressions of coming here were seeing mountains of receipts and cash sheets.

The travel business was highly competitive and there was a general awareness that all their competitors were preparing to introduce automated systems and that they had to do the same to remain competitive:

The market was and is becoming more competitive, so one must continue looking at ways of achieving the result at a lesser cost. If you are going to remain competitive this is the direction you have to move because it is obvious that the multiples are moving in this direction as well, and if you don't you are going to lose, you are going to become totally uncompetitive.

Their main overhead cost was staff costs and it was clear that the main aim of any system would be to free these expensive staff from administration and to give them more time to sell holidays and raise staff productivity:

If the staff were becoming in relative terms more and more expensive, what we had to do was to come up with a system which could release these staff ... to sell more holidays ... rather than their time being taken up with administration, so it was very much an attempt to improve our productivity.

A secondary aim was to raise the level of business activity without increasing staff numbers.

Rapid growth through takeovers throughout the 1980s had left many of the branches running hybrid systems. Branch automation was a way of imposing discipline and standardization on the branches and imposing a unification on the company.

Communications within the company were inadequate because head office did not have confidence in the accuracy or currency of their management information. The inaccuracy of the existing manual system was leading to uneasy relationships between the branches and the central accounting function as it was commonplace for head office to make several telephone calls a day to one branch alone to sort out errors in the accounting returns. Frequently these errors could be months old and difficult to trace. Consequently the prospect of automating these processes and eliminating the manual system was generally welcomed throughout the company, both at branch level and at head office.

There was a general anticipation that the company would be able to offer a much more professional service to their customers:

It would certainly improve one's image if nothing else ... the customer's perception has to be better.

So there was a general acceptance that the rapid expansion of the company had not been matched by an equivalent modernization of administrative systems, and the general objective of improvement in this area was accepted throughout the company.

The priority given to lower level objectives varied according to the particular management level within the company – branches, regions and divisions having slightly different objectives to head office.

The branches wanted more staff time available to sell holidays and reductions in the crushing amount of time spent on form-filling after each holiday transaction. Some branch Managers also welcomed the prospect of a more formalized and standardized system. They also hoped for an improvement in communications both vertically and horizontally. But at the same time many Branch Managers were reluctant to lose their autonomy and freedom of manoeuvre afforded by the level of errors in the manual system. Branch managers were not enthusiastic about losing some of their independence in the cause of total company efficiency, but few of them initially saw the branch automation system in these terms. Most saw it simply as a way of cutting down paperwork and freeing staff to sell more holidays:

> I think it will be fantastic; it will really cut the paperwork down. If that was the case you could use the whole staff to sell holidays rather than have to take them off from time to time to catch up on paperwork.

Regional and Divisional management were responsible for the overall efficiency of the Region or Division. They were responsible for branch manager recruitment, training, marketing, sales analysis and setting up new branches. Many of them had little knowledge of the system or its potential before it arrived in their area and had few expectations from it.

Senior head office staff saw the logic of generally cutting paperwork and time spent on administration, as it was in the interests of the whole company that more holidays were sold. There were additional objectives that in some ways conflicted with those of the branch. Head office also felt it was essential to impose a uniform administrative system on the whole company allowing less leeway for the individual manager to develop their own way of running their Branch. Where many branches expected the computer system to adapt to their existing business methods, in fact head office were determined that branch systems should conform to a company-wide automated system. This would have two beneficial consequences from head office's point of view. First, taken-over firms would be fully assimilated and no longer running their own administrative systems. Second, the information received from the branch would be in a standard-ized form and the disciplines built into the computerized system would mean that the information was current, reliable, accurate and comparable. The level of errors would be rapidly reduced by establishing firm central control on accounting information from branches:

> we are finding that paper is never a standard system – there are always different ways you can handle paper. You can always choose to fill in a form or not to fill it in, choose to complete a box or not ... you will find the system employed in each branch is a hybrid of their old system and our system ... they all have their own variations of the system. I think there is an expectation that automation will finally provide the disciplined system that people must adhere to.

The main formal requirements of the new system were:

- to reduce paperwork in the branches and at head office;
- to minimise the processing cycle;
- to eliminate errors;
- to improve security (cash and data);
- to facilitate banking;
- to satisfy business travel and retail requirements;
- to improve information service and communication between branches and head office.

The requirements during the implementation phase were that any new system should interface with existing head office financial systems and gradually eliminate the manual data handling.

The main requirements of the system held by the people working for the travel company were:

- any new system should be easy to operate;
- the system should be user-friendly and have no adverse effect on customer service;
- provide diary prompts;
- should eliminate manual reporting;
- provide a capability to develop credit account status information;
- should allow the creation of local databases of client information and branch performance.

In return for providing a solution to these problems the system should have realistic costs and show benefits by improving the service to the customer, reflecting a more professional image and improving financial control.

The practical considerations of selecting a solution included the need to interface with the existing TRAVICOM and viewdata equipment, and with existing head office computer systems:

> I think we recognized that we were not going to be able to change what we had. The industry was based on viewdata – we are talking about the leisure industry here – the leisure industry was based on viewdata so that was hands-off. They had to work with that and the same applied to TRAVICOM. We had also paid for these viewdata sets ... so that was also a consideration, just purely financial.

The system also had to be introduced into branches without disrupting customer service, and had to be capable of accommodating further growth of the company.

The cost justification of the system was difficult as many of the future benefits were impossible to quantify. Some senior managers did insist on the production of some kind of commercial justification for the cost of the system. The benefits as seen by the study group included the saving of:

- forty-four posts at head office previously employed manually checking the paper system;
- stationery costs of £140,000 a year;
- £110,000 saved on telephone and postage;
- £47,000 on the maintenance of redundant computer systems;
- an annual cost benefit of £130,000 by reducing outstanding debts;
- £75,000 saved by the earlier collection of cash balances at the branch;
- a 5 per cent productivity increase which would add £790,000 earnings.

The cumulative effect over a 5-year period was expected to be nearly £4,000,000. The strategic benefits were much more important and much more difficult to predict:

> It was very much 'finger in the air' ... and I almost ducked out in terms of increased productivity, efficiency, benefits of efficiency and so on.

In reality final Board approval for the whole project was not forthcoming until 2 years after the original pilots went live. The company had grown so quickly in the 1980s that some of the more long-serving managers still had many of the attitudes characteristic of a small family business. Many wanted to be able to appreciate the return on investment the system would offer in a fairly clear-cut way. They were reluctant to make the 'act of faith' necessary to let the whole project involving a huge capital outlay go ahead with their full backing. In fact once the system had been piloted and the costs became more widely appreciated cost justification became more widely demanded by some head office managers.

Summary

1 The main objective of the branch automation system was to reduce the amount of paperwork.
2 The company felt it had to automate to compete in the travel market with its competitors.
3 In reducing paperwork it was hoped to increase staff productivity by increasing business without increasing staff numbers.
4 The company also needed to improve the quality of management information available.

5 Automation was also seen as a way of imposing discipline on the branch processes and improving the assimilation of taken-over companies.

6 It was seen as important to present a much more professional image to the customer.

7 Cost justification proved to be a problem as many of the benefits were strategic, but many senior managers were uncomfortable about giving approval without a traditional costing justification.

THE PROCESS OF CHANGE

A study group was set up in 1986 to set up and oversee the branch automation project. The study group consisted of a sponsor (the director of the retail sector), the systems development team, a Regional Manager, a member of the branch staff, three representatives from IBM and a telecommunications consultant who had previously been employed by IBM. Once Holidata had been selected, a 'walkthrough' of branch processes was undertaken to make sure all essential aspects had been covered. During the study period the group undertook a limited survey of branch staff opinion in six branches which identified head office reporting as a major irritant. It also identified the number of telephone calls from head office, especially the accounts department, trying to sort out queries due to inaccurate information, as another major source of stress. The study-group then produced a projected implementation plan and a detailed business case. The report was then presented to the sponsor who in turn presented it to the Board.

As well as dealing with the technical aspects of the project, the study group also addressed the social and organizational problems of introducing branch automation and made some recommendations. They recommended the early communication of company strategy on branch automation to all staff and that branch managers should be involved in the detailed plans for automating their branches. They recommended that a Project Manager should be appointed with appropriate resources at their disposal. The introduction of a training strategy was considered essential to ensure consistency. It was suggested that an implementation team should be established and a training manual and package be developed. They felt that two key personnel from each branch should be trained centrally, they should train their own branch staff and that the whole branch should have a period of hands-on familiarization before going live. A technology-awareness event was suggested for senior management and the directors of the company and the establishment of an Information Centre at head office to provide access and training for head office staff at all levels.

The initial time-scale envisaged all regions on-line within 2 years. Although IBM personnel on the study group thought this was practicable, the travel company staff did not. The original idea was to spend 3 months on familiarization, then select a small number of pilot branches and introduce the system into one pilot branch every month. Following this, one Region a month would go live until the whole company was on the network. The study group emphasized:

a successful pilot is crucial to the success of the whole project.

These then were the recommendations of the study group that set out an ideal implementation plan. The actual implementation process differed in a number of ways from this ideal.

The implementation

Quite soon after the decision to buy the 'off the shelf' package it became obvious that the software vendor company did not have the resources to undertake and implement such a large project and that they were in extreme difficulty. The viewdata link promised was non-existent and the travel company were forced to investigate alternatives from other manufacturers, and the systems development staff proceeded to develop the physical cable link and necessary supporting software themselves.

Five new systems development staff were recruited including a PC development manager. Most of the new people had both PC experience and formal IT qualifications. The search for training premises took 18 months to find suitable accommodation. A Project Manager was not finally appointed until the project eventually got Board approval 2 years after the first pilot system went live.

The pilot

The system developed and adapted by the company's technical staff from the original 'off the shelf' package was introduced into a small number of branches throughout the country from Aberdeen to the City of London, with variable success:

We have got the manager who is enthusiastic from the word go and his or her enthusiasm stays and they carry their staff with them. You've got the other manager who is enthusiastic to begin with, but because of their way of working they get slightly turned off, but with a bit of work they can be turned round. Then you have your third type, the people who have automatic resistance from the word go and were never enthusiastic.

The experimental introduction of the pilot system and the training of the staff in the pilot branches was undertaken by two staff from head office. They took the PC and the software to the branch, installed it, set it up, got it running and then trained the branch staff 'on the job'. Sometimes the PC arrived a couple of weeks before the date set for going live and the branch staff were able to experiment with it in a non-live environment. But equally often the PC arrived at the same time as the implementation staff arrived in the branch and went live immediately. As a general rule, no training was given at head office during the period of the pilot, although some of the staff from the pilot branches located near head office had been able to go and see the system in operation before they received their own systems. Once the system was in operation and the implementation staff had left the branch, problems were mostly tackled via a telephone help line. Some pilot branches had few problems and seldom used the help line, but others had many problems and made constant use of the help line. In some cases the implementation staff had to return to the branch to provide further assistance with the system.

In the cases where there was resistance to the implementation of the system, head office enlisted Regional and Divisional management to encourage branch acceptance. In general, the further away the branch was from head office the more likely there was to be resistance, but there were other factors like the level of staff turnover, the volume of business (although one of the busiest branches also had one of the most successful implementations), whether the PC had been present in the branch for some time before the system went live, the level of support from Regional and Divisional Managers and, probably most significantly, the initial attitude of the Branch managers themselves.

At head office the main concern was that the administrative staff who were involved in checking branch returns had not had enough training in the use of the system at first and were not particularly well prepared. Senior management regarded the system as a success from the branch point of view, but had reservations about the levels of security and control within the system. They gradually became enthusiastic about the potential level of management information which would be available from the system:

> That really fires me with enthusiasm, I can see that just computerizing what we do at present has almost incalculable benefits for us ...

but when my mind begins to range over the additional information I could perhaps ask for ... !

Changes in implementation policy

After the first year all the branch managers from the pilot branches were invited to head office to discuss the system and how it had worked in the first year. This meeting was the foundation of the Users Forum which eventually became the main filtering mechanism for amendments to the system in the light of experience gained during the pilot. It also provided a forum for problems to be aired and solutions offered by managers who had experienced successful implementations. Enthusiastic managers had a strong positive effect on those who had not been so positive in the beginning. It became a valuable mechanism for establishing 'ownership' of the system and making the Branch Managers accept responsibility for its success or failure rather than blaming head office and expecting them to sort out problems. The systems development team also arranged a 'technology awareness' event for senior managers to show them some of the potential benefits of the system from their point of view.

The pilot also ensured that realistic targets were set for the 'roll out' to the whole company. A decision was made to iron out the initial difficulties and bed the system down before extending it further. It also became obvious during the pilot that the training and implementation policies would have to be re-thought and re-planned. Renewed energy was put into finding suitable training premises in the vicinity of head office, and a further nine people were recruited for training and implementation work. It was decided that the next phase of the roll-out would be the Region nearest head office rather than a whole Division as originally envisaged, and would contain a pilot branch with a working system so that it would be easy for staff from the new branches to see the system in operation before it arrived.

Changes in training policy

It was decided that training should be done centrally with a fixed 2-day programme and that the Branch manager and one or two staff from the branch should be trained and then train the rest of the branch staff themselves. Once convenient training premises were obtained and resourced, three senior staff were appointed to be training and implementation officers. Subsequently they were both called 'project leaders'. These staff came from a variety of backgrounds, both from the technical and the business sides of the company.

Evaluation

The evaluation of the pilot system was done mostly in consultation with the managers of pilot branches. They drew up a list of desired enhancements and corrections and a User Forum met quarterly to discuss progress. Attempts were also made to measure increases in productivity at branch level in terms of turnover and commission earnings per employee or pound of salary cost within a given branch. But evaluation was not seen as a crucial function, as automation had been accepted at all levels within the company both as the only way of keeping up with their competitors, and also to enable them to expand at the rate they planned:

> Again we come back to the great imponderable of increased efficiency and increased productivity and how you measure that. We do have some tools that we use to measure productivity in terms of both turnover and commission earnings per employee, and I would think we will tend to adopt the same measures post-automation, but we haven't given a great deal of thought to that.
>
> It's quite wrong I suppose, but you get the gut feeling right throughout the company that automation is essential if we are to expand at the rate we would like to, if we are to stay ahead of our competitors and give us competitive edge.

Summary

1 The study group undertook a limited survey of branch opinion while they produced the requirements analysis.
2 The study group made a series of recommendations that addressed the social and organizational problems of introducing the branch automation system.
3 The implementation was hampered by lack of support from the software vendor and the lack of a project manager.
4 The pilot system was introduced into a small number of branches throughout the UK, some were much more successful than others.
5 There were several changes in implementation policy as a result of the pilot, including centralizing training rather than training in the branch.

CHANGES TO STRUCTURE, CONTROL AND WORK ORGANIZATION

Although the introduction of computer networks has facilitated a more flexible and flatter organizational structure in many companies (e.g. Kwik-Fit, see Chapter 7), there was no evidence of any significant structural change being contemplated within the travel company during the period of the case research. Other companies have found it possible to eliminate layers of middle management (see ScotRail case study, Chapter 3), but for the foreseeable future it seemed that the network system would conform to the existing patterns rather than bring about structural changes at least in the short-term. From an external perspective the network system took over some of the functions of Regional and Divisional management within the travel company, e.g. aggregation and analysis of branch data within a region and/or a division, but political considerations made it unlikely that there would be a swift elimination of these layers of management. For example, some of the Divisional Directors were previously Chief Executives of taken-over companies and to threaten their position would not have been politically acceptable or aid unification of the company. Regional management offered a promotion path within the company for successful branch managers and to remove this opportunity might have significantly reduced motivation for branch managers.

Even in the early stages of the introduction of the network it became obvious that there was an important shift in control patterns between the branches and head office. The formal nature of the computerized system meant that the branch had far less control over decision-making. In addition, as the quality of information received by head office improved, they became increasingly able to make many more decisions centrally about prices, promotions, foreign currency holdings, credit ratings and so on. It was hoped that as more of these decisions were made centrally the company would begin to behave like a homogeneous whole rather than a collection of individual branches.

Most of the staff originally employed to check the manual returns from branches were technically redundant following the implementation of the new system, but nearly all were either retrained as implementation staff or absorbed in the continuing expansion of the company. There was also a high turnover among these employees and the company hoped that a large proportion of the redundancies could be dealt with through natural wastage. Apart from these jobs it was not anticipated that the new system would have a large impact on employment within the company. It was hoped that the main effect would be to allow the company to deal with increased business with the same level of staffing, so that staff costs would not rise. It was also hoped that the ratio of staff costs to sales would improve giving a significant rise in productivity.

The introduction of branch automation did not immediately change any reporting structures within the company. It made an immediate impact on the way people worked within some of the branches. Previously each branch had developed its own way of working, each developing its own variation on a basic theme, some actually letting the system fall into confusion. These branches often found the introduction of computers most difficult, and were among the most resistant. Automation meant that all branches had to work in the same way, working practices being rationalized and made to function efficiently. Branch staff found that it did not change their individual ways of working too significantly, but it did lead to dramatic reductions in the amount of paperwork they had to do. While some branches had previously had an invoicing desk to help with administration, this post was eliminated, and all administration done by sales staff through their PC. A 'procedure group' was set up to standardize procedures.

Summary

1   The travel company made few structural changes as a result of the network system.
2   The introduction of the system led to much more centralized control of information and decision-making.
3   Branch procedures and working practices became more uniform and predictable.
4   The amount of paperwork was reduced and more time was made available for the staff to sell holidays.
5   A User's Forum was set up to review the system and suggest enhancements.

CONCLUSIONS

The travel company was in a competitive holiday retail market with outlets throughout the UK. The company went through a phase of rapid growth mainly by taking over smaller but similar travel companies. As a result of this growth, the administrative burden of paperwork had become unacceptable. To deal with this the company introduced the branch automation system which has gradually been extended to the whole network. This process took a number of years to complete. The company needed the system to maintain its competitive position in the marketplace.

The main objective of the system was to keep administrative costs as low as possible in order to release the branch staff to concentrate on selling holiday packages to customers. The branch automation system would allow head office to take over most of the administration, and greatly improve the quality of the management information available.

IBM PCs and a letter-quality printer were installed in each branch, and the PC's telecommunications facilities were used to connect to head office mainframe computers. During the day the branch staff used it to produce invoices and itineraries, and at night the details of the day's transactions were moved to head office where they were processed.

The system took six years to implement fully and there were several problems along the way. Some of the branches were initially more enthusiastic than others, some branch managers were antagonistic at first. The setting up of the Users' Forum helped to overcome initial resistance. The pilot scheme led to changes in training and implementation policy.

Head office imposed considerably more control on branch processes as a result of the system and became far more important within the company. The system helped the company improve its efficiency and foster a more professional image. It also allowed branch staff to spend more time with the customer than on paperwork. The company benefited as the same number of staff could cope with increasing business.

The new system also increased and improved the amount of management information available to senior management and aided their decision-making and enabled them to impose closer control.

Senior management were not entirely convinced of the advantages of branch automation and at first it was promoted by the Systems Development Manager with support from the Director of Accounts. The software supplier provided little support for development or training. The system was developed by a small team some of whom had more experience on mainframes than PCs, with little input from branch managers. A pilot system was tested with mixed success in a small number of branches and then was gradually introduced to the rest of the branch network, over a period of years.

The network system had little effect on the structure of the company, although the system took over many of the responsibilities of regional and divisional managers. Branch managers lost considerable autonomy as the system imposed discipline and uniformity of procedures and head office took control of information and could monitor branch performance on a daily basis.

The initial lack of commitment of some senior management influenced the progress and outcome of the network system. Some were reluctant to make a complete financial commitment and until final approval was given about 2 years into the development process, there was no Project Manager, no centralized training premises, and limited staff commitment to the project. The slow progress of the implementation of the network system can be related directly to the lack of enthusiasm and drive from the top. This makes an interesting comparison with the outcome of Kwik-Fit's network project (see Chapter 7) and the contrasting attitudes of the senior management of the two companies to essentially similar systems are notable.

3

SCOTRAIL

'Omega': a network-based administrative reorganization

SUMMARY AND LESSONS

ScotRail is the Scottish Region of British Rail. It has been used as a pilot site for many of BR's computer systems. In the early 1980s rudimentary computer networks were introduced to all of ScotRail's ten Administrative Areas and enabled dramatic reductions in waged staff. In the late 1980s a more sophisticated computer network system was introduced to underpin a radical structural reorganization nicknamed 'Omega'. The original ten Areas were reduced to five and over 200 salaried jobs were lost at middle management level.

The aim of the system was to facilitate reorganization in the short-term and to work towards privatization in the longer term by increasing efficiency and productivity. Subsequently similar changes took place throughout BR.

These objectives were rapidly achieved. In the early 1990s, all the Areas were eliminated and their functions devolved to station managers. Networked computer systems were a major factor in making these dramatic changes possible.

Although the objectives of the implementation were political and long-term, the Omega process illustrated some useful lessons in how to manage a large-scale, complex project that had threatening implications for staff at all levels:

Some of the lessons learned during the process were:

- the importance of involving the technical staff as well as operational users in the analysis and design of the system;
- the significance of previous experiences of IT projects and their impact on internal attitudes to change;
- the importance of central IT resources to coordinate, resource and implement a network project and organize the training and retraining of staff;

most of the impetus for change was at regional level, nevertheless the main centres of resistance were also at regional head quarters:

> That is where the organizational block is, despite the fact that the organizational change is coming from them, the inertia is always with them as well. All they can do is talk and write papers ... there is too much talk going on and not enough decision-making ... the debate is about themselves and no-one likes committing hari kari! It is biting very close to those sort of people who have to make those sort of strategic decisions ... for the first time in a long while.

Certainly one of the main aims of Omega in the longer term was to reduce the role of the regional HQ to a small 'rump', so much of the regional managers' apprehension was fully justified:

> take this building for instance (ScotRail House – the Regional HQ) we have got maybe 1,500 people in it, it is a hell of a lot of people when you think there are only 13,000 left in ScotRail.

In contrast, the management at Area level were less vulnerable to redundancy and had a bright future in terms of promotion and security within the larger BR system. There was a general feeling among Area management that it would be difficult to ensure that Regional HQ actually allowed the devolution of power to the Areas and that a power struggle would ensue between those Regional Managers who wanted devolution and saw their future in the wider BR system and those regional managers who were losing their power to Area management and feared redundancy:

> The Areas are still afraid that the Regional bureaucrats will try and stop them doing what they want to do and the HQ bureaucrats will try their hardest to do just that.

The rest of the management grades could be divided into those who hoped that the reorganization would bring them promotion and those who hoped for a generous early retirement golden handshake:

> People have two attitudes in a sense ... there is one group who say 'how quickly can I leave?' and take the benefit of redundancy, and they are switched off because they know they are going to go anyway ... and there are the other lot who are saying 'let's get on with it quickly because when those so and sos go I am going to get promotion out of this'. All of them are uncertain and therefore not delivering of their best.

At lower staff levels a certain degree of cynicism coloured reactions. Many would say that there had been 'a reorganization a year' for the last 10 years and the rationale behind the changes had been communicated to very few staff, although many realized the need for change:

> most of them have gone through it in one form or another before in previous jobs further down the tree, so they are a bit cynical about it and just carry on.

> Staff on the ground usually say 'Oh no! Not again!

The loyalty and attachment of virtually all ScotRail employees was an important factor in times of change. Many had worked for the railway since they left school, many had fathers and grandfathers who also did so. This tended to mean that although morale was at times extremely low, and though a considerable degree of cynicism existed, the basic loyalty of most employees meant that they were determined to make the reorganization work for the sake of the railway itself:

> It will sort out in the short-term by people doing each other's work for them. The discipline is that we have to keep the trains running 24 hours a day and everything the railway does is geared to that, and the people who do that are professional enough to accept any sort of pain.

Consultation procedures

Any reorganization of ScotRail would have needed to go through a mandatory set of consultation procedures established by BR at a time when the rail unions were far stronger. These procedures were designed to allow the staff side in each of the Areas represented by their Unions to be informed in detail of the proposed changes and to make amendments to them. Regional management then had to attend a series of meetings in the Areas listening to and answering objections and making changes where appropriate. At one time change on the scale proposed by Omega would have been subject to powerful staff action, but this time the consultation procedures though lengthy and comprehensive had become something of a ritual; time-consuming and bureaucratic, but no longer a serious barrier to change, an indication of the unions considerable loss of power during the 1980s. The railway unions had shifted their focus from creating new jobs and protecting existing jobs, to upgrading the posts that remained:

I think you know the trade unions are now in a situation, they'll accept virtually what you are proposing numbers-wise. What they are looking for is gradings. A few years ago the consultation processes would have changed the original plan beyond recognition, whereas now it went through as originally planned.

Nevertheless the procedures took 6 months to complete following the introduction of the Omega proposals and generated an immense amount of paper, which was a serious consideration as the timescale imposed on the reorganization was so short.

Grading structures

ScotRail had a very rigid job grading structure at this time which had also been introduced in times when unions had more power and was designed to protect the employees' earnings and status. In practice the grading structure meant that after every reorganization there was a long list of people looking for posts at certain grades and long vacancy lists of posts with certain grades attached to them. Linking the two without causing too many practical or personal problems was a long and complicated procedure for the Personnel Department with huge associated training and retraining implications. Following even large reorganizations like Omega, local managers had to more or less accept who they were allocated by the Regional Personnel Department and had little say on suitability or acceptability. The appointees had to be the right grade for the job rather than have the right technical expertise. This led to some strange anomalies after a period of change; people could be allocated to IT jobs with no IT experience, typing jobs when they could not type, finance jobs when they had no accountancy experience at all:

> the freight clerk is now the sort of typist. She's the one I told you about, the only one who can't type.

The changing organizational culture

Changes in the culture and style of ScotRail had been taking place in the years leading up to Omega and these formed important contextual factors for the reorganization. Ten years before the railway had been an 'appalling bureaucracy'. One example quoted was that:

it was necessary to consult the highest authority before changing the light bulb from 40W to 60W ... the guards did not feel able to change the failed light because that was the electrician's job.

The major changes in bureaucracy date from when Chris Green became General Manager ScotRail, but there had been a change of climate even before that. Nevertheless many changes had been attributed to him:

There is room for innovation, for the maverick. There is scope to be unorthodox.

You've got to know the old to know the new, We've got a credibility that we never had before. Its nothing less than a railway renaissance, in the eyes of the railway staff and the public.

ScotRail had been working hard at changing the culture of the railway for some years and this attitude helped greatly when it came to the implementation of Omega:

A few years ago I know for a fact that this railway would have been at a standstill if we had tried to do what we are doing now. There's been a great change in attitude ... and it's because there was that change in attitude and the change of attitude has become an accepted thing that Omega was possible.

Part of the process was sending managers away to Outward Bound Schools for management training. Here they were shown the need to adapt styles of management to suit changes in conditions, managing uncertainty, self-awareness, leadership styles and so on. In many cases these courses had a dramatic effect on the managers concerned:

we had half the people coming back with the intention of putting the world to rights and at the same time having managers that were prepared to let them do it.

There was also a sense that the general railway culture was a constraint on change processes. ScotRail staff were usually firmly committed to the railway as a way of life. This worked both ways. In some ways it worked against change because many loved the organization the way it was and they were established in the hierarchy. In another way, once the changes were a reality the staff mostly worked hard to make them succeed because they were committed to the efficient running of the railway. This generally meant that it was difficult to bring in changes, but once they had been introduced they were not sabotaged or run with sullen resentment.

Existing technology

At the time of the study, BR had many computer systems and hundreds of computer applications most of which are highly centralized and mainframe-based to ensure standardization throughout the organization. The Regions within BR all use central mainframes for most of their applications, e.g. payroll and personnel systems. This has led to complaints about their inflexibility and lack of responsiveness to differing local requirements:

> there are the mainframe systems which tend to be regarded as a nuisance, because they tend to demand that you do things rather than provide you with anything back.

At the beginning of the 1980s each of the then ten Areas within ScotRail had a network WAN installed based on a Novell file server and IBM PCs, which dealt with most of the day-to-day operational administration of the Area. The introduction of the Novell networks enabled the substantial staff reductions of the mid-1980s. The capacities of these networks varied and were progressively increased. Glasgow Queen Street started off with 75 megabyte and Glasgow Central had 120 megabyte. The applications mounted on these Novells included train crew rostering, direct data entry to BR mainframe systems, Multimate word processing, public complaints, Supercalc, plus a telecommunications server and a link to the High Speed Data Ring. The systems were essentially stand-alone and the Areas could not communicate with each other without using the High Speed Data Ring:

> if I wanted one network to talk to another, even if it was in the room next door, the message had to go down to the mainframe in London, Crewe or Nottingham to go onto that High Speed Data Ring and come back up to the other one.

All technical decisions involved in choosing upgrading and changing systems were taken at Board level by the Director of Information Systems and Technology (DIST). DIST had decided on the Novell file server and IBM PCs as a standard for the original networks in the early 1980s and these were introduced nationwide. All programming was done centrally. All software development had to be passed through a national software 'clearing house' to ensure standardization.

The reaction of the ScotRail staff to the Novell networks was mixed at first, but eventually became positive and enthusiastic. This was in part due to the way the implementation was gradually phased in and staff were given time to adjust to new ways of working without undue pressure to do so. This 'softly, softly' approach eventually created a demand for further refinements and development of the system originating from the staff themselves. Very little training was given initially and the staff were left to find their own way round the system without being pressured. Some uses were quite unusual:

> People were actually using Supercalc for word processing!

The level of interest in the system's potential varied between Areas:

> even 2 or 3 months after they had been there you could go up to Inverness and the dust cover was still on the machine!

Often the level of interest seemed to be related directly to whether there was at least one computer enthusiast, or whether there was a particularly obstructive personality in the Area office, who inhibited the rest of the staff. This was sometimes overcome by sending him or her on a training course:

> once we got the reluctant personality on a training course they changed overnight.

This reluctance to engage with the technology had a direct relationship with the union's fear of job losses due to the new technology:

> There was a sign on it saying 'do not use this machine' and because he was Chairman of the Branch everybody in the office believed in him no matter what the manager said: 'no ... the union man has told us to leave it alone.'

But the majority of ScotRail staff quickly saw the advantages offered by the Novell network system, and by the late 1980s were making more than full use of them.

> The vast majority took to them like a fish to water.

Partly as a result of the successful 'demand-driven' style adopted for the Novell networks rather than an imposed 'top down' approach, by the time Omega and the accompanying changes in network technology was mooted in the late 1980s most staff were enthusiastic about the potential of IT network systems and realistic about how essential they had become to the efficient working of ScotRail:

> But now we can't survive without them ... we couldn't pay the staff, we couldn't roster the staff ... it is as fundamental as that.

Summary

1   ScotRail was the Scottish Region of British Rail which had undergone a series of reorganizations since the early 1980s.
2   Staff morale was low because of the rapid change and continuing uncertainty.
3   Trade union power had been undermined and no longer offered much protection for the workforce.
4   Grading structures were outdated and led to structural employment anomalies.
5   The railway culture had become far less bureaucratic since the early 1980s.
6   In the early 1980s BR had successfully installed WANs in the then ten Areas of ScotRail.

THE OMEGA NETWORK SYSTEM

The main purposes of the Omega network system were: to enable the Area to function efficiently at an operational level and to provide the Area Manager with the appropriate management information. It was also to provide a direct communications channel between BR at Board level and the Areas, largely bypassing the Regional organizations.

The responsibility for designing the Omega networks was shared by the Regional IT group, who were responsible for the computers, and the Signals and Telecommunications Engineers who were responsible for the linking telecommunications technology. Both groups had recently undergone drastic reorganizations themselves which had reduced both the numbers of staff available to run the project and the level of expertise. The main problem faced by the IT network designers was that the networks had to be designed in response to the restructuring of the Area administration rather than the network technology dictating the pattern of change. They were left with the specification for the redesign of a large complicated network system to underpin the new Areas without having been consulted about the practicality or feasibility of the system from a technical point of view. Only a comparatively short while after introducing the original ten Novell networks they were faced with the prospect of:

> putting together five separate projects to build a new IT infrastructure for the five new Areas.

Each Area network had different and characteristic problems. Glasgow Central had remote links to Fort William and the busiest lines. Perth had remote links to Thurso and Wick plus the transfer of the headquarters from Dundee to Perth in a listed building that could not be changed externally. In addition, the decision to introduce 'Ethernet' LANs in each Area head office meant that the engineers were working with unfamiliar leading edge technology.

The existing ten Novell networks were reorganized in response to the administrative changes. This was accomplished by moving the existing Novell File Servers (e.g. the one originally based at Dundee was transported to Perth) and new communications links were established. Many administrative IT systems, formerly based at the Region, like Personnel and Finance were decentralized using the new networks and were then operated at Area level. Various formerly Regional systems were centralized to the BR Board using the mainframe systems. The networks made it possible for the BR Board to access, manipulate and alter data entered by Area and Regional staff. At the same time Regional, Area and Station managers found their freedom to access and amend data was increasingly limited:

> Once we started putting in networks and communication links, I used during interviews to ask a question 'what do you see as a long-term result of that?' Just to see if anyone would say 'well you get rid of Regional HQ'. Because the Board can talk direct to Area, because the technology has made that feasible.

At the same time as restructuring the IT network in response to the administrative reorganization, the IT Group took the opportunity to introduce more advanced 'state of the art' technology by deciding to install Ethernet LANs at Perth, Glasgow Central and Edinburgh Area headquarters and linking these to the remote Novells at Aberdeen, Inverness and so on.

Ethernets had been chosen by DIST to be the standard 'ring' network within BR to eventually replace the Novell networks. ScotRail were among the first Regions to introduce them, which caused some problems. The S&T had little experience installing Ethernets which meant that the process took rather longer than expected. Additionally, expectations of the potential offered by the network were raised and were not entirely satisfied once they were operational:

> we have taken the opportunity of developing in terms of technology and using Ethernets, rather than just having the Novell 'star' networks. We will have Ethernets at Perth, Edinburgh and Central. On to these Ethernets we will link the existing Novell networks and

these will be outbases. For example from Perth there will be outbases at Aberdeen and Inverness and we will leave the existing Novell networks there.

Summary

1 The new Omega networks were designed to service the five new administrative Areas.
2 The technical responsibility was shared by the IT group and the Signals and Telecommunications group, both of which had recently been reorganized.
3 The technologists were not consulted about technical feasibility before the new administrative structure was designed.
4 Each Area had particular technical problems to be overcome.
5 The Omega networks enabled the BR Board to communicate directly with the Area and bypass the Region altogether.

GOALS AND OBJECTIVES

Network technology offered the possibility of eliminating some administrative layers and staff numbers without reducing the effectiveness of the service offered to customers. Omega had two main stated objectives. The first was to reduce the number of operational Areas and the second aimed to devolve control and decision-making down to the lowest rational administrative level. Many previously Regional functions were to be devolved to the new Areas. Not only did this entail a radical restructuring of the administrative structure, but it also meant the loss of over 200 jobs. The general aims of the change were to make the organization more responsive to customer requirements, both individual customers and internal business customers like InterCity and Freight, and to continue the reduction of overhead costs started in the early 1980s. The imposition of government spending targets also galvanized attitudes on the business side and clarified BR's and therefore ScotRail's objectives:

> for the first time ever we actually got objectives from the government that were clear cut. Anything in the past was so woolly that one could drive a horse and cart right through it.

The changes were also meant to be a pilot for subsequent wider changes within BR nationally, leading to the whole organization being much 'leaner and fitter' in preparation for future privatization. The spectre of privatization loomed over every level of staff within ScotRail even during the main research period and there was an acute awareness that all the changes they were experiencing were leading up to privatization in the not too distant future.

The IT and telecommunications side of the Omega networks were not cost justified except in the very broadest terms. A global sum was allocated for the project, there were no funds specifically assigned to the IT element. The almost total disregard for the technical problems and costs of restructuring the IT system was a characteristic of Omega. It could be explained by the long-term strategic aims of the BR Board to streamline and make dramatic savings on overhead staff costs, which they felt would more than. compensate for any technological costs.

Summary

1 ScotRail hoped to reduce overhead costs by the numbers of salaried staff.
2 It was also planned to reduce the amount of bureaucracy by reducing the number of Areas from ten to five.
3 Another objective was to reduce the number of layers in the hierarchy by devolving decision-making to the lowest rational level.
4 A long-term aim was to reduce the role of the Regional Head Quarters.
5 A longer term aim was to prepare BR in general for privatization.

THE PROCESS OF CHANGE

The conventional view of managing large IT projects such as that implied by the Omega reorganization would be that it was essential to analyse the existing system in terms of information flows, compare this analysis with the new requirements specification and to design the new system in collaboration with the users. In fact the most interesting part of the Omega project was that all these 'rules' were broken and the IT element completely taken for granted. Neither the IT group or the S&T Engineers were consulted about the technical feasibility of servicing the new administrative structure: they were simply expected to produce the technology once the most rational administrative structure was established. The administrative designers assumed that technically virtually anything was possible:

> they have assumed computer systems would be there and enable jobs to be done.

Only towards the end of the administrative design process were the IT people brought in and then only in response to repeated requests that they should be involved:

> we didn't really get involved until the autumn and by that time the plan had virtually taken shape.

Even then they had no influence on the eventual shape of the reorganization, virtually no changes were made as a result of this minimal involvement, except for minor alterations like substituting fax machines for remote telecommunications links in two or three cases:

> I spent about 4 months talking unofficially to them, trying to tone down some of the remote links ... 'are you really sure that we can justify the cost of it?' and then they just said: 'well the technology will be there when we want it.'

The managers designing the new structure admitted:

> It must be admitted that we did not set sail with any thoughts of Information Technology.

The administrative reorganization

The new administrative structure was designed and planned by a small team of administrators who reported directly to the Deputy General Manager (DGM). They travelled extensively throughout the Region, visiting virtually all staff locations within ScotRail, analysing the work of each individual post and establishing whether that post was essential or dispensable. They refused to accept any input from staff at any level:

> I had to say to everybody, 'I am sorry. Leave this alone. Don't interfere with us until we get the draft memorandum otherwise we will never reach the end of the road.'

> Certain people tried to influence us, but we refused to listen to them.

It seemed to be part of the cultural background of BR to view consultation as a potential battleground rather than a source of ideas or a way of checking viability. The whole process of designing the new structure was done on a pragmatic basis, no formal design methodology was used:

> rule of thumb! If we had done a formal analysis it would have taken an ungodly amount of time.

The whole process led to a considerable amount of trepidation and fright among the staff being studied. It was generally felt that the team were in effect studying each person's work with a view to dispensing with their services:

> It was terrible. They would just sit there and make notes while people were working.

Once the regional analysis was complete a draft proposal for reorganization was drawn up and made available for discussion:

> There was absolute horror! The original document took absolutely everything into the centre (the Region), a total centralization. It was bombed out! It took out Area Managers. I suppose they were taking devolution right down to station manager level using the all singing, all dancing networks.

The initial document created such a storm that it was unanimously and summarily thrown out

> The Businesses flung it out, the Board flung it out and then we had a bit more active debate, which to me was feet-dragging ... this eventually produced the existing structure.

The fact that the Board and the Businesses effectively vetoed a plan generated at regional level indicated that strong centralized control was still exercised within BR, and that devolution of important decision-making to lower levels had not yet been achieved. It also demonstrated the significance of internal politics, and the power of the regional managers attempting to preserve their power base:

> The first version was their survival document.

The proposed structure would have preserved the Regional HQ and run the rest of the railway network through the station managers, eliminating the Areas altogether.

A second version of the document was produced after a few months discussion and, at the insistence of the Board, this reinstated the Areas, whilst dramatically decreasing the power of the Regional HQ. This was seen within ScotRail as a significant struggle for power within BR when the Board's 'hidden agenda' emerged leading to the beginning of the end of Regional control:

> The Board has now taken the Region out as the unnecessary bit in the middle.

Once the new plans were agreed in detail, Project groups were set up in each of the five new Areas to set up the new structure, make the necessary new appointments and generally coordinate the change. At this point for the first time, the IT group and the S&T Engineers became involved in the change process. The Project Groups were led by the new Area managers designate.

> Once the initial Omega concept had been produced, five project teams were set up by appointing an Area Manager Designate for each of these Areas, who then formed little teams which were appointed internally.

Many of the practical tasks associated with the implementation of the reorganization were the responsibility of the Implementation Officers who subsequently became senior members of the Area Managers' administrative team.

The top management sponsor

Although the main forces behind the initiation of Omega were national economic and political factors at Board level, the individual personalities within ScotRail had considerable impact on both the detailed nature of the changes, and the way the process of change was handled. General Managers, especially the high-profile Chris Green, have had a strong effect on the climate of opinion and changing culture within the Region. This was an important factor as Omega was to an extent trail-blazing as a pilot for similar reorganizations in the other BR Regions. The success or failure of Omega depended to some extent on the strength of personality of those managers most closely identified with it within ScotRail and the extent to which they felt their interests and future career lay within ScotRail or at Board level.

The original basic concept underlying the Omega project was developed by the DGM of the time in 1988. He was a manager of great experience with a reputation for original ideas and had been at ScotRail throughout the 'Chris Green' period. The details of the reorganization were worked out by two highly experienced administrators, with backgrounds in Work Study, who between them had 56 years experience of working within ScotRail at various levels. During the period of Omega, the previous Regional Finance Manager was Acting DGM and given charge of the management of the project. His political skills were indispensable in pushing the reorganization through despite all the doubts, difficulties and resistance. As he said at the time:

You have to galvanize those who matter in terms of delivering the thing. There are different ways to motivate different people ... you have got the self-starters, those who need oil in the wheels and the other ones who need a good kick in the backside and being told to 'get on with it'.

The Manager of Management Services who was in charge of the IT element of Omega was another highly experienced and politically aware 'railwayman' whose acumen and 'people skills' were invaluable when the IT implications of the reorganization became apparent. He played a crucial role coordinating the IT and administrative element and acted as the DGM's agent.

The role of change agents in the Omega process was particularly interesting. Each stage in the process needed a different kind of sponsor starting with the conceptual ideas stage and moving through to the more political and power-broking problems of implementation arising from the obstructiveness of different interest groups, especially from fairly senior managers at the Regional HQ. The fact that Omega remained consistent to its original aims was probably due to the fact that ultimately the BR Board were acting as the 'Guardians of the Concept' and ensuring that political pressure from the various interest groups, especially the Region affected, did not cause fundamental changes in the basic concept. The original plan designed by Regional officials which centralized all operations at Regional level and eliminated Area managers reflected dearly the Region's attempt to protect its existence, and was thrown out by the Board and the Businesses.

The role of the technologists

The IT Group and the S&T engineers were left in a difficult position once the Omega reorganization proposals were approved. Both groups had recently undergone drastic reorganizations themselves, reducing both the numbers of staff and the level of expertise they had available. They were left with the specification for the redesign of a large and complicated computer network system without having had any input into the practicality or feasibility of the scheme from a technical point of view, let alone its cost-effectiveness. They were, in effect, told to 'get on with it'.

The IT group were middle managers who had worked their way up the railway hierarchy acquiring on the way some IT expertise. Few had any formal external IT training, but had been trained on internal BR courses. Their normal tasks were to test new applications packages, to train staff to use them and to install hardware and software throughout the Region. Recently their role had changed. Due to almost continuous reorganizations the IT group had begun to spend most of their time restructuring networks making sure they were functioning properly and retraining staff. The implementation of the Omega networks meant a large drain on their limited resources and their expertise was spread very thinly at times during the project.

Major problems were experienced with the establishment of the new Area based at Perth.

The Perth Area geographically is as big if not bigger than the whole of the London/Midland Region.

Perth had never been the centre of a Novell network; this had been based at Dundee. It was necessary to amalgamate three existing Area networks based at Inverness, Aberdeen and Dundee into one based at Perth. In addition the head office at Perth was a listed building which limited the number of internal or external alterations that could be made. Each Area had particular technical difficulties, but there were also problems of coordination as there was no overall Technical Project Manager. Both the IT Group and the S&T Engineers assigned staff to the Project but no-one was in overall charge of the technical side. As the implementation proceeded it became obvious that the telecommunications links were the most difficult part of the project to deliver in the timescale laid down:

> well a lot of the S&T didn't know whether they were coming or going. They had their own S&T reorganization as well. The timing of bringing in Omega was totally wrong.

> This has changed our problems from being ordinary hardware and software problems and applications problems to being telecommunications problems. Our friends in the S&T have got to become almost our colleagues and we have got to work together with them, because we cannot now do things in isolation as we could when we had little local networks.

The progress towards the implementation of the Ethernets was variable. Edinburgh's Ethernet was up and running and a great success long before the Ethernet at Glasgow Central. Even though it was installed before Edinburgh's, it took much longer to become operational, largely due to the character and experience of the respective IT clerks, as well as a general shortage of staff from the IT Group to assist during the implementation period. An incidental result of the delay in implementing the Ethernets was that it created a demand for access to the system from Senior Managers. This repeated the success of the demand-led implementation of the Novell networks but at a higher management level.

It became a major task for the IT group to make sure that they did not get the blame for the S&T's failure to deliver the telecommunications links. Nevertheless the prevailing railway loyalty ensured that the two groups collaborated closely enough to deliver practically all the original technical requirements, even if they did not quite meet the timescale in every respect:

> 99 per cent I think. It is only the odd isolated location that difficulty has been experienced.

Implementation and training

The chosen implementation style of Omega was definitely 'big bang' due to the tight time-scale imposed on the project. There was no time to experiment on a pilot site or use a prototype system. Not all systems actually went live on implementation day, but the essential systems like payroll were available from day one and thereafter systems were phased in according to their priority rating. There had to be interim arrangements because the telecommunications infrastructure had not been fully delivered:

> If the S&T had done their wiring we could have got the rest of it in … it would have been flat out but we would have done it.

The Ethernets in the Area head offices took longer to implement, but this made little difference to the way people worked because they were just new ways of mounting the same applications and were transparent to the user. In the end Perth took longer than the other Areas mostly because of the difficulties experienced in dealing with a listed building. Portacabins located on the station forecourt were used for 6 months until the conversion was complete.

It was impossible to train people in advance for their new roles as many posts were unfilled until 2-3 weeks prior to implementation and nobody knew who would be allocated to the IT posts. The most that could be done was to reserve the training suite at ScotRail House for the 4 months following implementation of Omega.

> I have allocated the Training Room from the end of April till the end of August for Omega. But I cannot tell you even next week what I will be doing in the training room because I don't know yet!

Evaluation of the process

The implementation of Omega achieved most of the strategic and operational objectives laid out by management at Board and Regional level. However it also left the majority of ScotRail staff feeling fairly gloomy and pessimistic about the future, though some middle management saw it as an opportunity for advancement. The senior management at Regional HQ who did not move to the new Areas felt that the devolution of authority threatened their future jobs and took defensive action:

> the whole thing has been pointed much more at Regional HQ ... so watch the power struggles between the senior managers, the rearguard actions, the empire building, the defence! We see it and I joke about it with my trade union reps, but actually to see senior management behaving in the same way ... !

The lower management grades and clerical grades suffered significant loss of morale following the levels of uncertainty that existed for six months before Omega came into operation. Even those who were sure of a job had no idea where that job might be situated. Many feared they would have to move their families some distance to obtain a suitably graded job within the ScotRail system. Mostly they did not know where their new post was until 3 weeks before implementation:

> Well the implementation date was 22 May and I was officially informed on Monday 9 May ... it was all rumours up to that date ... so it was exactly 14 days before implementation that I was made aware that I was to be Support Services Manager for 2,100 staff ... and I had 14 days to get my show on the road.

ScotRail was determined to have no compulsory redundancies and managers nearing 55 were offered generous early retirement packages. In addition there was already a vacancy list of eighty jobs before Omega. The main reason for the loss of morale was the lack of communication between those in control of the change and those affected by it:

> It all boils down to one thing which was that communications were abysmal. The communications from top to bottom in the whole thing were terrible.

The main effects of the strict application of the grading structure was that a number of people were placed in posts for which they did not have the appropriate experience or expertise, and a large retraining requirement.

Summary

1 Neither the IT group or the S&T engineers were consulted about the form of the administrative reorganization.

2 The original reorganization was designed by Regional administrators and eliminated the Areas, preserving the Region and using Station managers for day to day administration.

3 The BR Board and the Businesses objected and insisted on a rethink.

4 Influential senior managers at the Regional level promoted the new plan on behalf of the BR Board and used their influence to ensure successful implementation.

5 The political nature of the Omega reorganization led to particular technical problems for the technologists with the responsibility of managing the implementation.

6 The short timescale enforced led to problems of planning in advance for training and retraining staff.

CHANGES TO STRUCTURE, CONTROL AND WORK ORGANIZATION

An obvious structural change was achieved by the reduction of ten operational Areas to five and an equivalent reduction of the number of Area managers. It was more difficult to establish whether the objective to devolve decision-making down to the lowest rational level and give local managers more autonomy was fully achieved. Senior management indicated that the whole aim of the reorganization was to decentralize decision-making to the new Area Managers, but admitted that the successful achievement of this objective depended on the attitudes of both the Regional Managers and the new Area Managers:

> the expectation is that the decision-making will be decentralized, but I don't know whether that is really window-dressing ... I think there are people at head office that still want to keep their fingers on the button and make the decisions and ideally have puppets in their Areas.

> Personally I feel that there's an awful lot of people desperately breaking their finger-nails trying to hold on to that power at the moment.

The Senior Managers who had instigated Omega were aware of this danger and were prepared to intervene to prevent the Region blocking the devolution of power to the Areas:

It is up to us as senior managers to make sure that doesn't happen.

In reality, although it was true that certain Regional functions were being decentralized to the new Area Managers, in fact many of the functions of the Region were also being centralized to BR Board level:

> On the one hand you are saying devolution and delegation of decision-making and on the other hand ... bloody hell! are they not centralizing more rhubarb to London, Derby and Crewe!

In addition, much of the ultimate power over quality, professional standards, performance measures and so on were preserved at regional level:

> I see my role at Regional level in terms of standards, performance ... a sort of analytic role, pushing the business forward. The scheme is geared for decentralization of decision-making to the Areas and stations ... whilst at the same time accepting there are certain things that are going to be centralized at the Board. Nothing wrong with that ... there are certain things that lend themselves to centralization.

In effect, as many staff pointed out, the railway was coming full circle. Omega reinstated the Divisional structure last abolished in the 1960s, although the former Divisions were renamed Areas:

> well I have seen it ... I went through it 12 years ago. It is amazing how you come full circle.

> we should have left the Division, that is what we are putting back.

Although this was represented as a decentralization of power from the centre, power and control were actually being centralized at BR Board level, with the same jobs being done at lower levels by lower graded and less well paid staff. The people who were appointed to the new Area and Station Manager posts were younger and on lower grades than their immediate predecessors though they had similar responsibilities for staff and budgets. This represented a considerable cost saving for ScotRail in addition to the loss of 200 posts and the reduction of Area managers from ten to five.

Omega led to a considerable reduction of staff at middle management and upper clerical levels, especially at Regional HQ. The new network structure also made it possible for the Board to bypass the Regional HQ and work directly with the Area Managers. The Region was therefore reduced both in size and in power. As one Area Personnel Manager said:

My colleagues at Regional HQ are being missed out by the Board. They send them direct to myself ... which is another development. I think this may be the forerunner of the demise of Personnel at Regional HQ.

Middle management at Regional HQ were under particular threat and their future was doubtful unless they transferred to the new Areas:

> There has been a reduction of power and manning levels ... middle management have had the biggest hammering so far ... they are the biggest obstruction to change ... they have lost a lot of their power but they certainly fight a strong rearguard action to retain it or regain it ... the worst middle managers are those at Regional HQ who really haven't got a job unless they make one and that is a problem. Work expands to fill the time available.

An additional dimension of the change was that Omega was another stage in the progressive shift of power from the Production side of BR to the Business Sectors which were closer to the Board:

> The Businesses are a growing and developing organization both physically and in power terms: everything else and us (the Production side) are a declining side. They are obviously very close to the Board.

It was an assumption in the minds of many ScotRail employees even in 1988 that all the reorganizations they had experienced were in preparation for eventual privatization:

> There are long-term aims that are not really being declared whereby we are really doing two things at once, we are leaning towards an element of centralization at the Board for certain things and a decentralization of everything else to Area level. What will be left in the middle will be very small ... but no-one will admit that to you publicly. It is inherent in going towards either a privatized industry or a quasi-privatized industry.

Changes in the structure of IT management

The reduction in numbers and downgrading of posts within the IT Group and S&T Engineers at Regional level immediately prior to Omega rejected the general attempt to devolve responsibility from the Region to the Area. The general aim was that the responsibility for managing IT should be spread out to the functions and to the Areas leaving a very small resource at the Region and the main responsibility for selecting standard software and hardware at Board level with DIST. The result of this reshuffling of control led to two main problems. First, how to mobilize enough experienced staff when large region-wide projects like Omega are needed, and second how to deal with the massive IT training and retraining requirement resulting from such reorganizations.

The Omega process made it clear to Senior Management that it was desirable to retain a regional IT resource. Since its inception in the early 1980s when it evolved from the old Work Study Department, the IT Group initially came under the authority of the DGM, but then were transferred to the Regional Personnel Manager who at the time of Omega had little knowledge or interest about IT. During the process of Omega it became obvious to Senior Management that IT had become central to the functioning of ScotRail and the IT Group were returned to the direct authority of the DGM.

At a local level,within the previous Area structure there were full time 'IT Clerks' in each of the ten Areas. In the new Omega structure there were actually fewer people directly responsible for IT at Area level. Each of the five new operational Areas had a full time IT Clerk who reported directly to the Area Manager and was responsible for all IT systems. Considering that these IT clerks were not on management grades and were responsible for running sophisticated computer systems like the Ethernets in the Area offices it seemed surprising that a higher grade post had not been established to cover day to day running of the systems, further development and training. At the level of the station the only allocation of staff time for IT systems was that one member of the clerical staff devoted a notional 10 hours a week to IT 'housekeeping' tasks. Another problem was caused by the grading system. Some staff who had responsibility for the IT system in the old Area structure and were enthusiastic and knowledgeable were not the right grade for the new IT post and could not carry on the job. Conversely, some new IT Clerks might have been the right grade for the job but had little enthusiasm or experience for IT. This was particularly problematic when the Ethernets were introduced, as there were few central IT staff available to train or support these reluctant and sometimes panic-stricken IT clerks:

> if we'd had the choice we would have had the enthusiastic individuals, but we didn't have the choice.

The installation of these networks and ScotRail's increasing dependence on telecommunications links certainly meant that the relative importance of the S&T Engineers increased. The Signals side of the S&T was always recognized as a vital part of the railway system, but more recently the telecommunications side had had a much higher profile:

> yes it is becoming more important ... but it is as if their own department don't realize it ... the telecomms had always been the poor relations ... but now the comms and data links are: becoming more important.

At that time the telecommunications provision was entirely in the hands of the S&T which was only second in size to BT itself and actually supplied Mercury with its long-distance lines. It was a frequent matter of speculation whether the S&T could well become a separate privatized company from whom BR would then have to purchase services:

> we are actually the largest telecommunications organization outside BT, we provide all Mercury's trunk lines for example ... but the way we are likely to go is to run that as a totally separate entity ... as a telecommunications business in our own right.

Summary

1 The number of administrative Areas was quickly reduced from ten to five.
2 The devolution of decision-making took longer, but eventually the Region ceded control of a range of operations to the Areas and Stations.
3 Other functions were centralized from the Region to the BR Board.
4 At the same time there was an increased shift of power from the production side of BR to the Businesses.
5 The Omega project made it clear that it was desirable to maintain a central IT resource for managing large network projects.

CONCLUSIONS

ScotRail had undergone a series of reorganizations since the early 1980s facilitated by increasingly sophisticated network technology. Omega was the latest reorganization and its priorities showed for the first time the importance of future privatization, and the priorities of the Board in implementing Omega reflected this long-term strategy.

The lower-level stated objectives of the reorganization and the introduction of networks were the reduction of the bureaucracy by reducing the number of Areas, the devolution of responsibility to the lowest rational level, and the reduction of overhead costs. The longer term strategic and less obvious objectives were the virtual elimination of the Regional Head Quarters and the search for efficiency in the run up to privatization.

The Omega networks consisted of five WANs centred on the main stations which were at the centre of the new Areas: Glasgow, Edinburgh, Perth and Fort William. The Area head quarters had Ethernet LANs installed. This system was designed to deal with the day to day administration of the Area and also data communications with the BR Board. The system enabled the BR Board to communicate directly with the Area or Station and bypass the Region. In the longer term it also enabled the BR Board to communicate directly with the Station and bypass the Area organization. The Omega reorganization proved to be a staging post in the BR Board's drive for efficiency. Whereas the main concern in 1988 was the devolution of power from the Region to the Area enabled by the network, in the early 1990s the same technology enabled power to be devolved from the Area to the Station.

After a few teething problems caused by lack of consultation between the designers of the administrative system and the technologists, the system was installed on time and was easily accepted by ScotRail staff who had become used to the Novell networks introduced in the early 1980s. The medium-term outcome was that the new Areas undermined the power of the Region. The longer term outcome was that the BR Board used the same technology to bypass the Area and deal directly with the Station manager. In effect, the more important administration was centralized to the BR Board and the less important operational administration was devolved eventually to the Station, the Area being an interim arrangement.

The longer term outcomes were certainly not predicted at the time of the reorganization, although privatization was certainly the spectre at everyone's elbow.

The change management processes employed were unusual in that the IT Group and the S&T engineers were not consulted about the feasibility of the technical implications of the Omega reorganization. Users were not involved in any sense. The reorganization was designed in line with the aims and objectives of the BR Board and the technology conformed with central BR requirements. ScotRail staff were not consulted or even informed about the details of the proposals. The trade unions had considerably reduced power and could offer the staff little protection. Middle management were only informed of the medium-term objectives of the change and in the longer term many of them lost their jobs as part of the long-term strategy of the BR Board. The whole process of change was driven by the Board with little consultation at local level.

The network system eventually changed the way people worked at all levels in ScotRail. This was not in any sense determined by the technology, rather the technology enabled wide-ranging and continuing structural changes within ScotRail. These structural changes were part of BR's long-term plans and facilitated by the technology rather than determined by it. In the longer term, network systems played an important part in preparing BR for privatization.

4

THE LIBRARY NETWORK

SUMMARY AND LESSONS

The organization is the largest library cooperative in the UK and was established in the 1960s. It sells specialized library computer systems. The Libraries become members of the Cooperative with access to the central database. This allows them to achieve considerable economies of scale. The library system has been continually enhanced and can now run the loan system, book acquisitions, serials, On-line Public Access Catalogue (OPAC), as well as allowing access for cataloguing via a WAN, to the Cooperative's centralized database. The case study shows that the same technical system when installed in different types of libraries has markedly different outcomes and clearly illustrates the importance of social, financial, geographical and political factors in determining the relative success or failure of computer systems. Some of the lessons learnt were that:

- it was essential that the parent institution provided sufficient funding for the library to buy an appropriate sized computer;
- it was helpful if the Chief Librarian was supportive and involved in the central decision making processes of the Cooperative;
- it was useful if the library established a systems librarian post and appointed somebody with the appropriate qualifications of both professional librarianship and computing;
- it helped if all library staff were trained in the use of the systems so that senior staff did not feel marginalized;
- the new system meant that some restructuring took place, eliminating a professional cataloguing function and downgrading the technical services function;
- the new system led to the increased importance of Reader Services and this was reflected in the new structure;

- the Library Assistant post needed to be upgraded in response to the skilling-up of their job;
- the Cooperative needed to provide sufficient support and training at the time the system was installed and continuing support if problems were experienced;
- the distance from the head office of the Cooperative was significant in that it affected the amount of support the library received from central staff.

INTRODUCTION

This case study looks at an organization, formed into a cooperative for the benefit of its members, and using computer network technology to link different types of library to a central database of bibliographic records. At the time of the study the Cooperative was at a decision point. The continual induction of new libraries meant the company had grown to over fifty members and the representative structures set up when it was a small friendly cooperative, were now unwieldy. The company was also debating how to maintain an acceptable balance between the commercial development and marketing of new computer systems to new members, and maintaining the loyalty and satisfying the demands of existing members. The case study shows how even quite similar libraries can react entirely differently to the same computer system depending on the financial, geographical, and political factors that affect their implementation. This chapter will first examine the Cooperative's view and then move on to look at the views of five of the member libraries.

BACKGROUND

The context

In 1967 the Office for Scientific and Technical Information (OSTI) published a policy statement concerning library automation. The policy aimed to support projects in three areas; to examine the necessary elements of library automation; to evaluate and develop new mechanization techniques that could be applied to libraries; and to promote cooperation between libraries particularly in the area of the new techniques being evaluated. The main area of investigation centred on the production and use of machine-readable bibliographic catalogue records. In the USA the possibility of producing machine-readable records was considered as early as 1963 and a group of sixteen libraries began to use machine-readable records in

1966, receiving weekly magnetic tapes of current records. This project was known as MARC (Machine Readable Cataloguing). In the UK the British National Bibliography (BNB) began to look at the possibility of using machine-readable records in 1967. The adoption of the international standards of cataloguing rules (AACR2) and the International Standard Book Number (ISBN) were important in paving the way for the development of machine-readable catalogues.

The Cooperative

In the 1960s, OSTI funded several feasibility studies to look at the co-operative use of BNB machine-readable records, and the development of computer networks to support the rationalization of house-keeping operations. One of these feasibility studies was based in Birmingham, and the original participants were three very different types of library: a large well established academic library, a modern academic library, and a large metro-politan library, ensuring that the findings would be widely applicable. This was the origin of the Library Cooperative's network.

From 1968–1970 the study group concentrated on MARC and the computer hardware and software necessary to implement the system. In 1970 OSTI granted a 2-year extension to the grant during which a costing study of the existing manual catalogues and the various computerized options was undertaken. From the results of the costing evaluation it became apparent that the least expensive computer output for the catalogue was on microform (COM). Between January and September 1972 MARC records were created for all new acquisitions and the first machine-readable catalogue appeared in February 1973. By the end of the first extension period, a database containing 14,000 records had been created. A further 2-year grant extension was approved in June 1972, during which time the first catalogues became available. There were also a series of feasibility studies on behalf of a number of libraries who were interested in joining the scheme. By September 1972 all BNB and Library of Congress backfiles were loaded onto the mainframe. This covered a further 100,000 items. A final grant extension was agreed in September 1974 for a further final year and the time was spent completing documentation and a short comparative evaluation exercise between the manual and automatic cataloguing systems. By 1987 the catalogue had reached three million records growing at a rate of 300,000 per year.

By the end of the OSTI grant period, the original membership of three libraries had grown to seven including one in Denmark, and by the end of 1976 the membership had grown to seventeen. As membership increased it became difficult to maintain standards of service, and in February 1976 the Council of the Cooperative set a temporary limit of twenty libraries, which was expanded to thirty in October of that year. The combined pressures of computerization and cooperation meant quite dramatic changes in ways of working both for junior and senior library staff. In the late 1960s librarians in the UK were passionately divided about the impact they felt computers would have on their profession. Even in the late 1980s at the time of the study, when computer systems were obviously successful, there were still librarians who felt that computer systems led to conformity, or were not sufficiently adaptable to local requirements and led to the depersonalization of the library service.

The evolution of the Cooperative company

In 1977 the Cooperative network became a limited company, a completely separate and autonomous organization. An unsuccessful submission to the British Library for further grant assistance meant that the cost of running the Cooperative had to be met by member libraries. It was felt that the development of new systems could only take place if the Cooperative took on independent company status. After considerable discussion, the Cooperative became a registered non-profit making limited liability company regulated as a mutually trading cooperative. A Board of Directors was set up consisting of seven librarians from the existing members who were elected at the AGM and the Managing Director who was also Company Secretary. The Board held its first meeting in October 1977.

During this period the Cooperative concentrated on developing new services for its members. The most important new services were: retrospective cataloguing of older catalogue records, data compaction techniques to facilitate storage and accessing bibliographic data and, most importantly, the development of an online cataloguing system. From 1979 onwards the trend was towards developing an integrated library package. Much of the development work concentrated on a circulation control module, and an online public access catalogue, and through these developments, a gradual evolution towards a total integrated library system. The final version of the integrated library system was available in 1986, whilst over the same period the membership had grown to fifty UK libraries. Each was a full member of the Cooperative and agreed to abide by the rules. All members paid an annual charge to fund software development, support and unlimited database access. New software revisions were provided at no extra cost. Hardware maintenance and microfiche catalogue costs were additional. A charge was made for the first 5,000 titles catalogued and after that titles were charged individually. In fact libraries did not have to become members to take Cooperative services; they could take selected services without having to contribute to the database.

Decision making within the Cooperative

There were five user groups representing each of the five main services: cataloguing, Online Public Access Catalogue (OPAC), circulation, acquisitions, and serials. The groups met about twice a year and two representatives from each member library attended. In practice this meant they had become unmanageably large. The groups fulfilled an important function in allowing the airing of grievances about the systems and expressing future requirements, but dissatisfaction arose when individual demands had to be sacrificed to the demands of the majority.

The Council of the Cooperative consisted of all the chief librarians of the member libraries or their substitutes, with the addition of the Managing Director and the three Executive Directors. At the time of the research the Council consisted of twelve University Library representatives, sixteen polytechnic, nine public, eleven college, one special and one national library representatives. The Director's report kept the Council informed about the activities of the User groups and product developments. The main business of the Council related to general issues like charging policy and the future direction of the Cooperative. The Chairman of the Board was also Chairman of the Council. The Council elected the Board which consisted of seven librarians who met with the Managing Director and Executive Directors of the company. The Board had both executive and statutory powers and dealt with confidential matters like staffing, policy and marketing. The composition of the Board reflected the composition of the membership and at the time of the study consisted of two university library representatives, two polytechnic representatives, two public library representatives and one college representative, plus four Executive Directors. The Board met six times a year whereas the Council met three times a year. The Board and the Council were seen as having quite different functions:

> We could take our marketing plan to the Board but we wouldn't discuss it in any detail with Council. We wouldn't discuss with Council whether we were going to place advertisements, or which segments of the market we were going to attack more strongly than others. I think there is some commercial confidentiality which does

distinguish between the Council and the Board, they get discussed at the Board and not at the Council.

The three Executive Directors were responsible for Customer Services, Marketing and Development, and Computing. The Managing Director was responsible for all the operations of the company. The Customer Services section was responsible for user support and they were all trained librarians with extensive experience of the Cooperative's systems. They were responsible for the telephone helpline, site visits, documentation, training and maintenance. The responsibilities of the Marketing section were divided into Sales and Product development. The Computing section comprised software development, technical support and operations. The staff were mostly trained programmers, systems analysts and operators, but also had an idea of library requirements.

Charging policy

As a Cooperative the company had always charged for services on the basis of 'fair shares all round' rather than directly relating charges to the services actually taken. The larger libraries with the bigger and more extensive systems paid more, but there were not differential rates for access to the database or the number of files accessed. Charging for connect time was considered and rejected because chief librarians on the Council wanted a simple, fair and predictable mechanism for sharing out the costs of the Cooperative. Charging for connect time or charge per title were not as predictable as a simple subscription related to the size of the computer system the library had introduced. Originally the subscription had been related to the number of terminals connected, but then it had been changed to relate to the size of the minicomputer.

Existing technology

At the time of the research the Cooperative was dependent on a large IBM mainframe (model 4341) located at its office. By 1987 it had 8 megabytes of CPU, 6 channels and a total disk capacity of 11.25 gigabytes with a further 5 gigabytes added in 1988. It held six million bibliographic records and the holdings of all member libraries, their class marks and the locations of all the different titles. This linked outwards through six Data General satellite processors to the telecommunications network. The network reached as far north as Glasgow and as far south as Brighton with Kilostream links to London and Manchester.

At the library end of the network, a Data General minicomputer was located in each member library. This could support from 32 to over 200 terminals, depending on the size of computer demanded by the library. It supported the OPAC, the loans systems, book ordering, serials control and was used to search the central database on behalf of the cataloguing system. On receiving new book stock, the member library would use their own computer system to search the central data base for the bibliographic record. When traced, it would be downloaded into the library's catalogue as a local record and the central database would register their holding. Libraries could run off-line batch systems which held daily transactions in a file and then transferred to the mainframe overnight, where the catalogue was produced in microfiche form. More often members ran on-line systems where each transaction was recorded and transferred immediately. As more libraries converted to on-line systems from overnight batch systems, the company envisaged that the use of microfiche would die out. It was also anticipated that the newer systems would use PC-based work stations rather than the more usual dumb terminals. Existing members were offered an upgrade path for their systems – more terminals, more memory, and more processing power. The company were also supporting research into an expert system to reduce duplication of records on the database, and a front-end intelligent terminal for the OPAC which adapted its interface to the level of skill of the particular user.

Future pressures

At the time of the research the Cooperative was at a crossroads. The company felt under pressure to concentrate on one or two library sectors rather than trying to cater for the full range, a strategy which could involve considerable compromises with system specification. Library cooperatives had moved from a comfortable sheltered 'family' stance in the 1970s to the highly competitive times of the late 1980s and 1990s. They had to be run as publicly accountable companies subject to the same financial pressures as more conventional companies. Nevertheless the company was still managing to remain recognizably a cooperative company. The most important distinguishing characteristic was their non-profit making nature and the fact that their members had a substantial voice in the decision-making and day to day running of the company. The primary concern of the company was still service to its members, but as the size of the network increased this became increasingly difficult to maintain, especially as the different types of libraries had increasingly divergent interests. In addition the company had still to ensure that its products could compete on commercial terms. This reality could in some cases work against the interests of long-term members who would have preferred to have existing services improved. The main disadvantage of working as a cooperative was the restricted level of investment in terms of manpower and money that could be devoted to research and new product development, as so much time had to be devoted to keeping existing members satisfied.

Thus the research study of the Cooperative was undertaken at a fairly crucial stage in the company's growth and development. It had reached a size where some of the original objectives of the Cooperative were being undermined by the number and variety of the members and their varying and increasing demands on limited company resources. The aims and the objectives of the commercial company were somewhat different to those of the member libraries. In addition, the aims and objectives of members varied with the type of library, the length of time they had been members of the Cooperative, and to some extent with the geographical distance of the library from the parent company.

Summary

1 The library Cooperative under study played an important part in the development of cooperative library computerization in the late 1960s.

2 Subsequently, the library market place has become far more commercialized.

3 Since the late 1960s, the company had changed from being a small friendly cooperative to being an outright commercial concern, bringing a number of pressures on itself and its members as a result.

4 Throughout it had been an innovatory and pioneering organization with a central database being the 'jewel in the crown'.

5 Most member libraries would comment on the responsiveness and helpfulness of the staff as well as the quality and user-friendliness of the systems.

6 By 1987 there were at least fourteen other suppliers trading in integrated library systems based on minicomputers.

7 This Cooperative had the largest share of the market – about 21 per cent.

8 The members represented a variety of libraries with polytechnic libraries being in the majority, but with few inroads into the small special library market.

9 It was also the largest of the four library cooperatives in the country.

10 In recent years there had been signs of the maturity of the market with numbers of new sales slowing down considerably.

11 As a result there has been greater competition in the market place, with a greater emphasis on costs and services, and new foci for sales like small special libraries.

GOALS AND OBJECTIVES

The company were in business to provide computerized systems to libraries; they had no other business interests at the time of the research and no plans to move into other business areas. They had made few efforts to move into foreign markets, but had considered the possibility of franchising their systems. They felt that their traditional library market was nowhere near saturation, as there were still many libraries running batch offline systems who would be looking to replace them with on-line systems. In addition, those libraries with on-line systems would be looking to replace or up-grade them every 7 years or less. Because they were a cooperative the company did not need to sell new systems to survive as a company, they 'Hosted' on their existing membership and did not need to meet a sales target. At the time of the research they were growing at about six new libraries a year, which was faster than the majority of the competing companies. It was important for the company to keep their existing members happy with their systems and satisfied with the level of service provided to ensure their loyalty to the Cooperative, whilst also making sure that they devoted enough resources to the research and development of new systems:

> every time I go out and sell I am not supporting and I am not developing, so it is a difficult balance the company is trying to steer.

The history of the company meant that library cooperation was the driving force behind the company and that computerization had been used in the first instance to improve that cooperation rather than being an objective in itself. The increasing size and commercialization of the company meant that these priorities were under discussion and being reconsidered. The company felt that there was a big enough market for both themselves and other similar companies to continue to thrive. They felt more commercial suppliers had not managed to force a big enough market share and might decide to drop out of competition. The cost of making sales was rising:

> a public library might well ask as many as six suppliers all to give up four or maybe more days on site for demonstrations and that is a lot

of money. There are a lot of people involved and these are expensive people.

So the main objective of the company itself was to maintain the solidarity of the Cooperative, making sure that the member libraries were satisfied with the services supplied. Although the quality of the database and network were critical factors in maintaining a happy membership of the Cooperative, after-sales support and the cooperative consultative structure were also important.

Summary

1 The company's main business was to sell computerized library systems to UK libraries.
2 They considered that there was still considerable potential in the market for new systems and upgrades of existing systems.
3 They were not dependent on 'new' sales because of the cooperative structure of the company.
4 Nevertheless they were still selling more new systems than their competitors.
5 The loyalty of existing members was very important to the company's future.
6 Success was a balancing act between selling new systems and keeping existing members happy.
7 Computerization was a means to an end in making cooperation efficient and effective.

OUTCOMES: THE COMPANY VIEW OF THE EFFECTS ON MEMBER LIBRARIES

The company felt that the combined effects of cooperation and computerization had brought considerable benefits for member libraries. The technology had improved library services and tightened control on budgets, especially in the book acquisition area. In the future management information from the system would also provide significant benefits. The advantages of cooperation were economies of scale and the cooperative structure which allowed the fast development of a sophisticated and flexible system. The system's flexibility allowed it to be used successfully by a range of sizes and types of libraries.

Another advantage was the on-going support provided by the company after the system had been installed and the access to new ideas and joint problem-solving between libraries, although the libraries themselves had somewhat different views in some cases. The company tried hard to foster the 'club' aspect of the Cooperative and did not feel that their members saw the inevitable loss of autonomy entailed in belonging to a Cooperative as a problem. They admitted that their members had lost some freedom of action and that if one member desperately wanted a particular development and no one else did, then the pace of development might seem very slow. This had led to a growing trend to establish a 'normal practice' instead of catering for individual needs:

> We treat every member individually ... don't try and drive a member into what we would consider normal practice, but there is a bit of a development in that direction ... we do encourage standardization, but we don't say to people 'you have got to have the same sort of loan system as everyone else.'

The company recognized that there had been some changes in the roles of librarians, especially a reduction in the numbers of professional cataloguers needed, but they felt that the effect was simultaneously skilling-up and deskilling. They had to skill-up to learn to use the computer, but their cataloguing skills were lost.

The power structure within libraries had been changed:

> One strand is that the professional staff no longer understand the way the circulation system works ... where they thought they understood the manual system and could do an evening duty ... they then can't work the computer ... it means that they can become alienated.

The Library Assistant role had also changed due to the fact that they made more use of the computer system, but there had been few cases of their grade or salary being increased as a result of this upgrading of their skills and importance. They also felt that the systems librarian had also become a powerful person within the library hierarchy as they had control over the system and management information. The senior professionals, especially the cataloguers and reference librarians, had found that their jobs had changed:

> Well it is not that people are not able. It is just that the system that they were used to has now changed. So they worked their way up through the system, and they really ought to work their way back through the new system, but they don't in most cases.

The computerized library system could raise the image of the library within its parent institution:

> The computer system is a major element here in the way the library services are perceived and marketed. The image of the university library here will change by virtue of the fact that you have on-line terminals. They will suddenly think you are wonderful.

Member libraries had different perspectives both from the central company and from other members, depending to some extent on the type of library, and to some extent on the distance from the Cooperative. This dissonance between the parent company and the members, and between different types of libraries had led to considerable discussion about the future direction of the Cooperative.

Summary

The Cooperative saw the advantages for members being:

1 Increased efficiency and economies of scale due to being part of the Cooperative.
2 Better management information.
3 Access to new ideas and joint problem-solving.
4 Only marginal loss of autonomy and local control due to the adaptability of the system to local parameters.
5 The effect on professional librarians was simultaneously deskilling and skilling-up.
6 The Library Assistant job had become more important as they made most use of the system.
7 The Systems Librarian occupied a powerful position in the library hierarchy.
8 The system gave member libraries a more professional image within the parent institution.
9 Member libraries had somewhat different perspectives to the central Cooperative company.

THE PUBLIC LIBRARIES

Research was undertaken in two of the largest public library members. A number of staff from all levels were interviewed on their views of the Cooperative's computer systems and the consequences of belonging to the Cooperative. One public library studied served a predominantly rural area with only one large town within its catchment area The other public library was dominated by two substantial cities as well as having a large rural hinterland. The first will be referred to as the County Library the second as the Metropolitan Library.

THE COUNTY LIBRARY

Background

The area served by the County Library is located in the Englsih Midlands. There were thirty-five individual libraries of varying size and mobile libraries. Of these, only the main central library in the largest town and four smaller libraries were on network, but they accounted for 70 per cent of the total transactions. The library's computer system was in the charge of a systems librarian who held the rank of Assistant County Librarian. At the top of the library hierarchy was the Director of Leisure and Recreation, immediately beneath him was the Principal Assistant Librarian and then below that came the Assistant County Librarians, the systems librarian being on the third level of the hierarchy. The systems librarian was a professional librarian, but in addition had advanced scientific qualifications (a PhD). She had also taken computer courses for her own interest. The library seized on this expertise when it came to appointing a systems librarian.

The County Library had pioneered many of the Cooperative's products and the systems librarian was on the committee that drew up the specification for the loan circulation system. She also had a good relationship with the County's Computer Department, partly because she had the relevant knowledge to enable her to communicate with professional computer personnel. The County Council was generous in its funding of the library.

The technology

In May 1989 the library's computer system was run on a Data General MV15000 minicomputer with 16 megabytes and four disk drives plus a rapid access disk for the OPAC indexes. The OPAC was then only available to staff not to the public who used the monthly microfiche catalogue. CIRCO was introduced in 1986, and the acquisitions system had been introduced in 1982.

Goals and objectives

The County Library's main reason for joining the Cooperative was that it was not commercially oriented, unlike most other library systems suppliers. Because it was non-profit making they felt this allowed them to have some impact on the decision-making process within the company and steer it in the direction that suited the goals and objectives of the County Library, especially in terms of developing a customized program. A primary objective of joining was to obtain access to the central database, but all branches saw the elimination of the unwieldy manual loan circulation systems as a second essential aim. It was hoped that the introduction of the system would free the professional staff to make more contact with the public and give them more time to help the users.

Staff involved in the company at a high level saw participation in joint problem solving in the Cooperative as an important objective, to be balanced with the loss of some local autonomy. The County was represented on the Council of the Cooperative, but no longer had representation on the Board although the previous County Librarian had been on the Board for many years.

Outcomes

The system had been embraced with real enthusiasm throughout the library service, with a few temporary exceptions. Many of the more junior staff felt that their job had been enhanced and their skill level increased. Some of the more senior professional staff felt that their professional skills had been taken over by the system and felt deskilled. The users, except for some of the older generation liked the speed of the system and felt the service had acquired a more professional image.

The process of change

The introduction of the computer network system caused few people problems, only one or two of the staff had resisted using the new system. These were not forced to use it, although new staff had to learn to use it effectively:

> We had two real nightmare people. Six months or so into automation two people just couldn't work it out at all and we had to find a seventeen-year-old girl who taught the existing staff all about it. They just got in a mental panic.

This appeared to be a very temporary phenomenon:

> Those that were originally most vociferous against the system are now most vociferous when the system is down.

Changes to structure, control and world organization

There were few organizational changes directly as result of the introduction of the systems except for the introduction of the Systems Department. This gained power within the organization at first 'in the thick of automation' but gradually lost this temporary gain of power as the number of service points still to be loaded on to the network dwindled:

> Ultimately the whole thing could be run by the Computer Department. A lot of the practical stuff is done by them now.

A supervisor post was created at the time the system was introduced, and each District had a liaison officer who trained the library staff in the use of the system, the trainers being trained at the central library.

The introduction of the computer network system allowed them to introduce a Union catalogue for the whole County system rather than every library having its own individual catalogue. In addition all other formerly manual systems were assimilated to one County Library system using the network, although at first a comment was made about the individual District Librarians:

> sometimes they resent the loss of their autonomy.

The Library Assistant's job at the bottom of the library hierarchy had been upgraded in terms of skill content. They seemed to progress more rapidly to new, better jobs, after the introduction of the system because they had acquired desirable and marketable skills:

> The library assistants are more skilled and have more status especially at the branches, but they don't get paid more.

The branches were on the whole very glad to get rid of their large and unwieldy manual systems, but one unexpected by-product was that borrower requests were dealt with much more quickly; as a result they had increased in volume and become a much more important part of the librarian's job.

At the level of the professional librarian the system had enabled the reduction in the numbers of more expensive qualified staff. On the whole the remaining professional librarians did not use the system much:

the professionals are getting further and further away from the real system.

The job of the cataloguers had changed. As a result of being able to use the central database the number of professional cataloguers had been reduced to one, and the jobs of the other non-professional cataloguers had changed:

I think the job is now less interesting because you are tied to a machine all the time. Before we used to move around doing different jobs. There is less room for idiosyncratic cataloguing now.

Further up the hierarchy, the Principal Assistant Librarian occasionally used the network system, but few senior managers used it.

The users liked the speed of the system and the professionalism of the service, though some staff felt that the older generation still did not like computers. Some users from rural areas had taken some time to come to terms with the system:

Three years on, things are OK, but it took at least 6 months before they began to accept it.

Attitude to the Cooperative

The County Library was represented on the Council of the Cooperative and the systems librarian attended many of the User Group meetings. The general feeling was that the representative structure was biased against public libraries:

I feel it is biased against public libraries, but it depends who has the loudest voice in the user group really.

We are outnumbered by academic libraries, that is one of the disadvantages of the Cooperative.

The County Library also felt that the Cooperative was not spending enough time or money on R&D, and the little that was undertaken was geared towards academic libraries:

They don't seem to spend enough time proving a thing before they put it into operational use. They say they do, but there are always bugs and you feel like guinea pigs. It needs more strenuous testing.

They also felt they came somewhere near the bottom of the priority list for developments and amendments:

A lot of good ideas get knocked on the head because there are not many public libraries in the group.

Nevertheless the County Library felt that the expansion of the membership of the Cooperative had to continue and that the loyalty of the existing members should be cultivated.

Summary

1 The system serves a predominantly rural area with a central large town.
2 The Systems Librarian was a professional librarian with computer qualifications.
3 The library had pioneered many of the Cooperative's products.
4 The main reasons for joining were to obtain access to the database for cataloguing and to eliminate manual loan systems.
5 They accepted some loss of local autonomy because it was balanced by the benefit of joint problem solving.
6 There were few human problems or changes in structure as a result of the system, although the small branch libraries lost some local autonomy.
7 The skill content of the Library Assistant job had been upgraded.
8 There had been a reduction in the numbers of professional staff.
9 The users generally liked the system.
10 They felt that the Cooperative was biased in favour of academic libraries.
11 The Cooperative was not spending enough resources on R&D.
12 They were in favour of continuing expansion.

THE METROPOLITAN LIBRARY

Background

The Metropolitan Library consisted of sixty service points and nine mobile libraries serving over a million people, but was dominated by the two very large City Libraries, located about 90 miles from Birmingham. The total bookstock was nearly two million volumes and the total yearly issues were about twelve million. The total number of registered borrowers was about half a million, the number of reservations was 87,000 per year and the number of overdue reminders issued was about 90,000. The Cooperative network system had only been introduced into a small part of the library system at the time of the study – the two main City Libraries and three smaller libraries. The first branch went live in 1986.

The Assistant Director of Community Leisure was in charge of the library service. Beneath him was a range of Principal Officers whose responsibilities were concerned with Area Libraries, the main lending library, the reference library, computer systems and bibliographical services. There was no designated systems librarian as such, this responsibility being covered by the Stock Control Librarian, a post created at the time of computerization, but not part of the management team. The occupant of the Stock Control post at the time of the research was a professional librarian who had learnt computing 'as she went along'. At the time of the research the whole County was undergoing dramatic restructuring and this led to considerable uncertainty and apprehension among the library staff, particularly the senior members whose posts were liable to disappear in the restructuring. This also meant that the responsibility for computer systems alternated between senior members of staff which added to the general atmosphere of uncertainty. It was also difficult to recruit staff as local government faced stiff competition from private industry for all levels of staff in this part of the UK particularly those with computer skills.

The network system

The library had a minicomputer-based system with a minimum memory of 48 megabytes and from this they ran eighty-seven terminals including the Online Public Access Catalogue (OPAC).

> The computer we bought is just not big enough, we can't physically run enough ports from it. We are always short of terminals, they are always all in use.

> We had no idea how many terminals we would need, we forgot about the behind-the-scenes jobs.

Any proposals to upgrade the computer system would have had to be funded from the Book Fund. They had no plans to upgrade within the 3 years of the completion of the research period, so the system was being used to capacity and beyond:

> We could squeeze more on but the thing would probably fall over completely.

They did concede that the Cooperative had warned them about the situation:

> They recommended a larger one; they were honest about the library's needs.

Goals and objectives

When considering buying the Cooperative's network system the Metropolitan Library was enthusiastic about the central database and the positive impact they felt it would have on the cataloguing function. In addition they wanted gradually to eliminate manual systems and to free up the time of professional librarians to deal directly with readers' problems.

Outcomes

Overall the Metropolitan Library felt that the systems were good but not good enough. Their main complaint was that the system's response rate was painfully slow at times. The cataloguing system, the loan circulation system and the OPAC were all subject to this criticism:

> Sometimes you wonder what on earth you keyed in, what am I waiting for? Really I could not remember!

> But the OPAC is very slow too, it is given very low priority on the system. The public get impatient and start pressing 'return' repeatedly, which just compounds the problem.

> At one stage we had people returning a book and they could go and choose their books and come back to the other side of the counter before the discharge screen had cleared.

It was strange that these shortcomings were blamed on the system itself rather than senior management's decision to buy a system with too small a capacity in the first place.

The major problem seemed to be that the computer system had not lived up to the expectations either of the staff or of the public:

> I think readers have such great expectations from the new system, they think it should be better, and when it is worse than the old system then they feel cheated.

Many of the readers actually worked with computers and often knew more about them than the library staff did.

Nevertheless the system did allow the library system to handle 40 per cent increased business without increasing staff numbers. Despite their reservations, the readers liked being able to see what they had out on loan, and the ease of making reservations. The branch libraries liked being able to tell what was in stock throughout the library system rather than just their own stock. It made the system much more accurate and cut down on staff paperwork like issuing overdue reminders.

The process of change

When the system was first introduced the Library employed a temporary Project Manager on a two year contract. He left long before the end of his contract as his computer skills were in great demand in private industry and he could command a much higher salary than that he obtained from the library service. The Project Manager had occupied a powerful position within the library while he remained, not only because he had skill that no one else possessed, but also because he lacked the skill or inclination to pass them on to anyone else:

> The trouble was that he did everything and didn't teach anyone else anything. It would have been better in some ways if we had been thrown in at the deep end and we librarians had had to find out about the system.

Changes to structure, control and work organization

At an operational level, it was generally felt within the library that the staff directly involved with the system had gained power within the Library relative to other staff. Two library assistants had been upgraded in response to their change of jobs following the introduction of the system. Professional librarians felt that they had been able to become more professional since the introduction of the system and that the job had a better image with the public now it was clearly involving work with computers rather than endless tickets and forms. Some staff did not adapt well to the system:

> Some of the older professional staff have not adapted, but mostly it is the older non-professional staff that haven't. Most professionals have adapted. Most of the top management can use the system except the Director and Assistant Director.

At a more strategic level there were more doubts. Some of the senior staff felt strongly that they had lost control of their library, partly at least because of the general lack of technical knowledge about the system, but also because of the system's lack of capacity:

> We have lost control of the library, the system is now controlling the way we work. The slow response time makes you feel stupid and the lack of terminals controls the way you work. The development of

the system is also out of our control. We have to plan round the terminals and their availability.

Attitudes to the Cooperative

The Stock Control librarian usually represented the Library on the relevant user groups and the Assistant Director of Community Leisure was on the Council, but the library had no representative on the Board. They felt there was a bias against public libraries in the representative bodies of the Cooperative, and felt that it would be a great improvement if there was a larger group of public libraries within it. They also felt that the Cooperative's staff were not always as helpful as they might be:

> I know they are stretched to the limit, but I wish they would be more honest about what they can and can't do.

> One slight gripe we have got ... is that their training wasn't really up to standard ... they promised the earth in terms of training, in fact we thought that someone would practically be in residence, but I think we had two and a half days.

The library thought it would be good idea for the Cooperative to become more commercial and to continue expanding:

> It is too cosy at the moment. It should become more professional.

They also forcibly made the point that the Cooperative would need to keep their existing members happy before they could safely expand:

> We do have quite a nice relationship. But if at the end of the day you are not getting what you need ... then it doesn't matter how nice they are. It isn't the niceness we want, it is the goods!

> They are in no shape to go out and make a living in the market place. They are making a living through a coterie ... through a special client relationship.

> It is a bit of a cosy relationship we have, like a club that events are passing by!

> It leans on the loyalty of its members because they can't get out. They are loyal only because it is in their interests to be loyal. I don't feel it is like a club; they feel it is cosy, but it seems smug to me.

But they did admit that the cause of some of their grumbles was that, first, they had not appointed a permanent computer manager and second, they had been forced to buy a computer that was too small for even their existing requirements.

Summary

1 The library service covered a large area including two cities, about 90 miles from Birmingham.

2 The Cooperative's system had only been introduced to the two main libraries and three smaller libraries.

3 There was no designated Systems Librarian; the temporary Project Leader left before his contract finished.

4   The library had not been able to secure sufficient funding and had been forced to buy a system too small for their needs.

5 They had wanted access to the database to assist cataloguing and the elimination of manual loan systems.

6 They found the response rate slow on all systems and the readers were intolerant.

7 Two Library Assistants had been upgraded as a result of working directly with the computer system.

8 Some senior members of staff felt they had lost some control because of lack of knowledge of the system.

9 They felt that the Cooperative's staff were not as helpful as they could have been.

10 There was some resentment expressed about being 'locked in' to the Cooperative's systems.

THE ACADEMIC LIBRARIES

Research was undertaken in three academic libraries. One library served a large metropolitan polytechnic library 80 miles from the head office of the Cooperative, another served a small modern university library with an extensive rural hinterland and 150 miles from the centre of the Co-operative and the third was a very large ancient library which served a large metropolitan university. Interviews were conducted with a wide range of staff in all three libraries over a period of 2 years.

THE METROPOLITAN POLYTECHNIC LIBRARY

Background

The polytechnic was formed in 1972 as a result of a merger of several different colleges with different library systems and methods. The Chief Librarian appointed at the time of the merger set central library standards for the whole institution and made technical services a central library service. As a result the polytechnic library consisted of one large central library and six smaller site libraries mostly within 3 miles of the main library. Fifty per cent of the library stock was held by the central library and 50 per cent of library transactions took place there.

The Chief Librarian was in charge of the whole library system and beneath this in the hierarchy were two deputy librarians in charge of Reader Services and Technical Services. The Systems Librarian reported to the Deputy Librarian in charge of Technical Services and was on a par with site and 'floor' (or subject) librarians. She had no formal systems training, she was a professional librarian and had been deputy to the previous systems librarian. All technical services for the whole library system acquisitions, cataloguing, classification and serials – took place in the central library. The library was almost completely automated, having bought and installed all available computerized services from the Cooperative. They had also undertaken a number of pilots for the Cooperative's systems, finding it an advantage in that it enabled them to tailor the systems to their own requirements. The Chief Librarian had been on the Board for a long time.

The network system

The polytechnic's library system was based on a Data General minicomputer (MV15000) with all the Cooperative's systems except serials and short loans.

Goals and objectives

One of the main objectives of joining the Cooperative was to use the discipline of a centralized computer system to unify a number of libraries from different types of institutions into a coherent whole. The added advantage was in replacing a number of manual systems with one computerized system. This offered the polytechnic library the opportunity for considerable economies of scale.

Access to the central database was seen as important, but less so than the continuity and security offered by membership of the Cooperative and professional service from the systems staff.

Outcome

Centralized cataloguing had been taken over by lower grade assistant librarians instead of experienced professional librarians. This resulted in a great decrease in the turnaround time in getting books onto the shelves. They had no problems with response time. All the other systems worked very well and they were very satisfied with them. The systems allowed them to establish a great deal more control over stock movements, cutting down on duplication and allowing easy transfer of books between sites. Some users and staff found the system less personal than the manual system, and some did not like being 'dealt with' by a computer. But in contrast there were always queues of users waiting to use the OPAC. The system released a lot of professional time and had contributed to a notable breaking down of the barriers between the users and the librarians.

The library users were generally very pleased with the system:

> They are much happier with the library, it is now in the twentieth century. The old system dies with the old attitudes.

> I think they probably feel we are more friendly ... it is all important ... the image, they view you as more professional.

Changes to structure, control and work organization

There had been changes of organizational structure as a consequence of setting up the polytechnic and these were not attributed directly to the introduction of computer systems, but they had played an important part in assimilating several colleges to form the unified polytechnic. The post of Systems Librarian had acquired considerable power as the use and efficiency of the computerized systems became so central to library operations.

Following the introduction of the computer system professional cataloguers were gradually phased out to the point that at the time of the research there were no professional cataloguers employed at all:

> You need a staff with a completely different body of knowledge than the traditional library expertise. You don't need cataloguers with MARC and Dewey in their heads, you need different skills.

Rather than the staff being deskilled by the system they felt they were using different skills. They did feel that the traditional reference librarian could be deskilled because people had come to prefer to use the OPAC for themselves rather than ask a librarian.

Although the senior staff felt that some loss of autonomy and control was an inevitable result of joining the Cooperative, they felt that there were compensations because the flexibility of the system allowed considerable choice and some customization to meet the library's individual requirements.

Attitudes to the Cooperative

The stability and security of belonging to the Cooperative was a great attraction for the polytechnic. They agreed that the system was geared rather towards academic libraries and polytechnic libraries in particular, so it happened to suit them very well. This obviously followed from their involvement in piloting and testing new systems for the Cooperative.

> We will stick where we are, we are very happy with them. Many are offering the same and some say they are ahead, but when you really look around it is swings and roundabouts.

The polytechnic was quite happy with the structure and operation of the user groups. This was logical, as they were always likely to be with the majority if there was a clash of opinions:

> Polytechnics can always outvote the others ... only the Council and the Management Team can decide, but of course the Council is skewed too.

One complaint was that older members had difficulty in obtaining new developments and amendments to their existing systems because the Cooperative was preoccupied trying to attract new members to join:

> What about the old codgers? Been in 15 years, paying a large subscription every year and they put all their resources into getting new customers. But we gain when people come in.

> How they do the prioritization of their tasks is a mystery to us all ... everyone complains about being pushed down the list but nobody is at the top! Release dates are a complete fiction!

They felt that the continued loyalty of existing members was extremely important to the future of the Cooperative, but that it was very difficult to get out once you were in, in any case:

So we just put a brave face on it and say we are loyal!

There has to be expansion to survive in the market, but if they expand too much they may exploit members loyalty and loyalty is vital.

Summary

1 The library served a large metropolitan polytechnic in a city 80 miles from the Cooperative.
2 It consisted of one large library and six smaller libraries.
3 The Systems Librarian was a professional librarian with no formal computer training.
4 The library was completely automated and had bought all their systems from the Cooperative and piloted some of them.
5 Their aims included unifying a series of smaller libraries, economies of scale, eliminating manual systems and access to the central database for Cataloguing.
6 The security and joint problem solving offered by the Cooperative structure was most important.
7 All systems worked well, users and librarians were very pleased with them.
8 The computer system had facilitated changes in structure involved in forming the polytechnic.
9 No professional cataloguers were now employed.
10 Reference librarians had been deskilled by the OPAC.
11 They were very happy with all aspects of being members of the Cooperative, but agreed this might reflect an academic bias within the company.

THE MODERN UNIVERSITY LIBRARY

Background

The library consisted of a central library situated in a small rural city about 150 miles from Birmingham, with a single outlying library. There was matrix management structure with project groups being established for specific tasks like automation and retroconversion of old book stock. Computer systems were the responsibility of the sub-librarian in charge of automation who occupied the third tier in the formal management hierarchy. He was a scientist by profession, with on the job computer training.

The technology

The library had only bought the Cooperative's cataloguing system and had developed their own systems for OPAC, loan circulation control, book ordering, periodicals and inter-library loans. The cataloguing system was mounted on a Data General minicomputer (MV2000). In fact the recurring cost of their cataloguing system was not much less than if they had taken the whole range of the Cooperative's systems, as the charging structure ensured that it was more worthwhile to have the full range rather than just picking out one or two from the range available.

Much of their in-house development had been done in conjunction with their own computer centre with whom they had a good relationship. In the near future the library intended to move towards a fully integrated system, and had decided that the Cooperative's integrated system would be considered along with a range of other suppliers:

> We will consider lots of other alternatives as well, we are not locked in in any way, but the stakes are quite high. We have invested a lot of time and money in the Cooperative and have been very involved in the User Groups ... but at this stage all the doors are open.

Goals and objectives

The central database was seen as an important asset:

> The point is that no other system seems to have the same starting point, i.e. the Union database. The database is the most attractive feature.

Outcomes

The library was happy with the cataloguing system, felt that it had been cost effective and had allowed them to cope with a big increase in demand with a smaller staff. They had managed to achieve much greater stock control through the system.

The users enjoyed using the library far more since automation, especially since the introduction of the in-house OPAC. Not only did they feel the library was more user-friendly, but also gave a more professional impression:

> The great advantage from my point of view is that OPAC and automation in general has improved the image and standing of the library within the University. We look professional and hi-tech, we

are not as dry and dusty as we were. It is very important when you are trying to fight for funds in committees if perception of the library is changed.

Changes to structure, control and work organization

There had been no sudden change, but more gradual organic change. The major change had been the gradual promotion of those librarians with a strong involvement with automation to academic-related grades. The Chief Cataloguer's job had gradually become more technical as the system evolved and the post had been regraded as a result. In general the technical people in the library had gradually acquired more power within the library as the computer system became more and more central to library operations.

Only a few individuals had distanced themselves from the automated system:

> Now everyone has a micro in their office so they can try it out in private. There are two who said they didn't need it, but they are coming to ask for it now they see the potential of the system.

Because they had retained a variety of systems the library felt there had been little loss of autonomy or control, but they still felt part of the Co-operative, participating fully in the relevant User Groups and being instrumental in designing a projected new User Group structure.

Attitudes to the Cooperative

As the University was situated in a fairly isolated small city surrounded by as extensive rural hinterland, they felt that membership of the Cooperative had reduced their isolation:

> Keeps us from being the only one marching in step.

They did feel that the Cooperative was caught in a dilemma:

> In order to remain commercially viable they have to expand, therefore they concentrate heavily on new contracts and the existing customers end up at the bottom of the pile for developments and amendments.

They saw the future of the Cooperative as both expansion and looking after their existing customers:

> There are perceived benefits in expanding into Europe, because as

their user base increases they should be able to balance their resources better and put more into R&D and user support.

but with the proviso:

It depends on delivering the goods. They must adjust from being a little Cooperative to being a proper business.

Summary

1 The university library was located in a small city 150 miles away from the Cooperative.
2 It had only bought the cataloguing system and developed its own systems for OPAC, loan circulation, book ordering, etc.
3 They did not consider themselves locked in to the Cooperative's systems.
4 They wanted access to the central database as their main objective.
5 The library and the users were happy with the cataloguing system.
6 Automation had raised the library's profile within the parent institution.
7 Structural change had been gradual and largely involved the promotion of those most closely identified with the system.
8 Because of their isolated geographical position the library felt it was an advantage to be part of a Cooperative.
9 They felt the Cooperative should both expand and become more commercial.

THE METROPOLITAN UNIVERSITY LIBRARY

Background

This was one of the largest academic libraries in the UK, situated in a major city, less than a mile from the head office of the Cooperative. It was one of the few large libraries still running a manual issue system and a microfiche catalogue. This situation had begun to change at the beginning of the research period when a new University Librarian had been appointed who began to move purposefully towards automating all library systems. The automation project was a huge task, as there were about 1,600,000 book titles in the system and the whole of the loan issue system depended on three-part paper slips filled in by the borrower, separated and filed in three different places. The whole system was overloaded and subject to a great deal of delay and inaccuracy. As a result there was virtually no resistance to the idea of completely automating the system among the staff:

Perhaps library schools should make a tour of it ... you will find all over the Reading Rooms young people filing paper slips in wooden boxes. That is a sight I have not seen in 20 years. It is not a sight you would see in something like forty-four other university libraries!

There are no problems in terms of staff willingness or systems support from the university. I think it is a kind of historic burden!

The new University Librarian had set up a management team consisting of himself, the deputy, the heads of Reader Services and Technical Services and the two Site Librarians. This team met weekly or fortnightly to discuss progress. The Head of Technical Services was the equivalent of a Systems Librarian. He was a professional librarian and his computing experience had been gained on the job rather than through gaining formal qualifications. Part of this experience had been gained by working with the Cooperative for one day a week.

The technology

The library had a Data General MV15000 minicomputer which carried CIRCO and OPAC and 60–70 terminals of which about 50 were available to users. They were constantly upgrading the system to improve response time.

Goals and objectives

The chief objectives of automating library systems were to eliminate costly, labour intensive manual systems and to provide a professional, speedy and efficient service to individual users and the university in general.

Outcomes

The main outcome that the library had to cope with was a rush of enthusiastic users to use the system, queues to use the OPAC and as a result the response time collapsed:

we were swamped!

After the initial rush the automated system almost immediately provided a more accurate and faster service for users. It also made the job of the Library Assistants much more interesting than the never-ending filing involved in the manual system. On the other hand they realized that they had become totally dependent on the computer system:

You realise how vulnerable you are, it is catastrophic when the system goes down, you swap one kind of vulnerability for another.

Changes to structure, control and work organization

Shortly before the new University Librarian took up his post, the university appointed a new Vice Principal in charge of automation generally throughout the university:

> This man's brief is to encourage us. If you persuade him on a Monday then you have the money on Tuesday, which is not the normal way universities function ... he was told he could have a million pounds to start off with, which was a change!

An added bonus was that the two men got on together very well on a personal basis:

> The Chief Librarian gets on well with the Vice Principal in charge of IT developments.

The new University Librarian gradually introduced some structural changes, but these were facilitated rather than caused by the computer system:

> The Librarian wants more emphasis to be given to Reader Services and taken away from Technical Services and this means restructuring ... the balance is shifting.

A new post was created during the period of the research which allowed the library to appoint a designated Systems Librarian as a separate post, but for a professional librarian with computing experience rather than for someone with only computing qualifications. There had been some restructuring of Library Assistant grades, but this was not a direct result of automation:

> Library Assistant grades might bear looking at and it might be restructured, but it is nothing to do with automation.

Most of the changes in work roles were linked to those most closely involved with the introduction of the system and as such were probably temporary changes. The main change was that much of the routine clerical work was no longer necessary. Some felt that the secretarial staff would now have more power within the library, unless the professional staff made strenuous efforts to learn how to use the system to its full potential:

So I say 'I want all the information about this' and they say 'sorry you can't have it' and you can't contradict that unless you know more about the system than they do.

The role of the Library Assistants too had changed and become more powerful:

They will become more knowledgeable than their senior colleagues, but the Systems Librarian and secretarial staff have their hands on important corporate files and can become much more powerful.

The library had made great efforts to train all levels of staff in the use of the system so that professionals were able to use the system even it was run by non-professional staff:

I do think it is important that no senior should be in a position that they don't know what to do and a Library Assistant next to them has to do it for them.

Cataloguing tasks had already been allocated to non-professional staff before the advent of the automated system:

Quite a lot of the skill has gone out of professional cataloguing anyway; because 40 per cent are on the database now.

Attitudes to the Cooperative

The University Library's attitude to the Cooperative was almost that of the close family member especially as they were located 'just down the road' from the main offices and had been one of the original three members of the Cooperative, but were realistic about the benefits and disadvantages of being part of a Cooperative. They admitted that there would have to be an 'amazing reason which we can't think of' to make them leave. It was not surprising that they expressed no resentment about standardization or loss of control and autonomy, because they had participated in setting the standards in the first place:

It is fine at the moment, but the balance may change to our disadvantage. At the moment it is just the right size, the right balance. If they became more or less successful it might not be so good for us.

They participated fully in the User Groups and, like all other libraries, recognized that the informal meetings in between the formal meetings were the most valuable, and that the formal meetings tended to be dominated by one or two vociferous individuals. Despite their privileged status they seemed to suffer in the same way when it came to getting the Cooperative to amend their system or develop particular modules:

> The biggest disadvantage is that if you have asked for something that not everybody wants then you become bottom of the heap for getting things done.

In contrast the library had such a close relationship with the Cooperative they had participated in working parties designing some of the modules which led to an element of customization to their own requirements. Compared to some of the other members their criticisms were mild. As they were located so near to head office they were able to obtain immediate help with problems, a service not available to more distant members:

> I suspect we are fortunate because we are sitting on top of them. We also meet socially and this helps relationships.

On the whole they were very satisfied with the user support they had received:

> In general we get the answers needed and are happy with the level of help we receive.

They were very positive about the future of the Cooperative and had no doubts about them moving to a more commercial stance:

> I would have thought that they have the lion's share of the business now ... they have the advantage of the database and they have the lion's share of influence at government level. I would like them to be more commercially oriented, and wouldn't mind if they expanded abroad.

Summary

1 The library was one of the largest academic libraries in the country still to be running manual issue systems.
2 As the existing systems were so overloaded there was practically no opposition to automation.
3 There was a new University Librarian who drove the automation project from the top.
4 The Systems Librarian was a professional librarian with computer experience and had worked for the Cooperative.
5 Both users and librarians were enthusiastic about the new systems.

6 The new systems allowed the emphasis to shift to Reader Services from Technical Services.

7 The Library Assistants had become more powerful.

8 All staff had received training in using the system.

9 Cataloguing was done by non-professional staff.

10 They felt like a close family member of the Cooperative and found it difficult to imagine leaving.

11 They were enthusiastic about the Cooperative continuing to expand and become more commercial.

CONCLUSIONS

The Cooperative was in a competitive market, selling specialized library computer systems. It had the advantages of the cooperative structure and the central database to which all members had access for cataloguing. The company had gone through a period of rapid growth and was at a decision point: should they continue expanding and become more commercial, or should the company spend more time consolidating its success and making sure the existing members were happy?

The computer systems installed in the individual libraries and linked to the central bibliographical database through the network allowed members to automate all their housekeeping systems and share data permitting considerable economies of scale. It also allowed the library to spend more time on reader services because of the reduced paperwork. The centralized cataloguing system meant much more efficient stock control.

Minicomputers were installed in each member library and ran the loan system, book acquisitions, serials, and OPAC. These minicomputers were linked by a WAN to the central mainframe at the head office of the Cooperative, which held the huge bibliographical database. This central database was used for cataloguing. As member libraries acquired stock, the titles were checked in the central database and, if present, a local record was directly downloaded on to the library catalogue. The systems needed constant upgrading as business increased. Some libraries found it difficult to obtain enough funding from the parent institution for a computer with sufficient capacity. The library itself retained control over most of their operations, but cataloguing became centrally standardized.

Similar systems were installed into the five member libraries studied but had different consequences due to a variety of reasons. These ranged from the type of library, the distance from the centre of the Cooperative, the influence of the Chief Librarian, the status and experience of the systems librarian, the size of the system chosen and the funding available to the library from the parent institution. Despite these differences, in general the computer network systems were successful, eliminated considerable low-level administrative work and allowed economies of scale. The image of the libraries became much more professional and respected within the parent institution.

The Cooperative provided training for staff using the system, but the members varied in their assessment of its effectiveness. After-sales support and upgrading advice was freely available. The amount of support varied according to the distance away from the centre of the Cooperative and the size of system chosen. The Cooperative's development staff were a mixture of professional librarians and computer personnel, so the systems were well designed for library requirements.

The computer systems had initiated some changes in work roles. The Systems Librarian and Library Assistant posts grew in importance within the library. The number of professional cataloguers decreased as the availability of cataloguing data from the central database enabled non-professionals to catalogue stock. The emphasis within most libraries shifted from technical services to reader services, from administration to customer satisfaction.

There were minor changes in structure. The establishment of the Systems Librarian created a new post in most libraries and in some the Library Assistant post had been upgraded. The cataloguing department had disappeared in many libraries, and in one the whole technical services function had been broken up and distributed to reader services sections. Some Chief Librarians felt that they had lost some autonomy and control to the Cooperative's central organization, but they were in the minority.

The whole question of the balance between the autonomy of the individual libraries and the central control of the Cooperative through the database and setting priorities for the development of systems was unresolved at the time of the study. The Cooperative had to develop mechanisms for allowing local control as well as providing members with democratic representative structures so they could influence the future of the Cooperative.

5

GENERAL INSURANCE
A network linking branches and
head office in insurance

SUMMARY AND LESSONS

The company was founded in 1972, and had established a strong position in its market. That was becoming increasingly competitive, and the management began a process of changing the way the business operated so that it was more customer-focused and responsive to new needs. Branches were given greater autonomy over many aspects of performance, and were to be supported in this by a computer network linking branches and Head Office, based around a powerful Policy Management System (PMS). E-mail had also been introduced.

- The branch autonomy policy was not at first supported by all Head Office Managers, and aspects of policy (such as auditing) conflicted with branch autonomy. The computer system was also felt to have many features more suited to Head Office than to the autonomous branches. Branch Managers at that time did not feel clear what was expected of them.
- The network system had been intended to provide better management information at all levels, and to give customers a more effective service.
- The monthly reporting system was regarded as a good tool which helped Branch Managers to identify problems and opportunities, understand business trends, and take timely and appropriate action.
- The main complaints about the computer system at the time of the study concerned the number of complex, unexplained and unused reports, screen displays which were difficult to interpret, and the inadequacy of stored information on commercial policies – branches still depended on paper files.
- The increased availability of branch performance information had made branch management more participative, with staff becoming more involved in planning and problem solving.
- Branch Managers felt that they received from Head Office groups too

many requests for information, which increased the administrative load on Branch Management and other staff, but did not affect branch performance.

- The dialogue between systems development staff and branch staff, necessary for the development of useful management information and customer service tools, was not managed effectively, with poor contact between system and branch staff.

- Branch staff felt that they wasted considerable time keying information that was not used into the computer system.

- The increased availability of branch performance information improved understanding between branch and other levels of management. Discussions were based on figures, not 'feel'.

INTRODUCTION

This case illustrates the evolution of an organization and its technology over more than a decade. The organizational and technical changes were introduced in response to competitive pressure, but it is clear that there were differences of view within the organization about what that response should be. Branch managers were therefore sometimes receiving conflicting signals about where to concentrate their efforts, and the computer systems received a mixed response.

BACKGROUND

At the time of the study, General Insurance was an Australian insurance company which had grown rapidly both in the volume and in the types of business handled. The company had opened for business in 1972 and offered policies both to individuals and to businesses, policies being sold through a network of branches. By 1987 there were eighteen branches, and these were planned to develop the corporate image and improve competitive advantage. Branches were located where possible in or close to major shopping centres, and were well decorated and furnished. A strategy to give branch managers greater autonomy was instituted during the early 1980s, supported by heavy investment in computer systems at Head Office and in the branches.

Between 1981 and 1984, management accepted that there had been a comparative lack of emphasis on the customer. The pressures which attracted management attention had concerned internal administrative changes and developments. Since 1984 the company had become considerably more sales and marketing driven, with a clearer recognition of the importance of the client, and the need to introduce and actively to sell new products.

The company had followed a policy of product diversification, and premium income had risen strongly. In 1987 it employed about 560 people, about 70 per cent of whom were under 32 years of age. By then it had issued about 250,000 policies, mainly in the domestic and motor vehicle area. During this period the company strove to build its corporate image, and management worked hard to make the company a household name.

There were five assistant general managers, and a deputy general manager who reported to the general manager. Activities in the branches were coordinated at head office by the branch sales division, headed by the Assistant General Manager (AGM) for general insurance. This division also included staff working on product development and supporting services. Figure 5.1 shows the general structure of the company in 1988.

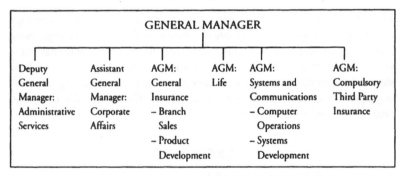

Figure 5.1 Structure of General Insurance

Throughout the 1980s the role of branches was redefined and expanded so that they could offer customers a total insurance service, instead of operating simply as sales outlets under strict head-office guidelines. At the same time, some branches had begun to handle the large commercial customers, whose business was more competitive and potentially profitable. Greater branch autonomy became necessary, and was encouraged by senior head-office management, and by the mid-1980s the branches had developed into profit centres. The employee handbook stated:

> Each branch is the front-line contact with our existing and prospective policy holders. Branches operate autonomously so that the particular needs of each area can be identified. Branch managers play an important role in budget planning, so that the targets set are achievable and performance can be measured against the final result.

The job of the Branch Manager prior to the decentralization programme had been mainly administrative, with no control over budgets, targets or business planning. Traditionally, managers working in the insurance industry thought of themselves as providing a valuable professional service to the local community. They spoke the language of 'writing business' for 'clients'. The language of 'selling' and 'products' and 'customers' was not part of that professional image. Both these languages were now used in the company. By 1987, managers had considerable influence on the profitability of their branches. They could accept new business on their own initiative, write commercial risks, and had some latitude on the rates charged in order to get new business. They were writing their own business plans, and setting their own revenue and expense budgets. Their autonomy was limited, however, with respect to premium setting, capital expenditure and staffing, which had to be approved at Head Office.

A member of head office staff said:

> we want Branch Managers to feel that they are running their own business, preparing their own business plan, budgets and sales strategies, with local responsibility for profit and performance.

Branch Managers were expected to analyse their own market, claims, loss ratios and other key aspects of their business, and they had been given more computer-generated information and reports to support this shift in policy and help them in their new responsibilities.

The new sales orientation also meant that Branch Managers had to develop new skills to enable them to move effectively out from the branch office, to relinquish their direct staff supervision function, and to become active salesmen with a visible presence in the local community. They thus increasingly became field workers, servicing in particular the needs of their large commercial clients, generating new business, and being more personally visible and known to the local area serviced by the branch.

These developments had different impact on metropolitan and country branches. The metropolitan branches serviced larger urban populations, covered geographically smaller areas, employed more staff, and could employ more specialized staff. The Branch Manager in this environment spent most of the time in the branch, and did not have far to travel to meet existing or potential clients.

The country branches in contrast generally had lower volumes of business, serviced smaller and significantly more widespread rural populations, employed fewer staff, and had no specialized staff. The country Branch Managers spent more time travelling around their area, reviewing existing business and looking for new clients, particularly in the commercial field.

As they had no specialist staff to cover particular products, they were expected to know more and to do more.

Branch Managers were expected to delegate aspects of their traditional administrative functions to the superintendents in their branches, and were expected to involve other branch staff in business planning and develop a genuinely participative management style which involved all their staff in the target setting and action planning process.

Head Office staff felt that, although senior managers seemed to endorse the new sales and results-oriented approach, the full implications of these changes in corporate culture had not been understood and accepted. Some staff felt that the policy of increasing branch autonomy was not supported by all of the assistant general managers, and that at least one assistant general manager resisted this change. Branch managers too sensed this ambivalence on the part of senior management, which was reinforced by other controls on branch management. The sales orientation encouraged the branch managers to pay less attention to administrative detail in running the branch, but in terms of branch auditing, this was still regarded as an important facet of the job.

This created a conflict of interest for branch managers. Where they had adopted the new approach enthusiastically, with less attention to traditional administration, they had on occasion received unfavourable monthly audits. These audits encouraged an emphasis on branch administration, perhaps at the expense of the more proactive, visible component of their work. The internal auditor reported to the general manager, pulling a lot of required information from the computer system, and examining whether branch management procedures as laid down in the company's manuals had been followed.

One member of the head office staff expressed a view that was generally felt:

> We need to give branch managers a clearer specification of senior management expectations. We haven't necessarily told them that.

Head Office unanimously appreciated that branch managers had come under increased pressure as a result of the shift in emphasis to sales and results. This was evident from the views expressed by various members of Head Office staff:

> I think it has made the branch manager's job more difficult. They used to sell insurance and keep their people in line. There was much less emphasis on long-term planning. But the computer system enables them to do that. They possibly had more personal involvement

in the business than they have now. They are more deskbound, with more piles of paper, under more pressure, and the business is more competitive.

But the process of change has been initially stressful. From the end of this year, the technology will all be in place; skills should be developed and proficiency established. Pressure has come from the learning process, and should be temporary, not a permanent feature of the job.

Most Branch Managers felt that their job had become more demanding. A metropolitan Manager, for example, said that:

> The job has become more demanding from an administrative point of view. I have had to cut the time I spend with customers by 50 per cent. A lot of my time, is taken up dealing with one of my agents. That's very time consuming, but then he is a customer and has big potential. Previously I spent about 20 per cent of my time with customers. Now that's down to 5 per cent.

The same manager, while appreciating the importance of the emphasis on business planning, felt that the new systematic approach he was expected to take to budgeting and to business and staff development was considerably more time consuming. But another metropolitan Branch Manager expressed a contradictory sentiment:

> There has been a shift in the Branch Manager's job objectives, and these changes have made it easier for me as a manager to meet my primary objective, which is to manage the branch. I need to monitor performance, and ensure effective operation. I also have to promote the image of the Commission in a manner acceptable to the local community. I think the Branch Manager is now taking a step backwards, delegating hands on responsibility. We talk responsibility and accountability now, and a lot of that can be pushed down to the superintendents.

This view of the need for client contact was supported by a country Branch Manager:

> We have had a shift in emphasis towards sales. We now put as much emphasis in that direction. A lot of my time is spent looking at new markets, and I am more out and about. We are looking particularly at commercial business. I have a clerk does a lot of administration – large slice. I am more of an 'up front' person, out and about. A lot of

branches have an inspector who does this. I haven't got one, so I do this myself. Over the last year, I have probably spent about 20 per cent of my time out of the office. Over the last two or three months, and into next year, I expect to spend 75 per cent of my time out of the office in selling and marketing. The other 25 per cent will be devoted to staff, claims, and other administration.

This attitude was widely shared. Another Manager commented:

I am happy about the shift away from the administrative tie-up. Now I can get out among the community. I have had several years of this and I find it quite enjoyable. I think the Commission had lost sight of where the business is; it's all with the customer.

The move towards a results-oriented role for branch managers was not triggered by computing developments. But the new direction was supported by computer-generated information that helped branch managers to understand the operation of their business more fully and thus to run their branches autonomously.

Summary

1 The company operated in the insurance market, which was highly competitive.
2 The company had grown rapidly by opening new branches, whose managers were traditionally concerned mainly with supervising staff and administering company policy.
3 There were significant differences in the roles of managers in city and country branches.
4 In the mid-1980s the company began to place more emphasis on customer service, and introduced a policy of greater branch autonomy, so that the branches operated more as autonomous profit centres.
5 Managers were therefore expected to spend less time in the office supervising staff, and more time with major clients.
6 This change in emphasis was not fully reflected in other policies, such as branch audit, which reflected traditional priorities – there was ambiguity in implementing the new policy.
7 Branch managers felt under greater pressure to perform, and to learn new skills.
8 This change was supported by enhanced computer systems.

THE NETWORK SYSTEM

The first computer system had been used when the company was created. Initially the system was based on a data processing facility within the parent organization, though in 1976 the company acquired its own system – a Honeywell mainframe. All existing software and systems were transferred to the new machine with only minor coding changes.

Processing was done in batches with paper Flowing to a central point for keying into the system. This meant that documentation was up to a month behind, and few useful statistical analyses were produced, and even less management information. In response to these problems a review of systems was undertaken, and management decided to upgrade its computer facilities.

By 1987 the company had a computer suite at head office, which employed sixteen people. This section was the responsibility of the assistant general manager for systems and communications, who reported directly to the general manager. The company was one of the first organizations in Australia to recognize the strategic importance of computing systems in this way.

The company had also started to develop a networked system, and by 1987 there were approximately 400 terminals in use. In some branches, the 'penetration ratio' (of terminals to staff) was one to one. Computer literacy was high, the network was growing, and was being reviewed and updated constantly. These systems were built around a policy management system (PMS) package, which covered almost every aspect of operations, from new business to payments, through standard statistics, claims, renewals, and so on. It was used both to store details of individual customers and to provide regular management information.

The PMS package was powerful. But management assessment of its effectiveness was mixed. Some regarded it as an excellent management tool while others saw it as poor and inappropriate for the business. The systems division in 1987 was aware of these perceptions, and was trying to reduce the problems.

With PMS a full client record could be retrieved by keying the policy number and customer number. This reduced the time spent on correspondence, and saved a lot of wasted time and frustration searching for information. Some branches also had their own personal computers, which were made available provided the branch could make a good case for them and had staff with the skills to use them. Computer literacy was high in the company.

The monthly reporting system revealed in detail where expenses were being incurred, and where revenues and profits were coming from. It showed market share, and where it was being gained and lost. In the latter half of 1987, a new report was produced, comparing branch performances on the basis of a number of key criteria. This was supported by a series of individual reports examining the performance, productivity and profitability of each branch in detail, including other statistics on, e.g. staffing and absenteeism.

This increase in the amount of available useful information allowed branch managers to set their own targets and budgets, and to justify them more realistically, making a case based on experience and judgement, but also supported by statistical analysis of the business performance and trends. The computerized analysis of the business also helped head office support staff and branch management to identify profitable new products, mainly in the commercial field. Branch managers were thus expected to take a broader view of business profitability, based on an increased understanding of the way the business functioned, and not merely to concentrate on gross premiums as they had done in the past.

There was however, only limited on-line access to management information. Monthly reports were sent to branches in various computer printouts. Some useful information could not easily be extracted from the database. Branch managers might have wanted, for example, to run a direct mail campaign to a select target segment. But they could not get the required information on clients directly from the database. To do this they would have had to use Easytrieve – a difficult procedure that was controlled by another division and was therefore not used at all. Most staff felt that the systems had to be easier to use.

The head office branch sales division provided a support function as well as having a management responsibility for branch operations. The computerized management information enabled them to scrutinise branch profitability more closely. This facility was used to help branch managers look at trends and examine future developments, and also to help them develop business. The branch sales division had a personal computer, which was used to set out model budgets, with graphs showing business summaries and trends.

Since the company's branch network was geographically dispersed, the exchange of information between branches, and between branches and head office, was critical to the operation of the business. The networked computing system gave each branch a new set of communications tools in the form of limited on-line information retrieval and e-mail. The latter might be considered an important new communication channel in this context, considering the time involved in sequentially telephoning eighteen branches in order to give or request the same information in each case. E-mail thus offered a significant improvement in the use of staff time.

With the development of networked systems and the increased number of terminals in branches, a pilot e-mail system was introduced early in 1987. This operated on the IBM 3270 network. It was installed as a 3-month trial, after which it was proposed that the facility be withdrawn, reviewed, revised, and a fresh decision would be taken concerning its installation as a production system.

But some branch and head office staff quickly came to see it as an actual system. They started to rely on it, and to reorganize their work around it. So they did not want to see it withdrawn. An updated version with new features was introduced in August 1987, but suffered from a number of flaws, and was not effective until November. The system was not expected to be fully operational until the end of 1987, and the systems division felt that, 'we really have lost control of it'. The e-mail system had 80 users; new users were allowed to join on request.

Summary

1 The company had been early to recognize the value of computers in its business.
2 By 1987 a network was in place linking head office with each branch, and most staff had a terminal WPC on their desk.
3 The main package was a Policy Management Systems (PMS) which was used for most aspects of the company's operations.
4 Transactions with individual customers were recorded on the system, and it was also used to provide management information.
5 Managers were now provided with detailed monthly reports on sales and other aspects of the business, which could be used to review and set targets and budgets.
6 By 1987, the system however provided only limited on-line access, and this was seen by branch managers as a major disadvantage.
7 Senior managers were able to use the system to monitor branch performance more closely.
8 An e-mail system had been introduced to link branches more closely.

GOALS AND OBJECTIVES

Management policy had long been to support their operations by computer systems. The parent organization's electronic data processing network was used initially, in batch mode, located at a nearby administration centre. That was seen as a means to an end at the time, and was seen as transitional.

That, however, created a longer term problem, as even when the company acquired its own system, it used one which could transfer the data from the original machine without change. Processing was batch-orientated, and the systems were limited and outdated in their capabilities. They were serving only in part the needs of the Commission. Paper had to flow to a central point, a key-to-disk procedure was used to input information which was then processed overnight, and some documentation was up to one month behind. The systems produced very few useful statistical analyses. There was, for example, a customer database with no claims information attached to it – and virtually no management information was produced.

The next step was to develop a corporate plan, with the help of a firm of consultants, and this was released in mid-1980. It provided strong directional statements, and provided what was seen as an effective basis for the data processing strategy. The corporate strategic plan was updated twice between 1980 and 1987, and was being reviewed again in late 1987. These updates and reviews led to some dramatic changes, particularly with respect to branch autonomy and the need to develop a strong management information and reporting system.

The corporate plan recommended a policy of developing the branch network, and the autonomy of branch management. Branches were to become accountable units of the organization, and not merely the insurance equivalent of post offices (which to some extent was how they operated in the 1970s). Before 1980, for instance, nobody outside the Chief Executive's floor had seen a budget. In 1987, Branch Managers were writing their own business plans, and set their own revenue and expense budgets.

It was recognized that these changes had to be supported by computing systems. In particular the company had to upgrade its transaction processing capability, as well as create effective management information systems to support the Branch Managers in their new roles. In the search for a suitable package to meet these requirements, a specification was designed, and presented to several potential suppliers. The Commission chose the Policy Management System (PMS). Most of the Commission's systems are now developed around the PMS software package.

In 1987, the Commission faced a number of uncertainties over the future growth of the business, and over the impact of these developments on the demand for computing resource. Legal changes affecting the business, and the potential growth in health insurance, were unpredictable. In planning for these contingencies, the Commission's systems strategy was to try not to limit the potential for growth, by developing systems that were too small, while at the same time striving to avoid spending too much up front.

Summary

1 The company had been early to see the benefit which IT could bring to the business.
2 The system was upgraded to support the branch autonomy policy.
3 It also improved service to clients.

OUTCOMES

Branch Manager's attitudes to the new technology by 1987 were diverse, but on balance positive. At one extreme:

> The computer systems haven't really changed the branch manager's job. We still get hard-copy reports which we have to collate and compile manually. It hasn't really helped us at all. Our systems have had no impact on the way management decisions are made. The computerized information system doesn't affect the running of the branch.

> I think our computer systems are disgraceful, and I have given up using them. We have an excellent opportunity to obtain information, but the system does not work in an understandable language. The output needs to be interpreted using a codebook. You can't just read it. I don't have my own terminal, and I have never had one. I have seen better systems that tell you what you want to know in a language that you can understand. I do my monthly reports by hand.

A country Branch Manager said:

> I use a terminal myself, mainly to authorize claims. As far as I'm concerned the job hasn't changed dramatically. As a member of the Commission's field staff, I was not involved with computer systems, so I had no prior experience before the last 2 years. I find that a lot of the reports duplicate each other, the system is not user friendly, it's difficult to understand, and it is not too easy to read. I only use a handful of the many reports which come out.

The system speeded up claims settlement as a Branch Manager observed:

> The system is efficient when it comes to dealing with claims in general. With motor vehicle claim it is now much easier for me to

authorize payment through the system which produces the cheque. Great! Fast and simple.

But there were problems, as one Branch Manager commented:

> We are making more use now of information technology,v. For me personally, the biggest change is that the systems doesn't really talk my language. And it doesn't talk the language of my staff or our customers either. For example, we offer buildings and house contents insurance, and we talk about the sum insured in each case. But the system gives buildings the code '441' and contents are '442'. The system deals with 'exposure', not with sum insured. A customer may ask me about building cover, so I look up '441'. But I have to key up another screen for the premium. There's a lot of little things like this, critical to our effective use of the system.

In the light of these comments, it is perhaps not surprising that some managers had a wholly negative view of the value of the new information system to their function. One branch manager dismissed its use, saying:

> The computer system has not had much impact. I decide whether or not to underwrite something. You can override the system – if you know the system, and understand how to make it work for you. But it doesn't do a lot for us. It is not flexible as a marketing tool. It has done nothing for our communications with Head Office.
>
> There has really been no change to our monthly reporting. We may use more information, but the reports are just the same. We didn't look as closely before at the detail of the business. Now we look in more depth, look at trends more closely. But we still have to do a lot of our own market research. We do it, Head Offices collates it.
>
> The system is limited as a market research tool. We can't get comparative information from it, for example. And whatever data the company has, is not given to us. Product development can do that. But the data is not available at branch level. Could be useful to us, though. And a lot of our hard copy is just stored. I want longer customer histories.

PMS was designed to assist in problem diagnosis and solution, future planning, identifying opportunities, and so on. There was a feeling at head office that Branch Managers were not using available information fully, but that by late 1987, they were 'now becoming more results orientated'. Head Office had arranged extensive training for Branch Managers in the interpretation of reports and in the use of the computer system, and made regular branch visits to reinforce this. As one member of Head Office staff explained:

> The Branch Manager has been told to 'run your own business', and to expect less direction from Head Office. They have been given local responsibility for profit and performance. They are expected to analyse their own market, claims, loss ratios and other key aspects of the business. So they are given more information and reports to support this, more analyses, and they are using this more fully. They have been given training, and Head Office have organized conferences to allow Branch Managers to share ideas and experience.

There was evidence to show that the increased breadth of information available to Branch Managers had increased both business understanding, and management confidence. One manager in Head Office commented:

> We have increased the emphasis on business understanding – the Branch Manager has to take a broader view of business profitability, where costs are being incurred, where revenue is coming from. Branch Managers can set and justify their own targets, and can make a case based on their own experience and judgement. In the past they would not have been expected to think or behave in this way.

An assistant manager in Head Office reinforced this saying:

> Personally, this has given me the opportunity to find out who's where and with what skills. Changes in branch staffing are all in the computer system.

> Then there was the example of the claims report, where we were able to tell claims staff how to interpret the information they were being given – on lack of movement on claims for example. There are opportunities here to improve results considerably, also personal learning of how to use the information, get a feel for how branches are dealing with the issues, a better feel for the size and scope of the business, and of staffing needs.

One branch manager stressed the benefits of improved access to information:

> The reporting system is very good. Our regular monthly reports are good. There are sometimes delays, but the reports are good when they are on time. It can save time. I write it down, someone else keys it in. It's a useful tool. And if some other report is required, I can get

the information and punch it into the system. We get information on gross premiums, claims, staffing – all monthly.

Access to on-line information at Head Office had made many people's jobs easier, as one clerk said:

> I enjoy it. I like working with computers. The Policy Management System has made clerical work so much easier. We used to key stuff in batches before, but we now put it straight in on key-to-disk. It saves time, and the information is better. We get better information about customers. The system used to tell you address and basic policy information, and you got the details from a manual file. Now it is all on the screen and comes up with a client record. Just key in the policy number and up it comes. Reduces mail correspondence, saves a lot of time and frustration. There is still some paperwork; maybe we can't be paper free. The information is on hand, which saves time.

This meant that staff could quickly check policy options, particularly helpful with the new and more complex 'package policies', and could check an individual customer's claims record through the terminal. This approach also helped to promote 'cross selling'; staff could easily look at the insurance bought so far by a customer, and identify needs in other areas of insurance. It was also possible to 'pull up' a limited customer history, showing business and claims. These records were based on client number, and this could be problematic if one customer had more than one number (which could happen if staff did not check the existing policies of that customer, or if the customer forgot to tell the sales staff about previous purchases).

The volume of paperwork circulating in the company was felt not to be as extensive as it used to be. But in the words of one of the Head Office staff, there had been:

> an increase in the number of computer printouts hitting the desks of Branch Managers. This has led to the possibility of management information overload consuming excessive amounts of the Branch Manager's time. Some Branch Managers also felt that the number of requests for information which they received from head office sections had become excessive.

At the time of this study, the e-mail system was suffering teething troubles. As one member of the Head Office explained:

> Branch managers began to gain confidence in the system, but then

the new version was introduced and crashed almost immediately. We need to re-establish that confidence which may have been lost.

Although the problems were not proving too difficult to solve, some staff had lost confidence in the system. It had been down for 6 weeks following the introduction of an updated and improved version which had not functioned as intended.

Despite what might appear in this context to be the obvious advantages of an e-mail system, the conventional technologies of telephones, memos, paper files, letter and couriers were still popular and indispensable. Many staff still preferred to use the telephone for contacting specific individuals and known colleagues, reserving e-mail for simultaneous transmission to larger numbers of people. A Head Office manager confirmed this view:

> E-mail is bad news. It's complex. It takes time to log in, and it takes time to move between enquiry and e-mail modes. It's not operating all the time, so people have no confidence in it. We used to use it a lot, but we have to phone and ask people if they have in fact received their e-mail! Some branch managers may only check their e-mail once a week, and tend to take faster action on hard copy. We need to develop the discipline of checking the e-mail more frequently, and many branch managers just will not do this.

Two branch managers expressed a widely shared opinion of the system:

> E-mail is hopeless. I don't use it, don't look at it. It doesn't talk to you. I shouldn't have to go and check. Messages should be on my desk or on my printer. It would also help if I could see a sign on my screen telling me there was a message waiting to be read. And with outgoing e-mail there's no indication that the message has been received.

> I have had no instructions in the use of the new e-mail system, and I have no time to sit down and find out either. It has only been available for a week, and I have only been able to log on once. We'd be better off with fax.

One down side of the change was that some Branch Managers felt that staff time was being wasted unnecessarily in providing the computer system with information which was then not used. One Branch Manager said:

> Far too much information is put into the system – in relation to what is used. Do product development need all this information?

Maybe this is their problem. I would like to see a reduction in the amount of information we key in.

On the proposal forms we use, for example, we have to ask for a lot of information, which all has to be keyed into the system. Nice to have all these details about swimming pools and types of air conditioning. But the information is not used. We offer 'Rolls Royce' policies – everything is covered anyway. A lot of the information we need to know to calculate your premium, but I don't think we then need to key it into the system, because it's no further use to us. Perhaps we need to use this as a checklist when offering insurance. But we don't have to key it in. It takes half an hour and needs to be more basic. The proposal forms need to be easier to read, and simpler to complete. A member of staff has to fill this in for the customer – it's too complex.

This comment may reflect a difference between head office and branch in information needs. Several users believed that they or their staff were spending too much time entering statistics, and queried the value of the information, and had no evidence that it was used:

The package provides us with a framework which we can adapt. I think we keep superfluous data, and that sometimes we don't keep the things we need. But our fund managers decided what they wanted.

Once again, comments from two managers in head office reinforce the concerns of Branch Managers concerning information input:

The Policy Management System is now moving to version seven. This has been a mammoth task. It has locked us in to this system for a long time. Takes a long time to key in the basic data – but what is the information really used for? Some is required by the product development areas, but is it used? Input is not fed back to support the Branch Manager.

Are we collecting too much information? Nice to have, but costly to capture and input. Our forms are too large. We are locked into developments taking place outside, through PMS, so we are not flexible and adaptable. Adjustments may take 6–12 months – by which time an opportunity may have been lost. These changes to the systems are too slow and costly – and so in some cases may not be done at all.

Summary

1 By 1987, Branch Managers' views of the systems varied from positive to negative, and were particularly critical of some of the reports they received.

2 Staff at Head Office believed that Branch Managers were not yet making full use of the information now available to them.

3 There was some evidence of greater understanding of the business and Head Office staff had more information on branch activity.

4 Claims could be processed electronically, and policy options could be checked, against a full picture of the clients position.

5 Branch Managers felt that Head Office required too much information, which was time-consuming to key in.

6 At the time of the study, e-Mail was not being used much, and there was support for this view from some Head Office Managers.

PROCESSES OF CHANGE

The limited use of the e-mail system, and the mismatch between branch activities and e-mail capabilities, may be explained in part by the apparent lack of contact between head office-based systems staff and branch employees. One branch manager said:

> What contact do we have with our systems people? We're lucky if we ever have contact. It's been at least a year since I saw one of them. We see the hardware people more often, when our branch sales division ask systems for ad hoc reports, but I don't use that facility. Will the new improved version of PMS help resolve some of these problems? I don't know a lot about it. Communications about it have been low-key, and I don't know what it will do for us.

Another said:

> Do I have much contact with the systems people? Never had a visit from them. The hardware people are very helpful though, very supportive. I wouldn't know our programmers if they came in the door.

It would, however, be unfair to say that their was no communication between head office systems and local branch staff. Head office systems relied on sampling branch experience rather than contacting every branch for every project. As one Branch Manager explained

> I was interviewed for version 7 – for the domestic and commercial working parties. I looked at the reports, and was asked opinions. On

the communications side, this enabled us to pass on information. The working party on commercial was active at the end of last year and the interviews were in January this year. The user representative on the working party [an ex-Branch Manager] came out to the branch to do the interview.

Another factor which might explain the concerns of Branch Managers about the inflexibility of the information systems, and other aspects of its operation, concerns the perceived lack of contact with systems development staff located in Head Office in Adelaide. Only four of the eleven managers interviewed mentioned this issue under this heading, but this seems to have been a widely shared concern. One Branch Manager explained this succinctly:

> There is little or no communication between systems people and users in the branches. The systems people live in their own world. I try to tell them what the branch problems are, but they don't really understand. They are not interested in coming and looking at what our problems are. This may be changing now. But the company still has to develop the ability to let people speak out.

Supporting this view, other Branch Managers said:

> I would like to see changes, if possible, in the way systems are designed. At the moment, the systems are designed and the users are told – 'this is what you've got'. It should be the other way around, with systems designed to meet our needs. And this is made more difficult because it is hard to communicate effectively with systems people. PMS was a senior management decision. No consultation with users. But that would have been complex, with so many different business functions and areas, all their different interests and needs. User involvement would be complex and take a lot of time.

> I have had memos asking about how we use reports – two or three times – but no action has been taken that I know about. I would like to see us get down to really meaningful reports. We never see systems people out here. There is a team investigating, doing alterations, making changes and so on. They're now working on our commercial system. I can't recall having spoken to them about this. They haven't been in touch. We need to look at all our reports decide which to keep and which not to keep. Must be accurate. Must give us what we require; need to discuss this with the systems

people. They have been told, but the reports keep coming. And some just get filed.

Another argued that systems staff determined the direction of IT development, and that this was not necessarily based on managers' requirements.

Further evidence of the lack of communications between systems staff in head office and branch staff in the field lies in this comment from another Branch Manager:

> From my side, these are management tools. But we need to refine the bulk of reports, scale them down into more definite information. There is a lot that doesn't relate. And the system is not geared up for the user. All the codes and the statistical information ... we seem to have been sold a system that's fantastic for systems people but not so easy for the people in the branches. Needs to be user oriented, needs to use our language. The computer system and the manual files should correspond, and they don't. But we have got to use this system.

And one final comment from another Branch Manager in support of this view:

> There are also some aspects of the system – useful capabilities – that haven't been released by the systems people. But staff can find out these, and other shortcuts, just through experience and sometimes through making 'mistakes' which reveal new and better ways of doing things. There needs to be more contact between systems people and the users in the branches.

Summary

1 There was evidence of poor understanding by systems staff of branch requirements, and system staff more rarely seen in some branches.
2 However, systems staff did sample branch experience during a project, though not all branches seemed aware of this.
3 When comments on reports were requested, branch managers doubted if they were used.
4 Some capabilities of the systems were discovered by branch staff themselves, rather than being announced by systems staff.

CHANGES TO STRUCTURE, CONTROL AND WORK ORGANIZATION

The systems had altered the relationship between branch managers and branch staff, and also between branch managers and head office management. Branch staff, who handled clients, had to be able to operate the systems to access and use information. They had developed new skills to enable them to do this effectively, and as a result they had achieved a high degree of autonomy from branch managerial supervision. One branch manager explained that he'd had to ensure his staff could work the system, as they were in constant communication with the customer.

Another branch manager confirmed this effect on staff competence and autonomy:

> These developments have restricted the need for communications between me and my staff. Only if there is a problem. They know their job, and they do it. It has made them more autonomous. The computer can answer many of their queries, or they can contact head office. We expect a lot more from them.

At least one Branch Manager felt that the company's information and communications systems had improved interpersonal relationships at different levels in the organization. The improved, shared information had not only improved communication, but had also brought about benefits in the area of management decision-making:

> Relationships with other company staff have become more harmonious and more meaningful, as the information is accurate and easier to get. Relationships with other branch managers have become more meaningful. We face similar problems that show up in our reporting system. We can spot absenteeism, for example, and compare one branch with others and with the company as a whole. We can monitor costs and try to alter them. We get better reports on branch performance.

> In June 1987 we started to get an individual branch productivity report. We can get a closer view of our clientele, our office staffing structure, who we are working with, and absenteeism, and we can compare this with the company average. So our conversations are more amiable, less stressful. Our budgets are based on precise knowledge, factual information, whereas in the past we worked on gut feel, hunch.

> This brings the branch manager and the more senior management closer together, because we have shared understanding of the issues,

and the same accurate information. It's easier to relate to each other. We get systematic productivity and performance comparisons. Different branches work in different environments, so comparisons are not simple. Now we take realistic account of the socio-economic differences which influence the business mix and performance of different branches. We get better branch profiles.

The volume of information and analyses available to both Head Office and Branch Managers had increased with the developments of PMS. This was the Commission's main computer system, and branch staff did a lot of their own input to the databases.

A Head Office manager said:

We have higher confidence in our strategy, decisions and action. We can convince senior managers more easily with sound plans and projections, particularly with long-term plans. So there is a mix of benefits, including strategic advantage.

A clerk in the Branch Sales Division in Head Office confirmed this:

Managers at Head Office are more confident because they have an up-to-date picture of the direction of the business in all areas, how the business is going. If things are working well, they might decide to reduce staff, recruit, expand, relocate, set up a new branch and so on. Having a true and accurate picture gives confidence.

Branch Managers in turn could see exactly where costs were incurred, as all staff costs, for example, were broken down in detail, so they could accurately cost specific management decisions. They also had on-line access to information. A customer might enquire about a premium and their claims history could be put on the screen. That meant that queries from customers could be dealt with on-the-spot, rather than by a time-consuming search through paper files.

A Branch Manager:

These reports do help me. They are a very good tool. I can look at expenses and see if they're getting out of hand. I can highlight items in the budget. I can then try to explain what's happening. The reports are triggers which set off a thought pattern and I try to analyse what's happening.

The reporting system gives you good indication as to how you're doing in the field, how things are going over the counter. If the actual profit figure is different from budget, it prompts the question, 'why?'. I feel that our premiums are expensive in some areas, but we're still selling. When that sort of thing happens, you can start asking questions. I don't have to rely on my feeling of how well we're doing. The gut feeling is important, but the figures confirm it.

Reinforcing these benefits, another Branch Manager explained:

> The main thing is having information in front of you each month, to see how you're doing, and take action. I can analyse, look at the direction we're taking, and maybe change that direction. It develops your whole business skills. You know where you're being successful. Decisions are clearly based on factual information, not on gut feeling – or you can back up the gut feeling with facts and figures.

However, there was still limited access to information, and this was one of the main perceived problems with the information system. A manager in Head Office explained:

> The Branch Managers now get monthly results – revenue, claims rations and so on – but this has not really enabled us to give adequate results feedback. The systems provide more information to help manage the business. But the Branch Manager has to wait till the end of the month for a status report. He cannot key in to get information on printout. There is no on-line access, though they could react earlier if the information was available. This has not developed as it should have done.

Another manager in Head Office complained about inability to extract relevant information:

> The information system gives me more information which I can use to look into branch profitability more closely. Problem is, I cannot get some information out of the database. The Branch Manager may for example decide on a direct mail campaign to a selected target market. But we cannot automatically go in to the database and get the information on clients we would need to do that. We need an altogether easier system.

Summary

1 The company's computing system had had positive implications for management decision-making.
2 It increased Branch Managers' confidence, by providing them with more information, which in turn improved their business understand-

ing. Branch Managers now had a clearer view of the impact of their decisions on profitability.

3 They used information feedback and analyses as a trigger for investigation and action. They were no longer dependent on intuition (or 'gut feel') as the basis of management action.

4 Customer enquiries and questions, particularly with respect to domestic policies, could be handled faster. There were remaining problems with commercial policies, however.

CONCLUSIONS

The company's market had become increasingly competitive, and management had responded to this by increasing the autonomy of the branches. This cultural change had been supported by a networked computer system, developed by staff at Head Office. The job of the Branch Managers varied between country and city locations, and a further ambiguity was that it was felt that not all the senior managers supported the move to give them greater autonomy: some at Head Office still wanted to retain control. This resulted in conflicting signals being given to the branch managers about their priorities (sales or administration).

There was a high degree of computer literacy in the company, as by 1987 a powerful network had been introduced, with terminals in every branch providing a link to Head Office. This was intended to smooth the task of administering queries and claims arising on existing policies, and was also intended to allow the manager to spot trends and opportunities in the market. They would be able to plan their budgets, and generally operate as a business, trying to meet the needs of their local community.

However the system provided limited scope for on-line access, and it was awkward for a branch to develop an application suited to their local needs. This entailed making the case to senior management in another division. As communication between widely dispersed branches was seen as critical, an e-mail system had been introduced but, although it had been billed as a pilot, it failed to work properly and the credibility of the system was undermined.

Views on the system as a whole were mixed, with some branch managers taking to it enthusiastically, while others were highly critical of it. They felt that they and their staff were having to spend a lot of time entering data into the system for which they received no benefit – perhaps reflecting differences in understanding and requirements between Head Office and branches. Some staff at Head Office recognized that the system was causing problems, and that the volume of paper still in the system was excessive.

Relations between branch staff and system staff was said to be poor, with the latter having little experience of how the branches worked. Systems were seen as being designed at Head Office, and imposed on the branches.

However, the information provided by the system had helped some managers improve relations with other parts of the business, and discussions were more likely to be based on fact than on guesswork. It had helped bring branch and senior managers closer together, with a shared understanding of the issues.

LINKS WITH STRATEGY

The increased availability of information had significant advantages, in supporting the strategy of branch autonomy:

> We are no longer just looking at premiums in the trend; now we have to look more closely at profitability. The aim is to concentrate on the more profitable areas of business. Computerized analyses helps us to identify profitable new product development, mainly in the commercial field. We think we have good prices, good products. And the sales force has good support.

A manager in head office explained other strategic advantages:

> Target marketing. With statistical information, we can identify more profitable markers. New products are a direct result of that. We identify areas of concern and turn them around (refuse or load a premium in an individual case for example). We can decide more clearly whether we want business and on what terms. We can look at the implications of our actions more closely.

> We are currently carrying a loss over 3 years on our health business, but projecting profits on investments in the future. Our personal computer-based projections enable us to compare with actual results, and enable us to decide action more quickly. In the past, it was more difficult to see the trends, and we reached decisions more on gut feeling.

Summary

1 The increased volume of information encouraged the spread of under-standing across Branch staff who now had the opportunity and ability to become involved in problem solving and business planning, consistent with the branch autonomy policy.

2 It enabled the Branch Managers to be more active in deciding where to target their effort.

3 Branch Managers were frustrated by the lack of easy access to some important and useful information held in the computing system.

4 The Branch autonomy was also undermined by auditing procedures, which were themselves enhanced by the computer network.

6

THE SCOTTISH AMBULANCE SERVICE

Computerization and rationalization in a public service

SUMMARY AND LESSONS

The Service provided ambulance services throughout Scotland, and had experienced a steady growth in demand. Financial constraints prompted a search for ways to economize, and this led to the decision to reduce substantially the number of control rooms, so that each would now allocate vehicles to tasks over a much wider area. At the same time, management and staff were aware of rising public expectations about the quality and timeliness of the Service provided. Finally, the hospitals which provided the bulk of the work were themselves undergoing major change, and there was no longer any certainty that they would look to the Service for their ambulance requirements.

A range of technological changes were made to enable the Service to support these new demands, including a control-room rebuilding programme, a new radio system, a computer-aided route planning system, a computer-aided command and control system, and an expanded management information system.

The systems were intended to fit together as a package, but delays and changes in circumstances meant that the projects were implemented over a longer period than originally intended. Many aspects of the system worked well and met expectations, but others continued to cause difficulties.

The main lessons learnt during this process were that:

- the scale and novelty of the planned changes were under-estimated at the start, and the project was also affected by unexpected external changes – these delayed the project, and increased the strain on staff and managers;
- the objectives and priorities of some parts of the project changed as new circumstances arose, and these had implications for costs and staffing;
- technical problems delayed the radio system, although the centralization of control rooms which it was meant to support went ahead on schedule –

the political obstacles were overcome more rapidly than the technical ones;
- the new management information system was based on networking an established financial management package, but it did not meet the needs of middle managers operating in a more commercial environment;
- it became clear during the project that an unexpected benefit of the computer system for planning routine journeys would be the ability to generate information for hospitals on the sources and costs of such provision – which could give the service an advantage over potential competitors;
- the most visible change in work was that control room staff spent more time keying data – which some managers saw as distracting them from their primary tasks of supporting current operations, suggesting that more effort was necessary to clarify the new roles after an accumulation of changes;
- the routine planning system was initially implemented in different ways in the separate control rooms which aided acceptance – but an enhanced version was expected to be applied in a more uniform manner throughout the service;
- there was no explicit discussion of these different experiences between the control room managers, and it was realized that an opportunity for learning had been lost – this was being addressed in later projects, to spread best practice;
- the organization had a strong commitment to training, and this was reflected in the resources committed to this in support of these changes;
- early experience in the project showed the need for both strong central project management, and for wider consultation with staff affected: both features were more visible in later phases, and were felt by management to have assisted acceptance;
- the command and control system deliberately retained the human element, and was introduced in stages to ensure credibility and acceptability;
- the opportunity was taken to modify quite radically the jobs and responsibilities of control room staff – made possible, but not determined, by the available technology.

INTRODUCTION

This case study reviews a programme of major changes in the Scottish Ambulance Service. There have been major changes in the Service and among its customers – and these have been accompanied by heavy investment in new technologies. The case demonstrates clearly the complexity which major linked projects can experience, and how technical and organizational considerations need to be seen together. It also shows the dangers of using networks to expand a system to new users when the original system had not been designed with their needs in mind. It also shows how a lengthy project offers opportunities for learning to take place, and how managers were beginning to use those opportunities.

BACKGROUND

The Scottish Ambulance Service is a division of the Common Services Agency (CSA), one of the operating units of the National Health Service in Scotland. The Management Executive of the NHS in Scotland is responsible to the Scottish Home and Health Department (SHHD). The Ambulance Service fulfilled two functions – the provision of an accident and emergency service (A & E) on a 24-hour basis, and the daytime patient transport service (PTS), mainly conveying patients between their homes and a hospital clinic or out-patient department.

Demand for both services was growing: A & E calls in 1992–93 were 7.2 per cent up on the previous year, and PTS journeys had risen by 3.7 per cent. Meeting nationally established ('Orcon') standards for the quality of the A & E service was a major concern of management. For emergencies, the standards varied according to population density – e.g., in places with a high density (more than three people per acre), 50 per cent of calls had to be dealt with in 7 minutes, and 95 per cent in 14 minutes.

Changes in the Health Service

On the PTS side, hospitals were becoming more demanding. They were expected to meet quality standards, and the performance of the Ambulance Service affected their ability to do so. They also wanted patients discharged as rapidly as possible, in order to save the costs of an overnight stay – and so wanted ambulances to be available at short notice.

The Ambulance Service was also affected by wider changes in public policy on the Health Service in Scotland. In August 1988 the Health Minister at the Scottish Office announced his intention to introduce competitive tendering for the non-emergency PTS work. A pilot exercise was carried out, in which outside contractors interested in providing the service were invited to submit tenders, in competition with the service. The contract was won by the in-house bid, and while further competitive tendering was not publicly ruled out, the emphasis changed. Following the example of the rest of the health service, the policy of separating the roles · of the purchasers and providers of services was to be expressed in service level agreements. The Ambulance Service was now required to reach such agreements with all its customers, specifying the volumes of work to be done, and the quality levels to be achieved. While in the past it had fifteen Health Boards as customers, there would now be fifty-five self-governing Trusts and Directly Managed Units. In due course these would get money for transport services from the purchasing health boards, and pass it on to the Ambulance Service, or another provider, in return for the service delivered.

This prospect obliged management to look closely at their service, and at whether vehicles and staff were being used efficiently. It also became clear that they would need information systems to log quantity and quality of work done – e.g. on the percentage of patients delivered within half an hour of their appointment time.

A senior manager commented:

> Before the competitive tendering thing started, the ambulance service really had no information. It had millions of log sheets filed away in cupboards, but there was no analysis. They didn't know how many patients were taken to a particular hospital last year, or why, or what it cost. Similarly the health boards had no idea. The consultants booked patients for the clinics and that was it. There was no information on either side.

Existing technology

In 1987, the service used very little modern technology. Ambulances were equipped with an old radio system, and reception was poor in some areas. They were based in 158 stations, and were controlled from forty-one control rooms, whose technology consisted of the radio system, telephone, and paper and pencils.

Some computer systems were operated in the headquarters and area offices, mainly for word processing. The service depended on the mainframe computers at CSA headquarters in Edinburgh for routine computing requirements. The Agency had recently installed a GE Millennium information system to process administrative and financial information from its various divisions, including the Ambulance Service. There were differences in local expertise and computer experience. In the Ayr control a direct computer link had been created with a local hospital long before the present national project was considered.

The organizational structure

When the computerization project began, the headquarters of the service was in Glasgow. There were eight geographical areas, each headed by an Area Chief Officer. A new structure was created in 1991, when the eight areas were grouped into three regions – North, South East, and South West.

A General Manager had been appointed (in place of the former Director), and under the new structure the Regional Directors and the functional directors (Logistics, Finance, Personnel) met as a board under the chairmanship of the General Manager.

The structure within each Region was different, but as an example, the West Region had three geographical divisions, each headed by an Operations Director. The Operations Director for the Ayr Division had two sub-divisions; in one of these the structure was as shown in Figure 6.1:

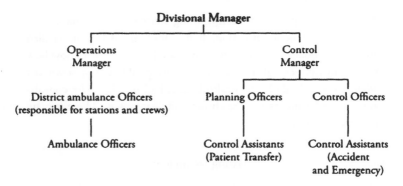

Figure 6.1 Structure of a subdivision in the Ayr Division, West Region

At the end of 1992 the service employed about 2,700 people, of whom 2,200 were ambulance staff. Operations staff ensured that vehicles and crews were available to deliver the service. Control staff deployed these resources to meet demand. The Planning Officer and one or more control assistants planned the schedules of the ambulances dealing with routine patient transport. Control Officers and their assistants handled the emergency calls, and despatched the vehicles. To operate a control room on a 24-hour basis was labour-intensive and there was pressure to reduce this cost by centralising controls into fewer centres.

Finance

Under the new funding arrangements for the National Health Service in Scotland, each hospital trust or unit would have much greater responsibility for managing their own budgets. They were moving to a system where they would be charged by the Ambulance Service for the use they made of it.

Similarly, by 1993, budgets within the service were being delegated to Regional Directors, and then to their respective operational managers and district officers. This was imposing new demands on information systems to support this delegated budgeting.

The quality of service was a matter of political sensitivity when complaints were received by members of parliament about the perceived quality of service. This was expressed by a Control Assistant:

> People sometimes get a bit worked up, and you have to try to calm them down and say you'll be there as soon as possible. The public always expect an ambulance immediately, even if it's miles away.

Apparent delays sometimes received critical media coverage and the staff were aware of public expectations of the service. The service was also seen to be competing for resources with other CSA divisions. The image of the service, and the perception of its needs held by ministers and senior civil servants was a matter of concern to managers and staff:

> We only have to make one mistake, and the papers are onto it in no uncertain terms – and rightly so.

Summary

1 The Ambulance Service provided two distinct services – an accident and emergency (A & E) service, and a routine patient transfer (PT) service.

2 The Service's clients were the fifteen area health boards in Scotland, soon to become the fifty-five Trusts and Directly Managed Units – and their expectations were rising.

3 In the course of the project SHHD announced the introduction of competitive tendering for non-emergency work, later changed to service-level agreements.

4 Prior to the current plans very little technology was used by the service outside of the headquarters, though some isolated computer applications had occurred.

5 The management structure of the service had been changed, in order to

emphasise local accountability for delivery of a national service. The service was politically sensitive and keeping quality up and complaints down was a ma)or consideration.

THE NETWORKED SYSTEMS

The modernization programme consisted of three distinct technical elements, which were combined with organizational changes to alter the services delivered.

Centralized control rooms

A major feature of the reorganization plan was to reduce the number of control rooms, by transferring their functions to eight new controls – one in each area It was argued at the time that this could not be implemented fully with the existing radio system, as it was not powerful enough to reach the whole of an area from a single point.

Improved radio and telephone communications

A new mobile radio system was therefore proposed to improve communication between a control room and the ambulances. The new system would be able to transmit data as well as voice to vehicles.

A second element in the radio plan was to create a microwave trunk system, connecting the eight control centres and the service headquarters. It would run from Inverness to Ayr, with spurs to the area control centres on the route. This represented a significant extension of the radio proposal originally suggested by the Ambulance Service. The SHHD took the view that as well as helping communications within the Ambulance Service, such a link would be usable by other organizations for which SHHD was responsible, such as health boards, police and fire services. As a member of staff at the CSA put it:

> that's a major benefit, and is probably the reason why the minister has approved it so readily. Because for a fairly modest capital outlay, there are significant benefits nation-wide.

Computer facilities

The third strand concerned the introduction of a range of computer facilities. A planning and scheduling package was introduced to support PTS work. All requests for patient transport would be entered into the computer, which would then work out the most economic route for the ambulance to take in collecting patients.

A computerized command and control system was introduced to support the A & E service, linked to the ambulances by the new radio. A control assistant receiving a call would enter the relevant information directly into the computer; since with the new radio the computer would know the disposition of the fleet at that time, it would be able to display on the controller's screen.

The final part was to be a management information system. This would take information from a range of feeder systems, such as a financial package, stock and stores control, fleet management and so on, to provide management at all levels with better information about the cost and use of resources.

GOALS AND OBJECTIVES

The changes were initiated by the former Director of the Service who was appointed in 1985. He had observed that the Service as a whole was not achieving the Orcon standards, and that additional ambulance crew members would be needed to reduce response times to the target level. With little prospect of additional funds from Government, they would need to come from efficiency savings within the Service itself Control room expenditure was an area which offered significant saving, if they could be provided from one control room in each area Staff controlling these larger areas would need to be supported by modern communication and computing facilities.

Another objective in the early days was to make senior officers more visible, both to their own crews, and to hospitals and doctors. By releasing senior officers from control room and administrative duties they could be deployed into operational work. A new grade of control assistant had been introduced who, with the aid of the new system, would carry out many of the functions previously undertaken by a (more senior) control officer. The latter would be able to spend more time supervising the management of major incidents and providing support and advice for the ambulance crew. They could also build closer links with the hospitals. This would help improve the visibility, status and image of the service.

The SHHD who financed the Service saw the benefits differently. They wanted the radio network to be the foundation for a system usable by other functions for which SHHD was responsible. Speaking in 1989, a chief officer pointed out:

The radio needs to be renewed but they're also putting in a micro-wave trunk. To me, that is the lowest priority in the programme. The trouble is that the department has decided to put the spine in first – so we'll be able to talk to other areas before we can talk properly to our own ambulances.

By 1992, there had been some changes in emphasis in the objectives held for the system. Service level agreements, and the growth in the number of hospital trusts, had made better management information more import-ant. It became critical to know the volume and quality of services being delivered, and what they were costing.

Interest then strengthened in obtaining such management information as a by-product of the PTS and A & E computerizations. This was seen as essential in establishing and delivering service level agreements:

> Another benefit they want from computerization is better manage-ment information, drawing together the statistics with the financial side of things, to really try and find out just how efficient the Ambu-lance Service is. We have to meet these standards, but how much resource do we need?

The information was also seen as a valuable competitive weapon in de-fending the service against new entrants. Hospitals were increasingly keen to identify the sources of their transport costs, i.e. who ordered ambu-lances, and the service wanted to be able to provide that better than anyone else:

> We are being asked for all sorts of information to be logged into the system, and so we're having to enhance quite significantly the system we have at the moment. If we can provide that information, it helps our competitive position, by making it harder for anyone else to offer.

Under increased pressure to cut costs and use available resources efficiently, Regional Directors within the Service wanted fast, accurate and summar-ized information, which they could interrogate easily to get detail on problem areas. They then depended on local managers taking action, for which again they needed information on the quantity and quality of services delivered, and on the efficiency with which resources were used. It became important to provide local managers with information which would support their decisions about, e.g., overtime, shift-patterns, or vehicle costs.

Summary

1 A new director had been appointed to the service in 1985 and had engaged upon a series of major changes to improve the quality of service provided, and the public image of the service.

2 This depended mainly on generating savings from within the service – and centralizing control rooms on one location in each area would enable better use of resources.

3 To achieve these objectives it was decided to support staff in the control rooms by computerized systems.

4 It was also argued that centralized controls would only work if communications to and from them was improved, by a new radio system, to which SHHD then added a microwave trunk to link the areas.

5 The objective of the management information system was to provide information on costs and performance. This reflected wider Government policy to introduce market forces into the public sector, to increase efficiency.

CHANGE IN THE PATIENT TRANSPORT SERVICE

Background

The APTC system to support the Patient Transport Service was introduced in 1992.

The traditional procedure was that a general practitioner or medical staff in the hospital requiring transport for a patient contacted the ambulance control room. They either sent a standard form (SAS1), or telephoned the control room, where a member of staff wrote the information needed onto an SAS1. This gave the patient's name and address, where they were to be collected, where they had to go, and their mobility. The forms were filed according to the day on which the journey was to be made. Requests were expected to be submitted by noon on the day before the journey.

The forms for journeys booked for the following day were laid out on a table, and sorted by the planning officer into runs for each crew to deal with the following day.

In making an efficient schedule, planning officers used their knowledge of the area, the ambulance resources available, and the appointment times and mobility of the patients. The outcome was a written schedule of patients to be carried. This was given to the ambulance crew, who then collected and delivered the patients. In some areas crews were given a schedule for the whole day, amended by radio contact if required during the day. Other crews were given one run at a time, reported to control when they were finished and received another run.

Medical staff sometimes requested additional or changed transport arrangements during the day. Control officers met these requests by 'reshuffling the cards', in the light of outstanding requests and their knowledge of where the vehicles were.

This well-established procedure was flexible and responsive. A disadvantage was that all records were on individual pieces of paper, so it was laborious and time consuming to produce management information about the activity, and little information was available about output or efficiency.

Goals and objectives

This was not a problem when the service was centrally funded, and free to the hospitals. But the introduction of service level agreements, each including ten or twelve quality standards, made better management information vital, and required the development of new information systems. Since the hospitals themselves were also wanting more information, the Ambulance Service had an opportunity to protect their competitive position against smaller transport firms.

The Finance Director said:

> We will be providing so much good information to them, to help them manage the system, that it will make it difficult for competitors. We will be using the information system to improve our relationship with a customer.

The technology

This prompted the search for a computer system to support the Patient Transport Service. Such a system, the Cleric APTC, had been acquired as part of the experimental competitive tendering exercise. The Computer Manager at the time was aware of the limitations, but took the view that they would learn so much by using this interim system, that they would then be able to specify confidently the system they really needed.

The most common procedure with APTC was that orders for transport continued to be received on, or entered onto, the SAS1 forms. The information from the forms was then keyed into the computer by the Control Room Assistants, on a continuous basis. Although this meant an additional data-entry task, the resulting information could be used both to support staff planning the following day's schedules, and for later processing into management information about the work done.

At about midday, the computer printed a list showing all the patients to be carried the following day, together with other relevant information from the SAS1 form. The Planning Officer took this list, and manually allocated patients to runs for a driver, by marking vehicle numbers on the print-out. A control assistant typed these allocations into the computer. This then printed a sheet for each vehicle, showing the relevant details of the patients to be carried the following day. These sheets were passed to the crews.

Outcomes

By mid-1993 staff in the eight control rooms had been using the system for almost 2 years; discussions were held with managers and staff in four of the eight controls. In three of these the system was working well, though with scope for improvement. In one significant difficulties had been experienced.

In Control E, staff welcomed the system, though aware of its limitations. They saw little difference from the old system:

> The only difference is that there is no hand written work – that's really what it does. It aids statistical information more than it does the planning, though it does take a lot of labour intensive work away from the planner – they don't have to write the log sheet out again, once they've planned it.

> The hospitals don't have to book any earlier; there's a standard guide of getting requests in by 12 noon on the day before the journey, though there is now some greater flexibility on late orders, because of agreements we've entered into with some hospitals, about the service we'll provide. We accept more after the 12 noon guide than we did in the past. The system is just as flexible as it was before.

Changes to structure, control and work organization

Staff at Control A were also asked to comment on the system. At the time of the initial interviews, the system was being used for archiving data about the requests received, but not being used for scheduling the ambulances. Staff felt they were doing more work to enter data from the SAS1 forms into the machine, but were not benefiting from this.

Under the old system, the crews were given one run, and as soon as they were clear, they contacted control. So the controller was constantly monitoring patient transport requests – and shifting priorities to deal with more urgent cases. So he would be constantly re-assessing priorities during the day – we call that 'hot seat planning'.

Whereas now you have to put the patient transport requests into the computer at 12 o'clock the previous day. And the ambulance crew is issued with the workload for the whole day – and he only calls us when he's eventually dear. It's not flexible at all, that's the problem. It lacks flexibility.

The introduction of the APTC system at A was followed by severe difficulties:

When we put the system in, complaints came in like confetti; and now we've gone back to 'hot seat' planning, complaints have dropped off. So all PTS work is done by the old system.

Although the hospitals were told in advance that they would need to book ambulances by 12 noon, they considered this to be a deterioration in the quality of service, and were not willing to cooperate. Ambulance service management recognized the dilemma, but did not feel they were asking for something unreasonable, given that the appointments were routine ones.

But it is perceived by the GP or the consultant as being unreasonable, that we've put in an extra step. The system requires the extra step of keying the details in, and you need therefore to have it earlier to work on.

In most control rooms staff continued to write telephone requests onto SAS1 forms, which they later keyed into the computer, though at Y, information received over the telephone was entered straight into the system. Management had decided at the outset that staff should not do the double work of writing and then keying:

They had to get the keyboard skills up, and the only way to do that was to take it from the telephone straight into the system. Because when command and control comes along, they're going to have to do that.

The pattern at Y also differed in that they had had their own computer-aided planning system before Cleric, and that they also had a direct computer link to a nearby hospital. Staff in Medical Records at the hospital received information from within the hospital on appointments needing an ambulance. They entered that directly onto the APTC system, through a terminal in their office. This was added to the ambulance database in the same way as their own control assistants would have done, and was then processed in the same way.

The Control Manager recalled:

> The planning officer and myself were very much involved in the configuration of how the system was going to work for us. The system that operates here is the exact same system as operates in the other controls. But how you configure your base information has a lot to do with how you get the plan out. The crucial factor is the zoning. If that is at all wrong, then you won't get a satisfactory plan. It takes about an hour to plan, after the first sheet is printed out. Fairly quick. The planners have taken to it very well.

Local attention to the definition of the system was said by managers at Y to have helped their system, as a lot of effort and local knowledge had gone into creating the zones, and in continuing to fine-tune them in consultation with staff.

Managers considered that staff could plan runs at least as quickly with APTC, and, except those in A, said that staff had taken to the system well. Regional management also stressed the benefits of the management information being provided, in that it provided a historical data bank, and much improved the information available.

Relations with the hospitals appeared to be a major feature in the success or otherwise of the system. At Y, the control manager claimed a close working relationship with the main hospital served. But control staff at A reported a difficult relationship with hospitals, who were seen as unwilling to cooperate, even though adequate warning of the changes had been given.

Summary

1 The manual planning system was flexible and responsive to changing demands for transport.
2 It did not provide any management information – and changes in the business environment were making this essential.
3 Hospitals too were seeking information about the sources of their transport costs, and the ambulance service could gain a competitive advantage if it could meet this need.
4 An interim system was therefore introduced, which would meet some of the needs, and be a basis for learning, on the way to specifying the next system.

5 The way the system was used and the operating benefits achieved varied between control rooms, reflecting differences in local conditions, and in the practice of local management.

6 In all cases the management information available improved significantly, though some local managers felt too much staff time was spent on data entry and similar tasks.

CHANGE IN THE ACCIDENT AND EMERGENCY SERVICE

Background

The primary task was to transport patients requiring emergency or urgent treatment to hospital. As each call was taken, an SAS1 form was completed, immediately altering the priority of outstanding jobs.

The control officers balanced transport requests against the ambulances available. Having decided which vehicle to despatch for a job (not necessarily the nearest one), they sent instructions to the crew by radio, or by telephone if a crew was on station.

One control officer described the job:

We keep information on resources on a log sheet in front of us. It gives us some idea of where they're supposed to be, and roughly what time they will clear. You're getting that information in regularly. Then I radio or phone the crew, and give them as much information as I've got.

So the crew gets the message, goes there, and radio in when they get there. So we'd log that they were in attendance, and after they've got the patient, they'll radio again, to tell me what they've got on board, and I'll relay that information to the hospital, so they know what's coming in. Then I'd note that time down, and then they'd radio attendance at the hospital; I'd jot down that time; and that's basically it, until they're clear. Then they're back into available resources.

If you get a lot of jobs coming in at once you have to work out the priority, and decide who's going to have to wait longer. That's my responsibility. That's a stressful area, when you don't have the resource, and somebody panicking on the telephone. And there's nothing you can do about it, because you don't have anybody to send. You just try and calm them down.

Goals and objectives

Communication between crews and the control officers was clearly a critical factor in the job. That process was obstructed if the control officer was already on the radio to another crew. That prevented the crew passing on their current status, so that control officers were not updated as quickly as they should have been. The radio was itself old and of limited range, and there were many places which could not. be contacted because of the terrain.

This problem had become worse as a result of the decision to reduce the number of control rooms from forty-one to eight.

It was also recognized that reducing the number of control rooms would increase pressure on control officers, as they would each be dealing with a larger number of calls – and reaching limits of what they could control by conventional means.

The command and control system

A project was therefore created to provide the A & E service with a new command and control system. This would consist of a new radio system to improve communication between control rooms and vehicles, a computer system which would improve efficiency within the control room itself, and a link between the two. This would:

- remove the need to complete an SAS1 for every request;
- automatically seek and recommend to the control officer the nearest ambulance suitable to be despatched to a particular task;
- communicate decisions and information between control and ambulance; and
- store activity data for later processing into statistical and management information.

The service selected the McDonnel Douglas 'Alert' system to provide the command and control system, and installed it first in the A control room.

Changes to structure, control and work organization

Control staff now received a call over the telephone, and keyed it directly onto the screen. Once they had enough information to activate a resource, they indicated this to the system. Although the case was now in the system, it remained live in front of the officer: if he or she did nothing about it in 3 minutes, it would alarm, to indicate a job that had not been allocated.

Each ambulance was fitted with a 'button box' which the crew used to record and communicate their status at any moment, without needing to speak over the radio.

The computer processed this information to indicate the resource that it was recommending. A control director emphasized:

> I stress recommending – the essential point is that the controller makes the decision as to who goes. It only recommends the deployment – we don't want this computer deciding. We will keep the human element in. The decision of the control officer will be transmitted via a screen, and the ambulance will get all the information about an incident that we have here.

A Control Officer agreed:

> The new system gives you a list of available resources, and it highlights the one it thinks is the most suitable. But most control officers want to retain the ability to make the decision. While it makes it easier by recommending a vehicle, there may be a valid reason why I, the control officer, don't want to use that one. So I can override the computer's recommendation.

The new system allowed control room managers to monitor their staff more closely:

> At any time during the day I, as the supervisor, can monitor the control performance on my screen and get the sequence of events in relation to incidents. All the actions taken in response to a call are recorded in the computer, until we decide to delete them.

> We'll also know how much time is spent at the scene of an incident by the crew. We may get an ambulance man who spends 20 minutes on the scene, whereas another only spends 5 minutes. So we are going to get comparisons.

A Control Manager mentioned the effect this may have on crews:

> Some of the crews may feel it's a bit as if Big Brother is watching them. But they should be telling us where they are anyway – the system will only work if crews do what they are supposed to do when they are supposed to do it – and I think we are going to have to be a bit firm to start with to make sure that message gets across.

The technology required new skills of staff in the control room, especially a greater emphasis on keyboard skills. This was a radical change, especially for those with long service.

Some of the distinctions between the work of the Control Officers and the Control Assistants had been removed. Either could receive telephone calls, feed the data into the screen, and despatch a vehicle. The remaining distinction was that the control officer still retained full responsibility for the allocations made by their assistant. The geographical knowledge acquired over many years by the control officer, would be much less important with the computerised system, as all physical features which could identify a location had been stored in the system.

No writing was required, as codes had been created for each type of incident. Automatic tracking of vehicles reduced much of the stress experienced by control staff.

The radio system meant that the ambulance crews needed to learn to use the button box to send data on their status, and to receive instructions in text form in the cab, rather than by voice.

Training of control staff involved learning to type at thirty words a minute, and to use the Alert system. A typing tutor was brought in so that staff could get their speed up, and they were able to practice during quiet shifts – evenings or at the weekend. They also needed to learn the Alert system, and extra resources had been provided for training. It would take 10 days for each two-person team, and had to be carried out alongside normal duties.

It had been decided not to start training until the system had been accepted, to avoid the risk of too long a gap between training and operational use. The system was accepted in September 1993, and the Control Manager and two other staff attended the training programme.

Plans were also made to provide strong support when the system went live:

> We'll have the computer experts here 24 hours a day for a month – so if they cannot find anything, there'll be an expert there to show them. And we've produced very simple guides on how to do it. And we all carry pagers. The staff will decide when this goes – it's the only way you can do it. The London trouble has helped slow things down, and that's a good thing for us.

There had been extensive consultation with management and staff in the design and adaptation of the Alert system, and this had produced positive attitudes:

The staff are looking forward to command and control – they can't wait to get their hands on it. My problem is keeping them away from it – they've had a look at it, and it's a superb system. But I do firmly believe it was because they asked the operators what they wanted.

Summary

1 The control staff on A & E work allocated ambulances to emergency and urgent calls, using a manual system.

2 The work was made difficult by the old radio system, and the decision to centralize controls.

3 A computer-aided command and control system, linked to a modern digital and voice radio system was therefore planned.

4 It was decided that the system would only recommend a vehicle to the staff, leaving the final decision to them.

5 The system would produce additional management information about work done, and would allow management to monitor staff performance more closely.

6 The work of control staff would now involve keyboard skills, and the distinction between officers and assistants was being reduced.

7 Significant effort had been put into preparing for the system – such as entering geographical information, and in consulting and training control staff.

CHANGE IN THE MANAGEMENT INFORMATION SYSTEM

Background

In 1989, managers in the ambulance service received little timely management information. A statistics department gathered information on activity and resources used, which was tabulated and passed back out to the service – usually many months later. There was little analysis of trends and comparisons and no attempt to predict demand and its effect on resources.

Goals and objectives

Major changes affecting the service and its customers made better financial and management information essential. Work was therefore undertaken to establish a comprehensive Management Information System, drawing on a range of sub-systems throughout the service. By 1992, the service had acquired about 180 PCs. Many of these were placed in divisional offices and control rooms, usually linked into local area networks. These were in turn linked by ISDN to the ICL mainframe computer at the headquarters of the Common Services Agency in Edinburgh.

The Millennium package

The core of the information system was to be a set of Millennium software packages, which would also be linked to the APTC and command and control systems. The Finance Director explained:

> The big project will be to bring all the systems together. We will have the financial management information system, a transport management system, the supplies management system, and there will be command and control, and APTC. We will need something in the centre which will take the appropriate information from all of those systems and present it as information that is meaningful to management.

The IS and Logistics Director gave some further insight into the background of the Millennium system:

> When we were both at the CSA, we persuaded the agency to adopt the GL Millennium Financial System. So when we arrived here the Ambulance Service was already using the financial management system and we have been developing the subsidiary systems that link to Millennium.

Salaries and wages were still administered by the CSA, and each month the staff costs were allocated to each cost centre or depot. Invoices for services supplied to depots (heat, light etc.) were authorized by local managers, and sent to Headquarters for payment. An interface was run each week, to move the data into the accounts for each cost centre.

Changes to structure, control and work organization

Activity information was collected at the divisional, or control room level, from individual transactions. Every request for patient transport was entered into the database. Information was also entered about patients actually moved, mileage incurred, quality of performance against the Orcon standards and so on. This was done by control staff at night, and also by administrative staff in the divisional offices, which were usually next to the control rooms. The data was forwarded to headquarters on floppy disk, where it was manipulated to produce the formal reports.

The IS manager recognized that this put an extra burden on staff in the control rooms:

> if you have more information about what you're doing, you need more people to handle that information, extract it, analyse it, which is in effect what we're doing.

All managers from Regional Directors down to Operations Managers in charge of a group of stations had access to their budget through a terminal in their office. They were able to examine it on a daily basis – to look at their salary costs, for example, or accounts payable – though they could not enter data.

They also received a monthly paper statement in more detail, which some found more useful. Regional Directors were asked what information they needed to support their work. One said:

> As a regional director, I want timely and comprehensive information about our performance in the emergency, urgent, and non-emergency areas. I also want the variances over time, and to see trends.

Another replied:

> I look for information that helps me keep tight budgetary control. In other words that we are doing what we need to do to meet our Orcon targets, as cost effectively as possible; that we are eliminating unnecessary overtime. So I need information to indicate to me where we may be wasting resource, and where we are doing rather well. We have a huge overtime bill to cover sickness, and I need figures to see where that is happening.

An operations director commented that he wanted to ensure that district officers, who were directly responsible for managing staff in the ambulance stations, had information which could be used as their tools of management:

> there was a wall, and nothing in terms of management information was going through it – so I've been knocking the wall down. What I want is systems that get management information down there.

Outcomes

Several points about the way the system was operating at the time of the discussions were made.

One concern was that control room staff now had to spend a lot of time on data-input. A regional director observed that the primary job of staff in a control was the service that they were giving out from that control. He believed they were being distracted from this by growing data entry tasks. It was also pointed out that as well as the cost of staff time, an equally serious problem was that these clerical duties were obstructing the leadership role which District Ambulance Officers were expected to perform in the new competitive climate:

> The General Manager's big crusade in the organization is to improve leadership, and management changes have been made by appointing leading ambulancemen to support district ambulance officers to be leaders. Now some of these guys are spending hours filling out forms that duplicate information – that's not what they are there for.

Senior managers wanted to be able to see a summary of the broad picture rapidly, and then to interrogate the system for more detail in the problem areas. This was not yet possible with Millennium:

> Once you get in, you're into large amounts of information. Typically what I want is to go to an area and see the total expenditure and then want to look at a station's salary bill. I could wait up to 30 seconds for that. And when it gets there, it gives the first page, which doesn't have the establishment, because it was set up according to finance. What I want is a screen that summarizes everything – but I've got to page down to the bottom and that takes another 15 seconds. I use it for the minimum possible period, to dip in for things I've picked up, and want to be aware of. I need to see the total first on the screen, but I never do.

Another commented:

> It was inherited from CSA, and imposed here. The problem is that it is essentially a financial system designed to pay wages and bills, rather than to help us manage. I think they should work from the other direction, of what we need to manage the business.

The system was not easy to use by staff away from the centre, who used it rarely:

Access is difficult. I have to write down the steps to get into it. I think it is something like fourteen different sets of commands, until I'm into a bit of information that is any use to me.

The information was only updated once a month, which reduced the incentive for managers to use it. That made it all the more important for the system to be easy to use, as occasional users could not recall how to access it.

The system did not provide information quickly – it was seen by one as too historical and too late. This reduced its impact on the way people managed their area. In order to check operational expenses, it was necessary to have rapid information about, for example, a district or control officer authorizing overtime or patient care equipment. This would only become available at that level of detail about a month later:

> If someone authorizes overtime, I wouldn't know about that through the system for about 6 weeks – too late. If I've got to take urgent action, I've got to know sooner.

The Finance Director had organized training for all of the operation managers and operations directors who would be using the system. This showed them how to access the financial management system through a terminal on their desk. They were also shown how queries were written and encouraged to ask the centre to provide information the manager wanted.

Several respondents commented that the system was being adapted in the light of comments and suggestions. Staff at the centre were seen as being willing to help in this, and having new features added was seen as a reasonably simple operation. One manager speculated that different people may be getting different things added to it:

> Clearly there's been creeping development, with individual operations directors getting things adapted. In a way that's a good thing, because you are getting what you want; the information is the same, but the menus are laid out differently.

Some system developments came as a surprise. A Regional Director observed:

> I've now got some new systems on my computer – I've got access into the Orcon programme, I've got access into the road-mapping system, and one or two others. I asked for one of them, but not the others – they just appeared! And I've never had any instruction in any of them.

My secretary has been given a new Windows program on her machine – but nobody knew it was coming, nobody has been given any information on it. My control manager has managed to get hold of a couple of computer screens, and my staff officer has got hold of one as well – I don't know how there was money for these, or who set the priorities – but actually our top priority in the office is another printer; but we can't get the money for that.

He thought the problem was a structural one, rather than a matter of personalities, in that the expanding computer department had not yet been properly integrated with the management process, and that there was a communication problem over priorities.

A line manager reflected on the overall approach:

I would say that our main need is for an information strategy that should have been there in the first place. What we are now trying to do is to link these things together, though as we are committed to so many things now, that it's going to have to be a pragmatic approach. And we really need to examine value for money on inputs and outputs. I can see a way through it with minor tweaking on the PTMIS and the Orcon. My major concern is on the financial information side.

Summary

1 Management of the service had received very little information about performance, but this became essential in the new, more market-driven, environment.

2 Management at the CSA had installed a Millennium Financial Information system, and this was used as the basis for developing a management information system within the ambulance service.

3 Some data was collected from the CSA systems, but other data came from the service's own activity records, putting an extra burden on local staff.

4 Information was available to local managers through terminals in their offices, though not yet to district officers.

5 Managers and Regional Directors were critical of the system, finding it hard to use, out-of date, in some respects inaccurate, and not providing the information they needed to run the business.

6 They acknowledged that it was a good financial system, but felt it was not an appropriate tool to provide management information in a competitive environment.

7 Training had been provided, and the system was being adapted in response to managers requests – but the basic Haws remained.

PLANNING AND IMPLEMENTING THE CHANGES

The project was large and complex, embodying several distinct but related changes – any solution had to be seen as part of a set of solutions, not as something standing alone. The context had also changed significantly since 1988. Moreover, the changes affected the business as a whole, and so had to be managed at three levels – in terms of overall direction and approval through a set of SHHD processes, at national level within the ambulance service, and at the local level of particular divisions and stations.

Since the service was responsible to SHHD, proposals for major capital investment had to be taken through an established evaluation and approval procedure. A senior manager who was at the CSA at the start of the project recalled its origin:

> We ended up with three projects, one on new controls, one to rebuild the radio system, and a computerization project which had various components to it. I found myself driving all three of them and trying to bring them together at an appointed time in eight locations. And if we started now I would doubt my sanity if I proposed that – but I suppose that's what we have done, with various problems along the way.

The procedures for project management had to cope with an inherently complex task. First, the project was technically novel, especially in respect of the radio and the command and control systems.

Second, the computer project was part of a wider change – the reorganization and centralization of the service. The interaction of these two elements was first mentioned in 1989:

> The management structure of the ambulance service has been entirely changed, and so the type of staff required has changed. The Director's moved ahead with the reorganization, and we haven't got these three modernization projects in place to match the organization he's putting into place – on the assumption these things will be there. I don't think anybody appreciated the magnitude of what was being proposed, and its implications. But I have to say, maybe there was no other way – if we'd known all that, maybe we wouldn't have done anything. Sometimes things have to be led from the front.

The same manager also commented:

> The fundamental problem we had at the beginning is that the management committee (of the CSA) took all these projects on board, probably without enough detailed consideration of all the implications. They almost said 'it's a good idea to modernize the radio system, to centralize to controls, and to use a computer system' – and then we've gone away and found what that really meant. And of course what it actually meant was that the ambulance service has had to be taken apart as an organization and then put back together again. It changes everything.

Third, the projects had to take account of what was happening in the Health Boards:

> That is unusual, in that normally any project is strictly within the Agency and usually within a particular division. You have to do more liaising, and despite that the time constraints are still there. I am having to watch in several directions simultaneously.

Finally, the ground-rules changed during the project, as competitive tendering, and then service level agreements, were introduced. Speaking at the time, a senior manager reflected the uncertainty it introduced:

> It's come in almost out of the blue, as a ministerial decision: and it's come in halfway through the procedure. But at this stage we're just having to bear that in mind; we can't assume anything really, we just have to wait and see how it goes.

The mobile radio project was originally intended to improve communications between each control room and its ambulances, in each of the then eight ambulance service areas. The project soon had another dimension added, at the instigation of the Director of Telecommunications, to link the eight areas by the microwave link. While this extension of the scope of the project was thought to have helped get ministerial approval, it led to delays and ambiguous ownership.

Centralizing control rooms had involved careful communication with the hospitals and GPs, a process helped by the appointment of a medical director in the service, who spoke the language of the consultants.

> When we closed down Law, we had to do a big exercise giving all the GPs and hospitals time to comment, voice any objections. We didn't get much response, but we had to give them the opportunity.

Although theoretically only possible with the new radios, most areas had in practice managed to reduce the number of control rooms ahead of that being available:

> The difficulties about rationalization were more about manpower and politics than about actual radio coverage.

Within the Ambulance Service itself, two formal structures had been created by 1989. At Headquarters there was a project team of three people – the Director, the Manager for Computing and Communication, and an officer from the Directorate of Telecommunications. In addition, an established committee of Assistant Chief Ambulance Officers, one from each area, had regular monthly meetings at which computer developments could have been discussed. This did not appear to have happened; 2 years after APTC had been introduced, a meeting was convened at headquarters of the control managers from each of the divisions, as part of the planning for the replacement of that system by PTMIS. It became clear that they had not sat round the table together before, and that for most of the problems which individual control managers raised regarding their use of APTC, another manager had found a solution – but it had not been passed on to the others.

Regional Directors also commented on their involvement in the project process. One with a particular interest in the MIS project commented:

> The Management Board as a whole hasn't really discussed computing. The only time we've focused on it was when we were doing the business plan, and that was when we identified that we needed an information strategy. We've never discussed it at the management board as such. Those at the centre have obviously discussed information strategy in terms of the command and control system, and where that links in. But as far as I recall we've not had a fundamental discussion at Board level on the long-term approach we want to take on our information. That is an omission, and I have tried to say that we should have that discussion.

To build the expertise required for the project, the service could draw on the experience of the CSA and of the Directorate of Telecommunications. Both however were there to provide support to other departments, had limited resources, and were inevitably limited in how much time they could give to Ambulance Service matters.

Later in the project, a senior manager commented:

> If I had known then what I know now we really should have put more staff on the ground. We probably should have had a project

manager for all this, possibly in each of the areas. Certainly on the radio project and maybe on the computerization side, we needed two individuals who were dedicated to it. Because I was trying to keep all the balls in the air, and so were other people, using staff resources who have other things to do.

I think that would be a lesson, it is a lesson that I tried to apply to a number of projects since – don't set off down the road with the project until you are satisfied that you have the resources to manage it. Its very easy to take these things on, and then find you're not getting the staff.

The planning structures for later parts of the project were more formally structured than the earlier ones, and used the Prince methodology. The project to upgrade the APTC system into the PTMIS system (like the command and control and radio projects) was guided by a six-person Project Board, intended to have overall control of the progress of the project. A five-person project team was to undertake the actual planning and implementation, while a Quality Assurance Team was to check performance against standards, and report to the Project Board. Membership was widely representative of the regions and levels within the service, though no representatives of Hospital Trusts or Units were included.

The Logistics Director commented that this need for formality was one of the big lessons of the project, as it provided a necessary discipline to guide the many separate activities. He also drew attention to the downsides – they took a lot of staff time, a lot of paper, and could slow things down if followed too meticulously.

Summary

1 The project was large, technically novel, and critical to the future of the service. It needed to be managed at three levels – national, service and local.

2 It was also part of a set of wider changes in the management of the service, and ideally the organizational changes would have been supported by the completion of the technological changes. The full implications of this had not been appreciated by the Management Executive, and the changes got out of step.

3 The ground rules of the project changed during the project, leading to changes in the emphasis placed on different objectives.

4 Capital expenditure had to be approved by CSA – and at one stage the

project was held up when a change in staff, with a different stance towards the project, led to an accepted case having to be renegotiated.

5 The addition by SHHD of a microwave trunk to the radio proposal led to ambiguity over who was in charge of the project, and perhaps to a problem of financial control. This was overcome when ownership was clearly given to the ambulance service.

6 Careful communications had been held with hospitals about the implications of APTC – though the effects of this varied; and was offset by political pressure in one area which delayed a change in practice which was planned.

7 Project teams had been created to handle the separate projects, though these became more formalized later in the project. There was no formal representation of the hospitals on the project teams.

8 It was commented that the management board had not formally discussed the information strategy of the service by late 1993.

CHANGES TO STRUCTURE, CONTROL AND WORK ORGANIZATION

Early in the project, organizational changes were introduced which were independent of the computerization project. These were intended to provide a dear line responsibility for the effective management of the different parts of the Service, and to reduce the costs of control functions.

Traditionally control rooms were operated by uniformed ambulance officers and a small number of control assistants. Agreement was reached to replace some of the ambulance officers, especially at the more junior level, by control assistants. This would produce some revenue savings, but a more valued gain was to keep more qualified ambulance officers on direct operational work. The intention was that with the appointment of control assistants many of these officers would be freed from routine internal work and would be able to play a more visible public role on behalf of the service.

Another organizational change was the centralization of control functions. This was to enable the total number of staff on control operations to be reduced, with those remaining being supported by new technology.

The number of control assistants grew substantially as the full centralization programme took effect. Some of those in the new control rooms were transferred from closed controls but others were newly recruited and trained telephonists and clerical staff. Their duties traditionally involved:

- receiving and making telephone calls, and writing orders onto SAS1 forms;
- helping the Planning Officer to prepare manually the journey schedules for non-urgent cases;
- answering queries about individual patients, or changing their arrangements;
- preparing statistical records of work that had been done.

The APTC scheduling package was expected to remove many of the repetitive manual aspects of this work. About one year after the system was installed, the effects on the work of control assistants varied considerably.

The control assistants on PTS work still took orders over the telephone, and in most cases continued to write these on SAS1 forms. They then did the new task of data entry into the system – only at Y was this done directly from the telephone. They also had the additional task of entering details retrospectively of patients who had already been carried, as this information was the basis of management information about the volume and nature of the work done. This was seen by some local managers as distracting control assistants from their main task of supporting current operations.

Staff had to spend less time on routine searching for patient details, as records were easily obtained from the computer. They no longer had to write the drivers' log sheets, as the lists of patients to be collected was printed out from the computer.

New operating practices were introduced along with APTC. In A orders for transport had to be submitted earlier, to give staff time to key requests into the computer. In control E the opposite happened, since following an agreement with hospitals on service levels, requests could now be submitted later.

In each control room there was a Control Officer allocating A & E vehicles, and supervising the work of their control assistants. The job was stressful, especially when the demand for emergency vehicles exceeded those available.

> Every call has the potential for a lot of subsequent calls, and a variety of decisions, which decisions can be wrong. To put a control officer in that position where they can take so many wrong decisions puts them under unreasonable pressure. Centralizing the controls will increase that pressure, until we have the supporting technology.

The command and control system was expected to reduce the pressure considerably, as they would need less reliance on memory. Automatic tracking of vehicle was expected to remove much of the stress experienced by control staff, who would also have less need for geographical knowledge. No writing would be required, as codes had been created for each type of incident, but keyboard skills would be required.

As the computer would only be recommending the resource to use, the autonomy of the control officers would be maintained.

Ambulance crews

The work of these staff was rarely mentioned in the discussions, and it was not clear how much consultation has been held with them about the proposed changes. It is possible to envisage their work becoming much more subject to control and supervision, if more precise, automated information is available to senior officers on their work load and pattern of movement.

The number of expert IS staff had grown sharply during the period of the project, raising many of the issues which commonly arise in such projects between system designers and users. Several comments were made that IS staff listened to users and their managers, and tried to incorporate their suggestions, although equally the results had sometimes been too complicated for infrequent users.

Summary

1 The plans involved reducing the number of uniformed officers on control room duties, and increasing the number of control assistants, and this change was taking place.

2 The reorganization depended on centralizing controls, and this was largely achieved by 1993.

3 The work of staff in the control rooms changed in different ways – some spent more time on data entry and other clerical tasks associated with the APTC and Millennium systems. Others spent less time – e.g. those taking orders and entering directly into the computer.

4 Control Officers spent more time using keyboards, and less time applying their geographical knowledge.

5 New operating practices introduced locally have affected the shape of the work of staff in the control rooms.

6 Both control and ambulance staff will be monitored more closely as the command and control system comes in. Control Officers are expected to experience less pressure once command and control is operating.

7 Operations and District officers have more responsibility for staff and budgets, and are expected to be using information from Millennium to

help them do so, although most do not yet make very much use of the system.

CONCLUSIONS

Following wider changes in public policy, the service was expected to provide higher standards of service, with limited resources. Control rooms represented a major cost, and a plan was developed to reduce the number of control rooms, and to support this change with a range of technological innovations, aimed at both operating and management processes.

The task of planning the patient transport service was previously done by hand, using information written on SAS1 order forms. This was a very flexible planning system, but it was impractical to use the information from the forms for management purposes. The Cleric APTC system was intended to record and store requests for patient transport, and then sort them in a way which would support the staff planning the ambulance journeys. The information in the system would then be processed and summarized to provide quicker and more reliable information about activity, especially on volume and quality.

The A & E service was expected to meet established performance targets, and was having difficulty doing so. The program to centralize controls would add to the pressure on the control officers who dispatched ambulances, and they would be covering a wider geographic area, with which they would be unfamiliar. A command and control system was to be installed, linked by the radio system to the vehicles.

Very little management information had been available to those responsible for the service in the past, especially in relation to the costs of delivering it. The only significant computer systems had been at CSA Headquarters. A new competitive environment, and the need to enter into service level agreements, increased the pressure to cut costs and use available resources efficiently. A management information system was therefore created, based on Millennium software, loaded onto networked PCs in the Divisions, which were in turn linked to the mainframe computer in headquarters. This allowed existing financial information to be loaded onto the system, before being processed and passed to PCs in the Divisional Offices of the service.

By mid-1994 the Patient Transport Service was using an enhanced package to help plan journeys, and the Command and Control System had been successfully installed in one control room. There were problems, however, with the management information system, as many managers claimed that they were not yet receiving the information they needed, though acknowledging that the system was probably very suitable for those in the finance function. Regional directors and their staff believed that too much time was being spent by control and station staff on data input, when their primary concern should have been the support of current operations.

The project was large and complex, embodying in effect three distinct but related sets of changes – any solution had to be seen as part of a set of solutions, not as something standing alone. The context had also changed significantly since the first inception of the changes in 1988. The changes had to be managed at three levels – in terms of overall direction and approval through a set of SHHD processes, at national level within the ambulance service, and at the local level of particular divisions and stations.

These processes were handled differently, and with varying degrees of success – with implications for other parts of the overall change. For example there were problems of project management and ownership on the new radio system, as a third party, SHHD enhanced the scope and cost of the system. This led to a delay of almost 2 years in commissioning. As the project to centralize control rooms went ahead on time, this led to temporary radio congestion in one area.

It was commented that the Management Board of the service had not had a comprehensive discussion of the information requirements of managers in the new structures, or of how the different aspects of the information processing fitted together. This was thought to have led to some of the unnecessary data entry tasks which were having to be carried out, and to lack of clarity about the priorities of the much-enlarged IS department.

There were different views among users over the way the initial patient transfer system had been implemented. There was comparatively little consultation with users over the system to be acquired, and some users, notably those most distant from the centre, felt the system had been imposed on them. There was a comprehensive and widely representative structure to plan the next system, and there were many positive comments about the benefits expected from the enhancement. There was also a very full consultation process in the design of the command and control system for the A & E service.

Prior to the computerization project, a change had been made to replace many officer posts by control assistants. Staff in this new grade undertook a variety of routine tasks, and the new systems affected their work in several ways. After the changes they spent less time searching for records about individual patients and writing out log sheets. It was also much easier to provide statistical summaries and other management information than it would have been without APTC. Some were entering requests directly into the system from the telephone, although others were still writing. On the A & E work, Control Assistants were expected to work on all stages of the process, significantly raising the variety and responsibilities of their job, though the Control Officer retained overall responsibility. The Control Officer was expected to find the job much less stressful once the command and control system was in operation, and early indications were that this was happening.

The number of expert IS staff in the service had grown sharply during the project, raising many of the issues which commonly arise in such projects between system designers and users. Several comments were made that IS staff listened to users and their managers, and tried to incorporate their suggestions, although equally the results had sometimes been too complicated for infrequent users.

7

KWIK-FIT

An electronic point of sale system in a retail chain

SUMMARY AND LESSONS

The company is Europe's largest independent tyre and exhaust retailer, created by Tom Farmer in 1971. In 1982 the company installed an Electronic Point Of Sale (EPOS) system, linking terminals in the depots to a computer in Head Office. This innovative system has been continually enhanced, and has been a major factor in the success of the business. The story contains valuable lessons for managers undertaking large networked computer projects.

The system was intended to solve the administrative problems which the company faced in 1980, as a result of its growth. It was intended to remove all administrative work from depot managers, cut administrative costs, and improve stock control – all of which would enhance the performance of the business.

These objectives were rapidly achieved – as subsequently were many more which were not envisaged at the start of the project. The system, based on the overnight transmission from each depot of details of all that days transactions to Head Office, also improved control over the growing number of depots, reduced excessive discounting, gave management rapid, accurate information about depot and product performance, and supported the creation of new lines of business.

Some of the lessons learned during this process included the benefits of:

- building the new system on well-established processes and systems, which had been refined to meet the needs of the business;
- directing the initial system towards automating clearly defined and structured administrative activities;
- having taken great care in selecting a supplier to design the system, which was a visionary adaptation of a fast-food system to a fast-fit business;
- a development team which worked closely with managers and staff at all

levels, to ensure that the system fitted established business practices and structures;

- designing a system which was robust and easy to use by staff whose skill was in using their hands for mechanical tasks in the depots;
- giving staff adequate time to become familiar with the terminals, and to be trained in their use;
- setting a tight implementation schedule, which energized the team, and was achieved;
- a clear willingness to experiment, and to change direction if necessary in the light of experience gained during the project;
- adapting the system to support managers in their new responsibilities, as the structure of the business changed;
- constantly searching for new ways of extending the system to enhance service, or to open up new areas of business;
- being a business that was run by a small, tightly knit management group, which ensured a close link between the business and the IT group, and therefore a consistent and coherent development path.

INTRODUCTION

This case looks at a pioneering application of an EPOS system, in a way that had significant consequences for the business concerned. The story shows how an initial imaginative decision helped to overcome a pressing administrative problem, and then led to the discovery of a range of new applications which had not been envisaged when the system was planned.

BACKGROUND

At the time of the study, Kwik-Fit was Europe's largest independent tyre and exhaust retailer. Tom Farmer had created the business in 1971, using the proceeds from the sale of an earlier company. Although now much bigger, the core business in 1993 was still the drive-in, 'while you wait', fitting of replacement parts, such as: tyres, exhausts, batteries, brakes, shock absorbers, engine oil and filter change, and child safety seats.

Tyres accounted for 45 per cent of sales, and exhausts for 35 per cent. Budget depots in Scotland offer lower-priced versions of the standard formula. The company had also entered the fleet market, offering the Kwik-Fit service to, for example, contract hire firms and large fleet operators. Services were delivered to customers through road-side centres, each staffed by a manager and a team of fitters. A customer arriving at a centre was met by the manager or a fitter, and stated their requirement. The fitter checked the fault, and that the parts were in stock. He then gave the customer a written quotation of the cost and, if accepted, did the work immediately. The customer then paid and left.

The vehicle aftercare market was based on transactions which were 'distress purchases' – no-one enjoyed buying a new exhaust. Customers would rather not have been there – and were usually facing unexpected expense.

The growing market

In 1991 the company estimated that it had 30 per cent of the market for replacement car exhausts, and 12 per cent of that for replacement tyres. Turnover that year reached £229 million, and grew to £254 million in 1992.

The aftercare market was rising long-term, with growth in the number of cars. It was also competitive. Two groups, ATS owned by Michelin, and NTS, owned by Continental, each had over 400 depots, and there were many local competitors. To build a dominant national position, the company had to provide a standard of service that would, in the words of the Kwik-Fit slogan, achieve '100 per cent delighted customers'. Factors thought to be valued by customers included, convenience of location, cleanliness of premises, speed and quality of workmanship, price, and availability of the parts required.

By 1992, the operation had grown to 599 depots – 459 in the UK, 122 in Holland, and 10 in Ireland. The customer would notice that there was no manager's office:

> By design our depots are open reception – because if you give a manager an office he will use it – and may never come out of there. So we expect the manager to be out there all the time looking after the customer.

A critical and costly aspect of the business was to have enough spare parts on hand to cope with the range of cars requiring service. Each depot's stock reflected as accurately as possible the types of cars likely to turn up.

The administrative burden

Transactions generated administration – notably to account for the day's revenue, and to replenish stocks. In the early years, the company used a manual administrative system. Records of transactions, receipts, and stocks were kept on paper in boxes and files.

There was a very small central management team, based at Murrayfield in Edinburgh, and led by Tom Farmer who had created the business, and his close business associate, John Padget. Farmer was seen as the entrepreneur, Padget as the organizer.

The centre had originally provided depots and their management with support in such matters as sales analysis, finance, advertising and marketing, training, depot administration, property management, stock control – though more recently, as we shall show, many of these functions had been devolved to the Divisions. The centre was also the hub of the computer network.

Kwik-Fit's structure was described by one insider as:

> a very flat structure, inasmuch as if we wanted to change something tomorrow we could do it – we haven't got a hierarchy that has to be gone through.

Farmer believed firmly in keeping the number of administrative staff as low as possible – with over 450 UK depots, it employed only about 90 staff at Head Office.

Organization and style

The main operating company, Kwik-Fit (GB), was organized into five geographical divisions. Day-to-day management was in the hands of a management board between the main board and the Divisional management. Management throughout the company was expected to be in direct contact with market conditions facing the depot managers and staff. They were expected to support the depots, not to dominate them:

> We're not a big organization – we're a collection of small businesses ... in our company culture, head office is seen as a support operation.

Tom Farmer stressed the key role of the (office-less) depot manager:

> The most important thing in Kwik-Fit is our depot manager. If the computer blows up tomorrow, we will still continue to make money. But if our manager is disenchanted tomorrow, then the computers won't fit tyres and exhausts, or talk to the customers. The attitude of people is critical.

Depots were grouped in 'partnerships', made up of three nearby outlets. A more senior manager, or 'partner', supervised two other depots as well as their own – and received a share of the profits each generated. This reflected the philosophy that staff should share in the success of the business.

These aspects of the structure were relevant to the operation of the computer network, and the scope it gave for central monitoring of the depots:

> The whole computer system is based around the depot manager as king. It doesn't restrict the manager in what he does – but he has to account for it.

A lot of effort went into ensuring good communications within the company. Since 1982 a weekly bulletin had been sent to all staff, announcing changes and events within the company – depot openings, suggestions for improving service, articles on aspects of the job, reports on current problems. A special edition of the Annual Report and Accounts was given to staff.

The company valued fast action – doing things today rather than tomorrow:

> It is part of the character of Farmer that things should be done fast in his inimitable phrase 'I want it done immediately. And that whole attitude stretches right through the organization.

Farmer's philosophy was that since continued success depended on the loyalty of customers, a high level of staff training was essential. All staff were trained to adhere to the Kwik-Fit Code of Practice, designed to ensure that every customer's vehicle received a high standard of service. Training also covered technical and product knowledge, depot management, sales methods and communications skills. In 1990 the company received a National Training Award in recognition of their commitment to training.

Summary

1 The company operated in the car after-care market, which was growing but increasingly competitive.
2 The company had grown rapidly since it was created in 1971, by opening its own new depots, and by acquisitions – its market share was rising.
3 The business was run tightly from the centre, and managers were required to follow precise company procedures in running their depot.
4 By 1992 more authority had been passed from the centre to senior

managers running the geographical divisions – but depots still worked to the standard formula.

5 All managers and most staff shared in the profits.

6 The original formula had been applied to related, but distinct, lines of business, such as Fleet sales.

7 The company valued fast action.

THE NETWORK SYSTEM

The first computer network system at Kwik-Fit was installed in 1982. It consisted of Electronic Point Of Sale terminals in each depot, linked to a mainframe computer at Head Office – initially ICL, but later DEC. A specially-designed point-of-sale micro-computer, known as a Management Action Terminal (MAT), was installed in each depot. These were robustly designed for use by the managers and fitters. Prices and descriptions of all 10,000 items in the Kwik-Fit inventory were held on the machine. The MAT could hold the sales and stock movement data generated by the average depot for about 2 weeks.

The keyboard was clear and easy to use, each key being marked with a system function – such as 'cash sale' or 'stock delivery. Pressing any key led the user through the process to be followed. Details of the stock held by the depot were stored in the MAT, and automatically up-dated as each transaction was processed.

During the day, the MAT performed administrative tasks within the centre:

- issuing quotations in response to customer enquiries;
- issuing instructions to the fitter about the work to be done (in effect, the accepted quotations);
- producing cash invoices;
- recording every transaction;
- recording stock received and/or transferred to other centres;
- recording the hours worked by staff;
- producing, at the end of the day, a daily operating report of sales against target for the depot as a whole, and for each main product group.

For a few minutes each night, the MAT became a terminal attached to the mainframe computer system at the head office in Edinburgh. This originally consisted of three ICL ME29 computers and a British Olivetti 'auto-dialler' computer (based on a DEC PDP 11/34), which controlled the dialling and data transmission functions. The British Telecom public network provided the link between head office and the depots.

The head office computer automatically called each depot in turn. Each MAT responded by sending data about the transactions made during the day to the mainframe; especially on: sales, payments, stock received and transferred, stock checks, and hours worked by staff.

This raw data was processed into management reports for internal use, and into instructions to suppliers and banks. The reports for head office use were printed out early the following day.

The telephone link which brought the data in from each depot was also used to send information back, on such matters as price changes (which were automatically recorded in the inventory details), information on credit limits, and which areas of stock must be checked that day.

The system was continually adapted after the initial installation. New facilities were created in response to business changes such as the introduction of the Divisional structure in 1985. Interactive services, allowing certain types of enquiry, had been added, as had an electronic mailbox system. Sales and other reports were automatically generated and put into them each night for Divisional management, who also had a menu of print reports which they could request.

Other facilities had been added as the technology became available, such as EDI. Major Heet customers received electronic invoices to a standard format agreed between the major companies in the industry.

By about 1987 it became increasingly clear that a more radical revision of the system would be needed, which resulted in a decision to change from ICL to DEC computers at Head Office, a change completed during 1991. In 1993 changes were made to the depot terminals themselves, including increasing the memory from 1 to 4 megabytes, and a larger display, to present more mainframe help information.

Summary

1 In 1982 the company installed an Electronic Point Of Sale system, made up of a Management Action Terminal (MAT) in each depot, linked to an ICL mainframe computer at Head Office.

2 Each transaction in a depot was recorded by the staff in the depot on the MAT as it took place.

3 At night, details of all transactions were automatically sent from the terminal in the depot to the ICL at Head Office.

4 The data was processed by the ICL overnight, and output sent to senior management (e.g. sales at each depot), and to some suppliers (re-ordering stocks).

5 The original system has been continually enhanced, to offer new features in the core business (e.g. credit card sales), to support new businesses (e.g. Fleet sales) and to support changes in the Kwik-Fit organization (e.g. a divisional structure).

6 The growth of the company meant that by 1987 it needed to up-grade the central computer system.

7 In 1993 the original depot terminal systems were still successful, though now with an extended memory and new displays.

GOALS AND OBJECTIVES

The Electronic Point Of Sale system had been introduced in 1982, in response to difficulties the company was experiencing at the time. By 1979, Kwik-Fit was operating in fifty-two outlets. In January 1980 it acquired Euro Exhaust Centres with fifty depots (including twelve in Holland) managed from headquarters in St Albans, and in September of the same year, acquired 180 sites from Firestone Rubber (eighty-one of which were quickly resold).

These moves nearly quadrupled the number of depots although effectively they were still operating as three separate companies. Each had its own Head Office, its own systems, its own coloured overalls – 'a real mess' was how one insider described it. The company began to experience indigestion problems, which affected performance – pre-tax profits fell from £4million in 1981, to £1.6million in 1982. The problems of welding the three companies into a single cohesive unit were proving more difficult than Tom Farmer had foreseen:

> we had an administrative structure that was good for fifty units, but not for 180 units – the whole structure began to creak.

Senior management decided that the only way forward was to automate the whole system, based on EPOS terminals in each depot, supported by a central computing facility. The initiative came from Farmer and Padget, who gave their fledgling data-processing department a challenging brief. The objectives which the Board set for the system included:

- to remove administration from depot managers;
- to centralize administration on one site;
- to allow painless expansion;
- to improve stock control.

To remove administration from depot managers

With the previous manual system, the depot managers had to carry out a range of administrative tasks, which were time-consuming and unpopular. They included checking stock manually, raising purchase orders and sending them to suppliers, writing out invoices and receipts for each customer, filling out cash reconciliation sheets, totalling daily sales and telephoning them to the area manager:

> The biggest problem was at the end of the day, closing the depot at six – by seven I might have managed to calculate how much business I'd done. Or you would cheat and start dosing the depot early so that if a customer came in, you'd say 'what a pain this is, why should a customer interrupt me when I'm trying to do my admin – I must get home tonight'. That was always a big criticism in the company, that people were still there at all sorts of hours, trying to add up bits of paper and send it off. It was just a mish-mash of bits of paper and stuff, especially with the three companies. The aim of the EPOS system was that no paperwork would come to head office.

Farmer himself explained that the system had been designed to take all administration from the depots, so that managers would not need to be concerned with routine paperwork.

Although the manual system was time-consuming, a lot of attention had been given to it – and it worked. This ensured a firm basis for the automated system.

To centralize administration on one site

The company had grown by acquisition as well as by opening additional Kwik-Fit depots. Newly-acquired companies had their own management and control systems, making it difficult to run the company as a single entity. Success had led to a growth in central administrative costs, which the system was expected to reduce:

> The main thing we wanted EPOS to solve was that after the other companies were bought in 1979 and 1980, we had three companies on the go, all doing their own administration – and we had somehow to bring them together and knit them together. We had three head offices.

To allow painless expansion

The depots were difficult to control. With the manual system, area managers were constantly checking that managers were running their depots in line with company policy:

> you always had to go back and do lots of checks on them. We had to count the cash, make sure the stocks were there, that no unauthorized discounting was going on.

They foresaw that such problems would become progressively more difficult as the business grew, unless a different approach could be put in place.

To improve stock control

Stock levels were a critical feature of the business. These had to be sufficient for staff to meet service requests on demand, without the costs of excessive stocks making the operation uncompetitive. Stock control had previously been done manually, with depots physically checking their stock, and placing orders directly with suppliers. This was very time-consuming, and a major aim of the system was to get better stock control.

As another manager explained:

> It's critical to the whole business that every depot has the right stock. You can't put the same stock in every garage, because the pattern is different between areas, depending on the cars people have. We needed to computerize because the information wasn't available sufficiently quickly. There was no method whereby any one person in head office, or at a given depot, could know what stock was in that depot.

Previously stock had been controlled manually, with depots raising their own orders, and placing them with suppliers.

While these were the primary objectives at the outset of the project, others emerged after implementation as the power of the system became clear.

Summary

1 The primary objective of the original system was to make the administrative processes more efficient.
2 It would allow depot managers to focus on customers, since administrative tasks were now handled automatically.

3 It would ensure that managers ran their depots in line with company policy.
4 Expansion would be easier, as depots could be added without extra administrative staff.
5 Stocks in the depots, a critical aspect of performance, would be managed more efficiently.

OUTCOMES

The EPOS system achieved the expected benefits – and many more as well. All administration was removed from the depots, and the three separate Head Offices were rapidly dosed, concentrating all administration in a new office in Edinburgh. Trading practices and reporting systems were also harmonized.

The system allowed automatic replenishment of stock. Sales were converted into orders which were automatically transmitted to four of the biggest suppliers overnight, giving a 48-hour cycle of delivery. By 1991, about 50 per cent of sales were being automatically re-ordered from suppliers through the computer, and 75 per cent of invoices received were received electronically, and paid the same way.

The system had supported growth:

It has allowed us to grow – there's no doubt that our expansion has depended on the system. We could have expanded without it, but we wouldn't have been as profitable, or as streamlined – it would have been cumbersome.

A newcomer commented:

Looking back, it eased the administrative aspects of growth. In 1981 there were 150 centres, which have grown to over 450 in the UK – but there has been no expansion of people at head office to cope with that. Acquiring businesses into Kwik-Fit is a very simple matter so all of this foresight allowed us to grow in a very smooth and flexible way.

As well as building their own depots, Kwik-Fit sometimes bought those belonging to another company. These were integrated by installing MATs and showing the staff how to use them, together with an exchange of managers between existing and new depots. Within a very short period the new managers knew the Kwik-Fit ways, guided by the Kwik-Fit technology, and could resume running their depot.

We run a very simple business. The only complexity in our business is size. MAT reinforces procedures in an easy way without being over-burdensome. It removes from the equation a lot of the complexity which our size and geographic dispersal could create.

The system also provided benefits which were not envisaged when the original specification was set. This was particularly true in the area of management information. The system had been designed to convert the existing (and effective) manual administration into an equally effective computerised one. Once that was implemented, managers rapidly realized that they now had a great deal of information about the business which had previously been unavailable. The IT Director responsible for implementing the system commented:

We totally underestimated the potential for management information; we got it wrong – and that applied not only to the DP team but to the company as a whole. When you switch an EPOS network on, you get flooded with mountains of data. It's live, current, happened yesterday – and you don't know what to do with it all! And you run around in a flat spin. 'How can I organize it? What shall I look at first? I didn't realize that was happening! what's going on there?'. We totally underestimated that, and didn't realize just how useful the data would be in controlling the company.

We were producing tables and statistics that surprised a lot of people. And they didn't know what to do with it: 'I didn't know that about the company' – but all of a sudden they had a tool that would let them find out.

A good example of that was discounting. We always knew that discounting went on in the depots, because we'd all been out there. But we didn't know the full extent until we got the EPOS data. Then we compared the actual selling prices with the prices that were in the MAT – the prices that they should be selling at. And we just about had a thrombosis: because we found that we were giving away about £5,000 a day in unauthorized discounts – about £1.5million a year. And that year we only made about £3.4million profit.

So we brought twelve experienced managers from the depots into the office for 3 weeks, and they sat with the print-outs for each depot in front of them, showing each exceptional transaction. They then phoned the depot manager, along the lines of – 'Fred, see that

Cortina exhaust you sold to Mrs Jones yesterday ... why did you knock a fiver off it?'

So we had them asking about what happened yesterday. That brought discounts down to about £300 a day, as a result of that 3-week exercise. People ask how quickly did the new system pay for itself? Reducing excessive discounting was one saving we got straight away, which we didn't expect to get. Nobody had ever identified this improvement in the original objectives.

In fact we never bothered to quantify the cost reduction, or the saving the system brought, because it was so obvious that we would save money in many areas – that being just one example.

As well as tightly limiting unauthorized discounts, it was believed that fewer sales were lost through stock-outs or through staff not being able to find goods that were in fact on the shelves.

More generally, managers at Head Office now had much more information available to them about performance across the whole of the growing company. For example, the sales director could review the following day how any depot had performed, in as much or aS little detail as required:

The systems have ensured that we have information to monitor what we are about – and every morning I have a daily update. It tells me for the company as a whole, through our major product categories, what we sold across all the depots, their value product by product, and the margin we generated. Those figures are compared with the same day last week, the week to date, the month to date, and the same month last year. And we could have an individual depot if we wanted to, but of course there are limits. It allows us to see whether we are achieving our target margin for individual product groups, or for the business as a whole, and whether we need to adjust prices to keep us on line. That is on my desk before I come in in the morning.

It gives us prices, margin control, and all the necessary monitoring elements. All this information goes to the manager as well, because they need to know how they are doing as well. So if I call a depot, and ask the manager how he is doing, he could press the key on the machine and would be able to say what he sold today, and what he sold yesterday. And that information is important because their earnings depend on how well they are doing.

It also provided daily forecasts of sales and margins against budget for the current month. This allowed managers to see whether they were likely to be ahead of target or behind, and to take remedial action quickly.

The system made it very easy to adjust prices across the whole group – and the effects could be seen in 24 hours. It allowed prices to be set for a particular area, reflecting the competition.

A manager commented that there were certain areas of the business, such as Fleet Sales, which would not have been worthwhile without the computer system. It enabled each customer's requirements to be programmed into the system, giving operators greater control over the work carried out on their vehicles. The company estimated that without automation the Fleet Sales business would have had fifteen people running it – whereas they had two.

Another unplanned benefit arose in 1985 from the use of new systems for data communications, such as a link to the Banks Automated Clearing System (BACS). The software in the MAT terminal was modified to capture and validate credit card numbers. The transaction details were collated centrally, and transmitted automatically to BACS. That meant the depots did not have to bank the credit card vouchers, and the money was credited much more quickly – 7 days from the date of sale. Controlling the batches of transactions down the telephone lines from the centres to the credit card companies was all done by one man. Without automation at the point of sale, and the data links to the card companies, it was estimated that five people would be needed, which would not be cost effective. It also allowed the company to introduce their own Autocharge card. The BACS link was one of several developments that were not foreseen, based on setting up the technical base, and building applications on top of that. The IT director:

> They weren't originally envisaged; we've inspired a lot of those as we've gone along.

The system allowed the company to produce the Annual Report much more quickly, and to announce half-year figures 21 days after the end of the financial period:

> it's just another example of the energy in Kwik-Fit, which the financial markets are invited to acknowledge. The press remark on it, as demonstrating the power of our systems, and the energy of the Kwik-Fit people.

Summary

1 The expected objectives were achieved, and some additional, unforeseen, benefits were also realized.
2 Administrative tasks were removed from the depots, enabling managers to spend more time with customers.
3 Head of fice administration was centralized, and overheads kept low.
4 Stock control was handled more efficiently.
5 A wide range of information about the operation of the business became available, which gave new insights into the company, focused management action, and enabled senior management to exercise tighter control.
6 Additional facilities were added to the original system, improving customer service (e.g. credit cards) and operating efficiency (e.g. using the BACS system to pay salaries).
7 New business areas could be entered, on the basis of the processes within the information technology system.
8 It helped to resolve a basic business dilemma between expecting managers to focus on individual customers, and at the same time expecting them to follow common company standards, procedures and policies.

PROCESSES OF CHANGE

The change was introduced in a way that matched the action-centred style of the company. It was driven by Tom Farmer. In 1980, the company had bought Euro Exhaust, which had developed a computer system to help run the business – indeed this was one of the reasons for acquiring the company. Tom Farmer recalled:

> We had been told that they had a very good computer system, their stock control was good, and all of that kind of thing. We thought we could just put that into Kwik-Fit. When we went down to see it, it was quickly obvious that it was not suitable for the way we operated.

Nevertheless, it showed Tom Farmer what such a system could achieve – and he persuaded the Information Technology Director of Euro Exhausts to stay with the merged company, move to Edinburgh, and to develop a completely new system for the rapidly growing business.

The then IT Director recalled that at the time the main proponents of the system were Tom Farmer and his close business associate John Padget. They were enthusiastic about the possibilities of automating the company

with EPOS and a central computing facility, and telling the IT Director
what they wanted to be done.

Although Farmer knew what he wanted, the technology to achieve this
did not appear to exist:

> It's a bit strange, but I do believe part of the reason for our success
> was our ignorance. We had no computer. Part of the reason for
> acquiring the other business was that we were told they had a good
> computer system. Just having the attitude was crucial – we recog-
> nized that we needed it, we couldn't continue the way we were.
> Management had to have access to instant information, to know the
> effect of making changes on our profitability.

Another manager recalled:

> After the merger, it was decided we had to have something to help
> us. But nobody had any idea what we wanted at that stage. In 1982
> it was just a way the company said they were going. Something had
> to happen to help us out- it could have been anything (e.g. micro-
> fiche readers).

It quickly became dear that there was nothing on the market that would
meet the company's needs. The technology didn't exist. They then discovered a system that was being used in a US fast food chain – and this served
as the basis for developing the Kwik-Fit system. A manager recently recruited to the company:

> There was a clear vision, a simple set of procedures and a simple
> process. Our business is not complicated. I think vision is very im-
> portant: one of the beauties of the system is that it is entirely robust
> and is clearly capable of operating in the relatively harsh environ-
> ment of the centres. When looking for point of sale equipment Tom
> didn't say 'what is available in the UK'? – he went to the USA and he
> found exactly what he was wanting.

He took a concept which was fast food, and applied a bit of lateral thinking with the fast food concept and applied it to our business which is fast
fit. Fast food doesn't have many product lines so they would always have
point of sale units with about forty pre-set keys. And each of these keys
was a particular product. They were able to have a simple operation, only
pressing one button and that recorded the sale of each product.

What Tom did was to take that, even though we have thousands of
popular products. But what we do have is only a few procedures so

instead of products having pre-set keys he made each one of these a procedure. The steps to be followed for that procedure are then shown on the screen.

One asset the company had was an excellent manual system which they knew how to operate, and how to monitor. They decided to retain that as the basis for the computerized system:

> That's what made our implementation of MAT so successful – it was really very easy to put the system into the depots.

Once a development team had been established, the US supplier of the system spent many weeks in the business, getting to know in great detail how it worked, and what information was needed. In addition:

> There was a big think tank or brainstorming session over it. Maybe twenty key people – depot managers, area managers, auditors – all levels of management were involved in it, and asked for their opinions about what they wanted from it. Especially depot managers, we hand-picked them. Not only those with good results, but perhaps also our worst depot manager was there as well, because he had an input.

Having developed the MAT system, the company did a pilot run in two branches – one in Edinburgh, the other in London. The manager did his administrative work in the normal manual way – and then put it through the computer terminal of the new system. This enabled the validity of the system in the depot to be verified. The information was then transmitted to the computer at Head Office and tested, which sorted out a lot of the bugs.

This phase of the project was handled in a way that reflected the company style. Implementation was very rapid. Tom Farmer recalled:

> We decided not to have a long testing period – we'd put it into two centres, and if it worked there, we'd put it into all the others. We went live very quickly. We kept the manual system going for about 6 weeks, and then dropped it off as quickly as possible. What made it easy for our centres was that it was very very user-friendly.

A manager closely involved expanded on this episode:

> The computer people initially wanted to put in six terminals a month, get the information, see if management liked it, and then move on to the next six. Tom Farmer posed the question – 'what would happen if we installed 180 (i.e. in every depot) at one go?

what is the worst that would happen'? We replied that probably 40 per cent wouldn't work. To which he replied 'put them all in – that would still be 60 per cent better off than we are today'. So on that one conversation, that's what we did.

In the event, 80 per cent of the MATs worked first time, and most of the rest within a few days. A few took a little longer, because of problems with electricity or telephone lines.

A deliberately 'matter-of-fact' approach was taken to implementation. They decided not to use the word 'computer', and no attempt was made to explain how the machine worked. There was to be a 'till' in the depot, and 'a piece of equipment' at head office. An installer explained that they used to leave the tills in the depots for a few weeks so that staff could play with them, until they were ready to go back and really install them.

All the depot managers went to Edinburgh to be trained on the system – and then went back and trained their own staff in the depot. At first the course lasted for 2 days, but this was later cut to one. Most staff in each depot soon learned how to use the system, even if it was only for a simple enquiry.

The rapid introduction also helped those providing a help-line, as they became very familiar with the problems which the managers were facing – which were often identical – and correspondingly easy to deal with. Head Office continued to help out if there are any problems in operating the system. This would normally be done over the telephone, though in practice problems were rare.

The process of change also reflected the initial emphasis on the importance of administrative rather than management information. In the early days, they now believe that they approached the development of the MIS in the wrong way, by asking managers 'what reports do you want'?

The managers didn't really know, and based it on what they were getting from the manual system – such as basic sales figures. This didn't seem very satisfactory, so we pulled together a seminar, with the sales director and all the other managers. Said to them – 'you tell us what information you'd need to run the company'. And they came up with all of these things, like the number of cars through the door, average sale value, ratios of all kinds. Then I asked 'what is the life of that information – when is weekly information not interesting?' Basically we then went away with that list, and instead of designing reports, we designed a database that was the size and shape of what they wanted to know.

Summary

1 Tom Farmer appreciated the benefits which IT could bring, and drove the design and implementation of the system from the start.

2 No suitable system was available in the UK, but he saw that a system used in fastfood outlets in the USA could be adapted to meet Kwik-Fit's needs.

3 An effective manual administrative system had been developed, which was retained as the basis for the computerized system.

4 The system was developed by a team led by Kwik-Fit's IT manager, in conjunction with staff from the US company developing the software for the MAT terminals.

5 Some depot managers took part in meetings to specify what they would like to see on the system.

6 A pilot system was tested in two depots, and then implemented very rapidly in all other depots.

7 Training was provided for all staff as the system came into their depot.

CHANGES TO STRUCTURE, CONTROL AND WORK ORGANIZATION

The company's underlying style of management has been described as relatively assertive and fast-moving. How, if at all, did the style change as the network came in?

In 1980, before EPOS, the company had about eighty depots. The managers of these depots reported to area managers, each responsible for eighteen to twenty sites. The depot managers sent information on performance directly to Head Office using a variety of forms and reports.

Depot managers had a lot of autonomy. Although there were company price lists, Head Office did not know what prices the depots actually charged: the information took weeks to reach them. Managers were also responsible for ordering their own stocks of parts, using their judgement about what was needed. The supplier delivered an order to the depot, and was later paid by Head Office.

The area managers had to monitor what was going on in their depots – which in some cases was extremely difficult:

> With a manual system, some depots needed a lot of hand-holding. You couldn't leave them alone, because you always had to go back and do lots of checks on them – count the cash, make sure the stocks were there. Discounts were very difficult to monitor – we didn't have a clue what was going on.

Before computerization it was uncontrollable. There was a price list, but we never knew if the depot was selling at that price, or at half of it. There was no method of looking at sales and controlling sales of specific items, and particularly looking at the discount, because there was no method of recording them.

Staff at Head Office were responsible for administering the company – receiving information on paper from each depot. Administrative staff had expanded with the business but by 1980 they were experiencing great difficulty in coping with the growing business.

The new system clearly eliminated some of the functions previously carried out by the depot manager. All administrative tasks were now performed automatically, with data on all transactions being stored in the MAT system during the day, and transmitted to Head Office each evening for processing. Stock replenishment was now done automatically from Head Office, on the basis of the information provided by the EPOS system about sales in the depot. Above all, accurate information about the performance of each depot was available the following day to managers at Head Office.

This significantly reduced the autonomy of the depot manager:

Now there is a lot more control at Head Office. The depot can still do whatever it wants ... the theory is that the point of sale system doesn't restrict the manager to do anything – he can still do whatever he wants. But he has to account for it. The whole system is based around giving the depot manager freedom in running his business.

The system enabled the company to monitor what was going on in each depot – in effect a small business – and at the same time provide them with support, by way of marketing, administration, and a constantly balanced stock.

I think it has enabled us to get the benefit of decentralized management, but with uniform procedures applied. And to be seen to be applied, and to be committed at the centre to intervene if there's a deviation.

Senior managers were able to monitor compliance with depot procedures. If things were not being done in the correct way, such as unusual discounts, or late banking, that would be visible at Head Office the following day. Depot managers came to realize that someone would be in touch with them very quickly and they did not repeat a mistake.

The system thus brought a sharper focus to the work of the depot manager:

> We have taken all of the essential elements of the Code of Practice over management procedures which were previously summarized on two sides of a single plastic covered A4 sheet (known as the Management Summary) and we have encapsulated all of that within the MAT software. So now the MAT focuses the managers' attention on doing things exactly the way Kwik-Fit requires them to be done. That really was the breakthrough. It still allows a degree of discretion on the part of management, but any discretion has to be accompanied by a reason, and these reasons are carried forward into our central systems.

> The Management Summary card has been in use for years and the company has great faith in it even today. If you operate your depot according to the procedures shown on the Management Summary you are going to have a successful operation: if you don't, you might succeed, but the chances are you won't.

Tom Farmer expressed the same point:

> Before we were computerized, to find out things that were wrong we had to check so much stuff- and we were always 8-10 weeks behind: and by then it wasn't much use speaking to the guy – it was too late to do anything about it. Whereas now we've got the information, and can talk about things that happened yesterday.

Similar views were expressed by another manager who had observed the change, which allowed senior managers to see much more clearly which areas they needed to attack. He saw it as being much more tightly controlled:

> I would say there is less branch autonomy – it is more uniform. The guy will act to the same guidelines, wherever he is in the country which again probably makes the company look a lot more professional, rather than each guy doing his own thing. It makes them more uniform.

> Head office have a greater command of the sales picture. They don't need to be in a depot to know how profitable it is – they can just tell from the information day by day.

Tom Farmer commented on the process of striking the right balance of control in the business:

We have gone through periods of centralizing and decentralizing. But with certain things like stock control, for example, we would never decentralize that. Whereas before it was left to every depot to look after their own stock, nowadays they have nothing to do with stock: that's entirely centralized, with automatic replenishment.

But there are other things, so we are not running a completely centralized operation. And one of the reasons is that you can't just run a centralized business – because you must make sure you don't lose the human element.

The management style is quite assertive – it always has been, and never changes, and hasn't changed as a result of the computer system.

He also spoke about how, in the early days, some area managers began to look at the figures rather than the business:

It went through a period when it changed for the worse – we had people out in the field who were all hands-on operators, and who had regular contact with the depots. And the first question they'd ask was 'what were your sales yesterday, why did this happen, why did you do that rather than this?' Now all of a sudden, they had the information available to them: and there was no need for the personal communication. So guys started to read the computer sheets, and talk about the contents, and analyse things – things nothing at all to do with an area manager.

Some guys actually started buying briefcases – became what we called the 'briefcase brigade'. They went from being hands-on operators, and didn't ask questions, because they had the information. There was a change in the management style, which was not of benefit to us.

So we stopped that. The guys out in the field don't get that information handed to them – they have to get it themselves. So before we had put viewdata in people's homes, to let them see what the depots were doing. We stopped that – now if they want to know what a depot's doing, they have to go to that depot and find out – purely to keep the personal contact.

He also emphasized that the data now provided was intended to support the depot managers, not intimidate them:

The other thing we have to watch is that we worked very hard to make sure it's not a Big Brother syndrome. We had to make sure that the only information we would be getting was information that would help the guys out in the field to do their job more easily. Anybody who phones a depot, or one of the area managers, and comes over heavy because they've picked up something that's wrong – that's not the way to do it. Everything is for support.

The structure of the company had not changed significantly until comparatively recently. There had been some changes: for example, in the early days, area managers supervising eighteen to twenty depots. This was replaced in the early 1980s by a system in which three or four depots were grouped as partnerships, with one partner controlling the others.

That apart, the system was seen as having allowed the company to grow as a relatively centralised business. At the time of the switch to DEC, consideration was given to decentralizing computer services to the smaller units then envisaged. However, the company did not actually follow this distributed computing strategy. Instead they built up Edinburgh as an international processing centre, providing a computer service here for the UK and the Irish Republic. It was felt to be more cost effective to provide the computer service from Head Office, especially when voice and data communications had become so good. They would continue to pull back data into this computer centre, process it, and transmit the results directly into a mailbox system in a division or associate company.

By 1992, however, changes to the structure were being made, in order to keep management close to the changing needs of the business. The five divisions were given much greater autonomy – they were not completely independent, but the Divisional Directors had full responsibility for the profitability of the division.

Speaking in 1992, a senior manager explained:

There was a large degree of autonomy within divisions but there were a number of things they had to refer back to the centre for approval. We have now decided that we don't really want to have a central core of people servicing these divisions. We would rather have the divisions as autonomous units.

To signal to managers that they were responsible, and had authority, the company eliminated various central departments and passed the work to the people in the divisions, with computerized support. In the past the divisions were mainly concerned with sales. Now all of the physical aspects of the depots, such as maintenance or equipment supply, which was formerly provided centrally became a depot responsibility:

If they create the problems they clear up the problems. So there is a distinct strengthening of the divisions.

To support this organizational change, the computer systems were revised to make them operate semi-independently for each of the divisions. Purchase ledgers, for example, were split into multi-company operations. The database was partitioned so that each division had access to their own data, but senior management was able to see the totality of the business.

One of the new Divisional Directors noted how this worked:

We have got here for example, the purchase ledger. We process the invoices for all of the purchases that our seventy-five centres make. They would previously have been dealt with at Edinburgh on behalf of the depots, but now the supplier would invoice the division here, and would be paid from here.

So we do all our own invoice matching, our own electronic checking, the reconciliation. Head Office still produce the cheques electronically and the payments electronically – but we initiate it. So we've got autonomy on the purchase ledger. And the same goes for new starts, payroll changes, training records. That was done by somebody from Murrayfield: we do it here now. We only depend on Murrayfield for two things – Marketing and Advertising, and Central Computer Services.

He pointed out that the information to give close monitoring of depots was there before – but it could be done better by someone managing seventy-five depots, rather than 400. Divisionalization enabled them to make better use of it. He had earlier been responsible for central purchasing and stock control. He knew there were problems of overstocks and understocks, but found it very hard to get to the root cause of the problem:

With the best will in the world, you couldn't get down the line, and get hold of it, because there were too many people to deal with. You couldn't phone a centre manager and say 'why are you buying too much stock?' You'd need to phone the divisional director – and he'd say, 'yes, I'll get something done about that'. But what he really meant was 'I've got more to worry about than how much stock I've got – I'm more worried about sales, and I need the stock to get the sales'. We couldn't get them to fully understand how important it was to hold the right levels of stock in the right situation. The computer system allowed us to see the problem, but not to get to grips with it.

Now, as a result of these organizational changes, and by taking local divisional responsibility, we've reduced the stock holding in this particular division, from something like £4 million to just over £3 million, in 6 months.

The EPOS system had a direct and visible effect on the work carried out by the depot managers. Previously they were required to complete a wide range of clerical and administrative tasks, such as preparing quotations and invoices for customers, banking the day's takings, checking and re-ordering stock, and providing information to head office. This ex-manager described part of the process:

I was the manager in Blackhall and we probably had 60 to 80 customers a day. I had to write every receipt by hand, then I had to put these receipts onto a master copy. I would then have to balance each product, whether it was a valve, a tyre, a shock absorber, or whatever. You reconciled what you had sold against what you had in stock, and made additions and subtractions because of stock coming in and stock going out. You had to balance it all to check that everything was OK.

With EPOS, information on each transaction was keyed into the system by the fitter – and the system then dealt automatically with all the administrative tasks. Managers and staff in the depot no longer had to spend time on paperwork:

because at the end of the day now when you press a button, everything is looked after automatically. There is no more walking out with sheets under you arm, sitting until 10 o'clock at night, especially in the big centres, trying to reconcile your figures.

This meant that managers were able to spend more time with customers. This was not an incidental by-product:

We expect the manager to be out there all the time right in front of the customer – they can see that is the manager, and if they have a problem that is the guy they need to see. This is by design, and you could never do this if they were sitting compiling receipts. There were times when I was guilty myself – to get a night out I'd do the paperwork during the day. If I was halfway through adding up an account, and a customer came in, I was very annoyed with them for interrupting. Whereas the computer knocks all that out, and you are glad to speak to the customers.

Another said:

> What it has really done is to leave the manager free to meet the customers rather than having to sit and do paperwork all day. He's basically seeing customers and motivating staff.

The terminals allowed staff to provide a quicker and more personal service, as they did not have to look at manuals and price lists, or to check physically whether an item was in stock. The customer could see the computer, and knew that the mechanic wasn't making up the price. And they could always read the bills.

This was felt to be important:

> The customer knows he is getting a national price, and again that makes it easier when dealing with Fleet Sales. The fleet operators are looking for the same prices across the country.

Staff found the system easy to use:

> It really is child's play to use a MAT – as soon as you have pressed a pre-set function key on the keyboard you are then locked in and everything you do for that transaction is prompted. It prompts exactly what information you need for each step, and that means a novice can pick it up and use it very quickly. The guys in the centres come in with a moderate educational background and their skill is in working with their hands – yet they can adapt to it very quickly. The combination of ease of use and being totally focused and allied to the procedures has been the success.

Although it eliminated some administrative tasks, EPOS did not reduce staff in the depots. The manual fitting work was still to be done, and the computer did not help with that. It was possible that depots had more staff, since the previous administrative burdens on the manager probably restricted the business he did. The growth in market share also implied more staff.

One consequence was that depot managers needed to be willing and able to deal with customers in the right way – which was not previously part of their job. There was also a new requirement for accuracy in entering data into the system.

The number and proportion of head office staff employed on purely administrative tasks had fallen. The ratio of administrative staff to depots has been cut from about 1:1 to 1:10. Conversely, more people were now employed on training, property controls, marketing – and all the other tasks associated with a growing business. The stronger divisional structure had resulted in some staff moving from Head Office to a divisional office.

Summary

1 Before the system was installed, information about activity in the depots took weeks to reach Head Office, giving depot managers a high degree of autonomy.
2 Area managers found it hard to manage the growing number of depots. 3 Head Office staff found it hard to run the administration, and senior management was losing track of business performance.
4 The EPOS system permitted closer monitoring of depot staff, sustained pressure or performance, showed up problems clearly and quickly, and instilled uniform procedures throughout the company.
5 An early experiment in providing area managers with direct access from home to information on depot performance was abandoned when senior management observed that area managers were spending more time with computer print-outs, and less time with depot managers.
6 In the early 1990s it was decided to introduce a stronger divisional structure, giving more responsibility for profit to local managers, and transferring many functions from Head Office to the divisions. This would allow the information provided by the EPOS system to be acted on more effectively, as profit responsibilities would be more clearly defined.
7 The system altered the work of the depot manager by significantly reducing the administrative load of their job, enabling them to spend more time with customers and staff.
8 Depot staff found the system easy to use, and no jobs were lost in the depots as a result of its introduction.

CONCLUSIONS

The company went through a period of rapid growth in 1979–80, and it became clear to management that this was imposing an unacceptable administrative burden. In order to grow and at the same time keep central costs low, management introduced an EPOS system into all their depots. This proved successful, and has been further developed since the original installation. The company has used the system to help gain a competitive edge in the market, and to offer new services to customers.

Tom Farmer believed firmly in keeping administrative costs as low as possible, and the system was originally seen as way of containing these costs as the company grew. EPOS was designed to take all administrative functions from the depot managers, so that they could concentrate on managing their staff and looking after customers. It would also improve stock-control and other procedures. These objectives were clearly expressed at the start, and helped to concentrate energies – as did the very stringent timetable set by Tom Farmer for introducing the system.

Specially-designed point of sale terminals, known as Management Action Terminals (MATs) were installed in each depot, and used by managers and staff to record all transactions. They also held details of all stocks and prices. During the day they performed administrative tasks, and at night were linked to the mainframe computer at head of fice. The original system was continually enhanced, with new reports and features (e.g. EDI, credit card transactions), and by the mid-1980s the ICL mainframe became overloaded, stimulating a change to DEC.

The system was installed on target, was easy to use, and was readily accepted by managers and fitters in the depots. It matched the way they had worked before, helped them do their job, and became a central part of management's strategy to grow in a competitive business.

The expected business objectives were rapidly achieved. A very tight administrative system, a strong company identity, and a focus on the customer had always been part of the Kwik-Fit approach. The computer system supported these.

Unexpected benefits were also obtained, particularly in the amount of information now available about the operation of the company. This gave new insights into the company, focused management action, and enabled senior management to exercise tighter control. Competitively important initiatives also became possible, and were used as a base on which to develop the business in new directions – which would not have been feasible otherwise. More facilities were added to the original system, improving customer service (e.g. credit cards) and operating efficiency (e.g. using the BACS system to pay salaries), and new business areas could be entered, on the basis of the processes within the information technology system.

Tom Farmer drove the design and implementation of the system from the start. It reflected very close working relationships with the supplier, who was chosen after a wide search. The system was developed by a team led by Kwik-Fit's IT manager, in conjunction with staff from the US supplier of the software and the MAT terminals. The team included some depot managers, who were able to specify what they would like to see on the system. A pilot system was tested in two depots, then implemented rapidly in all other depots.

The system had a clear effect on the work of depot managers, who no longer had to spend time on administrative tasks. This had previously been a major chore, and taking it away allowed them to concentrate on running the depot and dealing with customers. The ratio of administrative staff to depots had fallen, but more people were employed on activities which grew with the business.

The new system increased the control exercised by head office over managers in the depots. By transferring information overnight from each depot it permitted closer monitoring of depot staff, sustained pressure for performance, showed up problems clearly and quickly, and instilled uniform procedures throughout the company. But management also stressed the importance of maintaining the commitment of depot managers – which could not be done with an over-centralized system. Information was to be used to support depot managers, not to intimidate them. So although information about depot performance was available at Head Office, it was essential that human contact with the depot was maintained -and the system was shaped to ensure that area managers, for example, were obliged to visit depots to keep in touch.

The management style had always been described as assertive, and centralized – and the computer system was seen as reinforcing that. By the early 1990s senior management concluded that performance could be further improved by strengthening the Divisional structure, and giving them more direct profit responsibility. Managers in the Divisions would take over many Head Office functions, and would be better able to act on the information provided by the EPOS system, as lines of responsibiliy would be more clearly drawn.

8

THE PROCESS OF CHANGE

INTRODUCTION

Although the cases in this book relate to the introduction of large scale information technology systems, technical change and organizational change are increasingly indistinguishable. Most organizational change is either caused or enabled by technical change. Organizational downsizing, the flattening of management hierarchies, and the disappearance of middle management layers are facilitated by information technology systems. Introducing innovatory computer systems almost invariably implies organizational change in terms of strategy, work organization in the short-term and horizontal and vertical structural change in the medium- to long-term, but these changes may not be effective or successful. The difficulty of successfully achieving organizational change in response to technical change may underly some of the less successful computer applications (Miles, 1990, Hamilton, 1988, Kearney, 1990), and the initially low level of user-acceptance of many new systems. From the considerable documentary evidence available (e.g. Newman and Rosenberg 1985, Long, 1987), these failures are related to political, managerial and cultural issues rather than problems inherent in the technology itself.

Anyone wishing to change an organization has to go through a three-stage process of unfreezing old attitudes and systems, moving towards new attitudes and systems and then refreezing the organization in its new form (Lewin, 1951). In many ways the unfreezing process is the most difficult and, once achieved, moving and refreezing may follow more naturally. Change agents need to use techniques that develop a climate of change (Keen, 1981) or a perceived need for change (Kanter, 1983). A change involving a computer network means a fundamental change in the way people work throughout the organization and a considerable potential for designing structural changes. This involves an unfreezing of attitudes on a large scale. Many workers dislike the disruption or redirection involved in a major organizational change, feeling that their autonomy, skills, status and interests are threatened; their competence is invested in the old system and they dislike risk. Many of these reactions to change were initially demonstrated in the cases presented in this book. Collins and Mann (1988) write that an individual's reaction to change varies with their needs, their perceptions of threat, their needs for relationships, and their degree of reluctance to change. The techniques used in the past to prepare people for technical change have not always been successful, and may be even more inadequate faced with the large scale and interconnected complexity of network systems.

The computer network projects described in this book illustrate the complexity of the contexts within which the organizational change agents had to operate. The process of designing, developing and enhancing these systems took place over a considerable period and during this time the projects were affected by changes in market conditions, technological developments, changes in organizational structure and changes in key managers. ScotRail experienced changes of context as the government's policy of privatizing the railways became clearer, organizational restructuring took place in preparation and key managers were promoted to other parts of the railway network or took early retirement. Other cases demonstrated the difficulties of managing complex project in changing and unpredictable contexts; the Travel Company was taken over by a US company, the Ambulance Service also experienced the disruption of imminent privatization, Kwik-Fit experienced increased competition and restructuring.

The internal contexts of the network projects demonstrated interdependency problems due to the interdepartmental nature of the projects. Change agents had to wait for decisions from all the departments affected before progressing the project as well as waiting for multiple suppliers to provide equipment and expertise at the appropriate times. Most case projects experienced problems with delay due to prolonged decision-making processes and vendor supply. In addition some of the case organizations had to wait for decisions from parent bodies outwith the immediate organization, e.g. the Travel Company and the bank and, subsequently, the US parent company; ScotRail and the BR Board; the Ambulance Service and their sponsoring government department; and the public libraries and their local authorities.

Other internal contextual problems included unclear project management responsibility, which was in some cases not officially designated until late in the project, e.g. the Travel Company. In other cases the responsibility changed during the course of the project, as in one of the large public libraries. The attitude of senior management was a significant factor in the internal context, some expecting quick results and becoming impatient as in the Travel Company, others having unrealistic expectations from the new system for example many of the ScotRail Area managers who expected an 'all singing, all dancing' network. We will be examining the way the change agents managed the process of change, what techniques they used to cope with complex and changing projects and how the way they managed the projects affected the outcomes.

THE CONTEXT OF CHANGE

The introduction of computer network systems takes place within particularly complex and threatening contexts and presents particular challenges to managers. Buchanan and Boddy (1992) classify the context of change on a matrix using two dimensions. The first dimension is the perceived centrality of the change to the primary task of the organization (core ... peripheral) and the second dimension is the perceived scale and pace of change (radical ... incremental). This leaves four quadrants (see Figure 8.1).

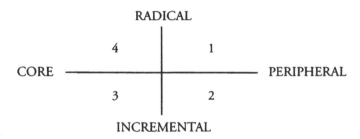

Figure 8.1

In the first quadrant change is perceived as radical, but peripheral to the main task of the organization. The personal vulnerability of the change agent is therefore low. ScotRail's network system probably fits into this quadrant. Quadrant 2 change is perceived as peripheral to the main task and incremental, and therefore presents few problems to the change agent. None of the cases fit into this category. Quadrant 3 change is an incremental departure from existing activities but affects the core of the organization's activity, and will more problematic to the change agent. Many of the library systems installed were essentially upgrades of existing systems and fall into Quadrant 3 as do those of the Ambulance Service. Quadrant 4 includes change that affects the core activity and is also a radical departure from existing arrangements, and will present the change agents with major implementation problems both organizational and technical. Penalties for failure and the vulnerability of the change agent will be high. The Travel Company and Kwik-Fit projects fall into this category.

There are added factors that elaborate this model. The pace of change can be significant and can add to the level of resistance if the implementation takes a long period as it did within the Travel Company. In contrast if the pace of change is rapid it can reduce resistance problems as it did with Kwik-Fit's implementation. Change projects can also move between quadrants, in particular the strategic potential of network systems may only emerge during and after implementation. For example ScotRail and the Ambulance Service's systems started off as Quadrant 1 and Quadrant 3 respectively, but as the importance of their information systems to future privatization plans became apparent both became Quadrant 4 projects. The varying contexts of the organizational change affects the level of vulnerability of the change agent. Obviously the scale and complexity of the problems involved in the change, the level of risk and uncertainty and the degree of resistance likely, are crucial, and computer network systems rate high on all vulnerability measures. The two extreme positions are summarized in Table 8.1:

Table 8.1 High and low vulnerability contexts of organizational change

High vulnerability	Low vulnerability
Unrealistic top management expectations	Realistic top management expectations
Fickle support	Solid support
Uncertain means	Certainty of means
Complex interdependencies	Few interdependencies
Dependent on third parties	Independent
Multiple 'ripples'	Self-contained
Conflicting perceptions	Shared views
Multipurpose changes	Single-function systems
Unstable goals	Stable goals
Confused responsibilities for process and outcomes	Clear 'ownership' of process and outcomes

Many of the cases demonstrate most of these characteristics of high vulnerability contexts. For example the senior management of the Travel Company expected the system to be implemented quickly and without disturbing the flow of business and as the project continued their support became less enthusiastic. They did not give final financial approval until late in the project and the formal appointment of a project manager was 2 years into the project.

CHANGE AGENDAS

In handling major network projects the change agent has to consider three main agendas. The content agenda addresses the technical, organizational and people aspects of the project, the technical constraints and opportunities offered by the hardware and software and the technical design methodologies commonly used in developing computer systems, as well as addressing implications for the organization and the people affected. The control agenda involves the full range of intervention strategies, project management planning, budgeting, and monitoring techniques. The process agenda demands a wide range of political skills where the manager is expected to be effective in communicating, consulting, influencing, negotiating and team building skills. The level of vulnerability of the project context dictates the change agent's agenda priorities. Although the importance of the control agenda is common to all projects the relative importance of the content and the process agendas will depend on the complexity of the project and the level of vulnerability of the change agent.

The content agenda

The definition of the content agenda can be technical or socio-technical. In the case organizations the dominant definition was technical, apart from ScotRail whose definition was organizational, the technology content of Omega being almost incidental. The content agenda always demands some technical competence, and experience of the potential and limitations of the technical system, but sometimes this technical competence can be a barrier to success. The rapid pace of technical change makes it difficult to keep up to date with the available technologies and skill obsolescence is a problem. For example at the start of the Travel Company project the systems staff were more familiar with mainframes than PCs, and none had telecommunications expertise. The skills acquired during a technical education and training can mean a rigid technical approach to what are essentially socio-technical problems. Examples of this type of problem are the design methodologies most often used to design and develop systems, and the communications problems inherent in the dialogue between technicians and users.

Design methodologies

The planning methodologies used in the past to design computer systems have had operational priorities and been system- and data-oriented, reflecting the domination of the content agenda by technical priorities. Computer network systems necessitate decision and information-flow oriented methodologies with a strategic focus. Most computer systems were designed to replicate existing information flows, rather than to change the information pattern in response to changing business requirements. This was partly due to the political implications of challenging the status quo, and partly because it was much easier to fit the system into the existing pattern. In general, IS departments have not been entirely successful in developing innovative design and development methodologies specifically geared to large scale complex strategic organization-wide computer network systems. The case evidence indicates that the most commonly used development methodologies were based on the traditional systems development life cycle and associated techniques.

Gunton (1990) describes the system development life cycle (SDLC) used by most organizations as a sequential linear process divided into a series of phases; investigation, analysis, design, development and implementation. He suggests that this linear process is now less relevant to systems that involve 'fuzzy' organizational requirements, which cannot be specified in specific quantitative terms, and which are subject to constant environmental change. The problem with the SDLC is that organizational change does not often conform to this 'rational-linear' model of change. The decisions that have to be made about technical and organizational change are seldom in accordance with the demands of the rational decision making model or limited to technical considerations.

Yadav (1983) felt that the usual methodologies used to specify information requirements (SSADM, Jackson, Yourdon) were not appropriate for specifying total organizational information requirements and that the tools in use had not generally kept pace with the complexity of the systems being introduced. He also judged that the older methodologies did not allow for the importance of understanding organizational issues and politics. He identified the possibility of the goals and objectives of each sub-unit within the organization being different both to each other and to the overall goal of the organization.

There was no evidence that the case organizations were making use of more innovative design and development methodologies. For example, none had attempted to use methodologies that include more 'soft' factors like Checkland's Soft Systems Methodology. This reflected the concentration on the technical content rather than the organizational or people content of the project.

Communications problems

Many operational users cannot specify accurately in technical terms what they need from a computer system or the technical potential of the proposed system. IT personnel often have limited knowledge of the business side of the organization. Few IT personnel have any training in interpersonal skills, and many have little interest in the human side of the essentially socio-technical systems that they design. Systems analysts have their own jargon, and their own professional loyalties. At present the systems analyst usually comes from a technical background, often having graduated from being a programmer and their aim in analysing the system is to reduce the users' real world into structures and processes. As Newman and Rosenberg (1985) describe it: conflict is structured into the relationship and Cooper and Swanson (1979) describe it as 'dissonance'.

This mismatch is most significant at the stage when the manager/user is attempting to describe the business requirements of the new system to the systems analyst and the analyst tries to describe the technical constraints and potentials. Considerable errors, misunderstandings and inconsistencies can be built into any system at this stage. Many of the cases illustrate this problem. Many users at the Travel Company, General Insurance, and the Ambulance Service complained that the systems turned out to be too technical and not sufficiently related to business problems, reflecting the tendency to regard network systems as technical rather than socio-technical projects. In contrast, Kwik-Fit's systems seemed to fulfil requirements closely, partly perhaps because top management was still so intimately involved in the business at customer level. ScotRail tackled the problem by designing the system at organizational level without consulting the IT people and then telling them to 'get on with it'!

The process agenda

The process agenda requires that the change agent has considerable competence in communicating, negotiating, influencing, team management, and a general ability to manage people during the introduction of the system. The type of people involved in the process of designing, developing and implementing computer network systems will affect attitudes to agenda priorities. If managers from the business side of the organization are involved in the design, development and implementation of the network system, this will ensure that the content agenda is socio-technical rather than purely technical. This in turn will ensure that the process of introduction is business and user-oriented rather than a technical exercise.

Any computer system, but particularly network systems, means a redistribution of information and control of information which raise potential political issues for the change agent to manage.

Information is a political resource within the organization. Any redistribution of information control affects the political balance and is likely to be resisted by interest groups. Networks have the potential, for example when linked to central databases, to significantly change information control between departments and between functions and the head office. They also have the power to formalize decision-making processes that were previously dominated by 'rule of thumb' or 'muddling through' or 'garbage-can' processes (Keen, 1981), and the computer system can be regarded as a criticism of the way decisions were previously taken. This was clearly seen in the case of the branch managers in the Travel Company, existing Area managers within ScotRail and professional librarians in the Cooperative where control and decision-making was, at least initially, removed to the centre. Top management support for the introduction of networks is vital as an overall organizational perspective has to be established to override the interests and political power-bases of departmental managers. Those case organizations which obtained active senior management backing for the project like ScotRail, the university librarians in BLCMP, and Kwik-Fit found the progress of the project greatly assisted. But the support of the chief executive has been used by many organizations as a substitute for designing innovative and creative change processes. This so-called 'commander-model' of change management has come under considerable criticism (Whipp *et al.*, 1988; Bourgeois and Brodwin, 1984) as a way of avoiding the time-investment necessary in both developing genuine user-involvement mechanisms, and negotiating between competing interests within the organization. The project role of both Alex Lynch of ScotRail and Tom Farmer of Kwik-Fit could be interpreted as using the 'commander-model' method to save time and effort and bypass the political sensitivities of functional managers.

AGENDA PRIORITIES

The agenda priorities of the change agent will vary with the context of the project. In a low vulnerability context the agenda priorities will probably be:

1 Content.
2 Control.
3 Process.

Managing the process of change in a low vulnerability context is generally less problematic and the relevant skills will be predominantly technical. Both the control and the process agendas will make less demands on the individual in charge of the project.

In a high vulnerability 'Quadrant 4' context like all those described in these cases the priorities of the project manager will completely change and will be:

1 Process.
2 Control.
3 Content.

In this case the project manager is highly vulnerable. The process of change is highly complex and interdependent. The control agenda is still important because the project is highly visible and strategic leading to considerable top management attention. The success of the project will depend less on technical competence and far more on political and interpersonal skills and competences. The change agent will have to provide top management and users with the conviction that the change is proceeding in an overtly logical, rational manner, whilst at the same time less open political activity will be vital to maintain support and overcome resistance at all levels. The content agenda is still important, but is best largely delegated to technical experts.

All the change projects in the cases fall into this category, but some organizations were better served by change agents than others. ScotRail, Kwik-Fit and some of the libraries in the Cooperative had change agents who managed the process agenda with a high level of political skill, but delegated the content and control agendas to others with the relevant technical skills. Others, like the Travel Company and the Ambulance Service, had to rely on change agents with mainly technical skills managing the content and control agenda, but ignoring, or unable to adequately address, the process agenda on the basis that it was not part of their job to manage people as well as the technology.

It is important for organizations to appoint change agents with the skills appropriate to the type and context of the project. In the case of computer network systems, which are high vulnerability projects, with considerable potential for strategic advantage and may attract considerable resistance, in many cases it will be inappropriate to leave technical people in charge of the project. The often unobtainable ideal would be people who can combine technical ability, business acumen and political and interpersonal skills. Where there is a choice, the individual with political skills and business acumen who will delegate the technical side may be the best choice. ScotRail used the Manager of Management Services, who had forty years' experience within BR, to manage the process agenda while the technical project was managed by a subordinate. One survey, (Ring, 1989) indicates a growing recognition that technical skills are not the first priority and may be a disadvantage in many cases: 'It is easier to teach a little bit of IT to a businessman than it is to teach business to IT people.' Certainly this is the model represented by the change agents within the case evidence, who were most successful in avoiding and countering resistance.

STRATEGIES FOR QUADRANT 4 PROJECTS

The development and implementation of computer network systems is a complex and uncertain process. There is a series of paradoxes between the logic of establishing 'ownership' and the logic of establishing the rational legitimacy of the system. There is often dissonance between the available skills of the change agents and the differing project agendas they have to manage. The vulnerability and visibility of the change agent is increased still further if the nature of change is in Quadrant 4, and it is advisable to concentrate on the process and control agendas and delegate the content agenda to appropriate experts. The high vulnerability context encourages the change agent to combine overt strategies aimed at generating feelings of 'ownership' and involvement, with more devious political 'wheeler-dealing' to muster support, manipulate opinion and threaten dissenters.

Two types of strategy are necessary for successful implementation of large scale complex technological changes in vulnerable contexts. Those promoting the change have to produce a 'public, frontstage performance' (Buchanan and Boddy, 1992) of logical and rationally planned change linked to widespread and convincing participative mechanisms. But they also have to actively pursue 'backstage activity' exercising power skills; influencing, negotiating, selling, searching out and neutralizing resistance. Kotter and Schlesinger (1979) identify a series of 'frontstage' strategies; education, participation, facilitation, negotiation but also 'backstage' manipulation and cooptation and explicit and implicit coercion.

Change processes within organizations have to conform to organizational 'theatre' to be successful. The users at all levels have to be convinced that they are genuinely involved in the change and have some influence on its outcome. Top management and systems staff have to be convinced that the change is technically rational, logical and also congruent with the strategic direction of the organization. In reality, it is difficult to achieve both, but the theatrical trick is to convince people that genuine user-involvement, technical elegance and strategic logicality are apparent in the change process. The skills necessary for successful change seem to be close to those manipulative skills identified by Pettigrew (1985), Kanter (1983) and Johnson (1990). Many involvement mechanisms can be seen as ceremonial symbolic acts or rituals which contribute towards a general feeling of participation in the unfreezing, moving and refreezing processes and a manipulation of the attitudes of people throughout the organization, rather than making a genuine effort to deal with real worries and anxieties which would be far too time-consuming. Hirscheim (1985) describes the commonly used participation strategies as inherently manipulative, Newman and Rosenberg (1985) describe them as pseudo-democratic.

In any case, there is considerable controversy as to whether the time investment necessary is really justified in terms of systems improvements. Although there is evidence that participative approaches to introducing computer systems are being designed and adopted (Hirscheim, 1985; Mumford, 1981; Eason, 1988, 1989), other evidence (Ives and Olson, 1984; Child, 1984) indicates that the benefits from such an approach have yet to be proved. There have been many attempts to evaluate the benefits of user-participation in terms of satisfaction with the system and its use (Tait and Vessey, 1988; Olsen and Ives, 1980, 1981; Franz and Robey, 1986) but with inconclusive results. There seems to be little direct evidence that participation leads to satisfied users.

The individual or group responsible for the change has a complicated and multiskilled role to play in this piece of organizational theatre. The change masters (Kanter, 1983) are both powerful and vulnerable. Their vulnerability is particularly apparent when considering their role in complex, large-scale projects such as the introduction of organizational network systems which imply wide ranging political implications and may take years to fully implement. It is difficult to maintain the public appearance of technical effectiveness and strategic rationality at the same time as in the background exercising a wide range of political 'fixing' skills over a long time period and in a organization-wide context, without losing credibility. Only two of the organizations in this sample can claim such a personality: Kwik-Fit and ScotRail. In these complex and changeable projects the emphasis on agenda priorities will change and adjust with changing circumstances and there will be constant iterations between the three agendas.

The most frequently advocated strategy to provide users with the conviction that they 'own' and feel comfortable with the change is to develop user-participation strategies, where users at all levels feel that they are participating in the whole process of change from inception to implementation. Newman and Rosenberg (1985) and Maish (1979) advocate that large projects should follow an evolutionary plan which accommodates the users' learning process and ensures that the organization 'learns' from the whole process. Swanson (1982) felt that users only benefit from any computer project 'to the extent that they understand the system as a whole'. Many writers (starting with Coch and French, 1948) have advocated making users feel involved in the process of change so that they feel 'ownership' of the changes once they have been accomplished, reducing resistance and increasing commitment.

The Quality of Working Life initiatives of the 1960s to 1970s, the Quality Circle movements of the 1970s and 1980s and the more recent High Involvement Strategies described by Lawler (1986) are all attempts to make employees feel involved in the management of their organizations. Much of current 'management guru' writing by Handy and Peters reflects similar concerns. As Kanter (1983: 277) says: 'participatory processes should be task-oriented, integrative rituals of high involvement and transformation – a way to engage many talents in the mastery of change.' Pettigrew (1985) categorizes the participative approach to system development as the 'truth, trust, love and collaboration' approach to change. Keen (1981) describes a method of systematic change he names 'UI' or 'Up and In' consisting of small groups, face to face involvement and participatory management, which he indicates works best for small projects. Kanter (1983: 238–9) feels that most 'failures of innovation are failures of participation.' But all these strategies can be interpreted as inherently devious as ultimately managerial objectives prevail.

Some writers suggest that there is a significant distinction to be drawn between token participation and genuine 'involvement'. Olson and Ives, (1980, 1983), Barki and Hartwick (1989), and Franz and Robey (1986) distinguish between token or symbolic participation and substantive involvement. In reality user-participation varies in degree and significance (Tait and Vessey, 1988). Participation can often be limited to the initial requirements analysis and to the implementation of the system, with little involvement in the actual design and development. Participation can be token, one user liaising with the technical department or on the steering committee (see Travel Company, the Ambulance Service, libraries, and General Insurance) and with little more than token attention being paid to them. Users have little control, sometimes not having the power to refuse acceptance when systems do not meet business requirements. In all these types of participation actual feelings of real 'ownership' of the system will be limited (Tait and Vessey, 1988). A comprehensive user-involvement strategy for a nationwide network system would demand substantial management time commitment, could result in unacceptable delay for the project, and is probably unrealistic considering the necessity to reconcile multiple competing interest groups within the organization.

For network systems, the need for users to have the perception that they are genuinely involved in the whole process of developing systems is at the same time both more necessary, due to the potential scale of resistance, and more difficult because of the size and technical complexity of the network systems themselves. None of the case organizations had managed to resolve this problem and few users participated in the development process. It is logistically difficult to involve more than a token few representative users, but the risks of users forming coalitions against the system and taking collective action to sabotage it is correspondingly high. This was illustrated by the initial reaction to the Travel Company system when coalitions were formed between some branch managers and their regional managers to criticise the system. It is important that the change agents develop 'front-stage' involvement mechanisms that make the users feel they they are playing a genuine part in the change process to avoid the phenomenon of 'counterimplementation' described by Keen, (1981) or tacit resistance to the system, followed by 'fermentation' and finally possibly sabotage identified by Leonard-Barton and Kraus (1985). This process was well illustrated by the Users' Forum introduced by the Travel Company and the Area Managers' meetings held by the Deputy General Manager of ScotRail during the course of Omega.

Large-scale projects like networks can encounter organizational inertia on a large scale and the choice of strategy adopted by the change agent is fundamental and can dictate success or failure. This organizational inertia was well illustrated by the initial reaction to the Travel Company's system and to that of the Ambulance Service. Keen (1981) writes that large-scale change may need an engineering approach named 'DO' or 'Down and Out', which involves direction from the top, lengthy design stages and a formal system for planning and project management. This approach is illustrated by the Kwik-Fit case where a consensus had been developed less through negotiation, coalition building, trust and love, and more through the impact of normative influence, and top-down authority and the sheer force of the personality of Tom Farmer on the attitudes of staff throughout the company. It is a substantial challenge for management to achieve a substantial degree of genuine involvement and 'ownership' when introducing organizational networks and may be too time-consuming and expensive to be justifiable. Child (1984) suggests that large-scale user participation strategies may be unrealistic because of the strength of clashing political interests within many large organizations. He suggests that for genuine participation to be a realistic option there would have to be no definite time limit on the project, the survival of the organization should not be at stake, the need for change not widely recognized, resistance minimal, and the power of the fixer strictly limited. Otherwise Child sees participation as a high risk strategy due to the potential opportunities for counter-implementation strategies and delay. Clearly most of the cases do not conform to Child's prescription and it is unlikely that any Quadrant 4 project would do so.

The role of the change agent in developing and implementing network systems is challenging, demanding a wide range of technical, organizational, managerial and political skills. From the evidence in the cases it would seem that the influence of dominant personalities within the organization can have a similar effect in creating a perception of 'ownership' and involvement with the new system for example ScotRail and Alex Lynch, and Tom Farmer and Kwik-Fit. The lack of dominant and inspiring 'champions' in other cases (the Ambulance Service, libraries and the Travel Company) seemed to have a negative effect on the feeling of user involvement with the new system.

FRONT STAGE TECHNIQUES

Organizational change agents have a range of innovative 'involvement' techniques at their disposal to create the perception of 'ownership' at all levels during each stage of the Systems Development Life Cycle: Initial planning, Investigation, Analysis, Design and Development, and Implementation. All these techniques are inherently manipulative and 'pseudo-democratic' because ultimately strategic and technical priorities have to prevail, but in facilitating the 'unfreezing, moving and refreezing' process these techniques may increase 'comfort' levels and reduce resistance problems at all levels of the organization and speed up the project's successful conclusion.

What was the primary orientation of systems personnel in the case organizations?

Perhaps the first step towards producing business-oriented computer network systems acceptable to the users is the reorientation of the systems analyst from a technical bias to a business-oriented bias and to encourage them to develop genuine interpersonal skills. Vitale (1986) found the more highly rated systems analysts are more concerned with user-involvement, managerial prerogatives and organizational politics. They regard hardware and software as constraints to finding a solution to the problems, rather than ends in themselves. Systems analysts can be recruited from a business rather than a technical background. Existing analysts can be trained in interpersonal skills and business needs. Users can receive IT training. Techniques can be used to improve user/analyst interaction. Maish (1979) found that there was a strong relationship between favourable user behaviour and positive user feelings about the quality of systems staff, thus reinforcing the view that it is vital to have systems staff who appear to be willing to understand user problems as well as technical solutions. Most of the people designing and developing these systems in the case organizations were technical by background, except in the case of ScotRail. The cases show that those project leaders who had a business background, e.g. ScotRail, Kwik-Fit, and the university libraries in the Cooperative, found the networks easier to implement.

What was the composition of project teams in the case organizations?

Project teams also need a wide range of skills, not limited to technical competencies. White and Leifer (198G) suggest that Jungian analysis using the Myers Briggs Type Indicator (Myers and McCaulley, 1985) would be useful and that a balance of types is vital for successful outcomes. Project failures have been associated with the lack of 'feeling' types in the project team. Particular personality types are more important at different stages of the project. In the cases the initial project teams were often composed of mostly technical personnel. This was the case with the Travel Company and the Ambulance Service, but not with Kwik-Fit and the libraries. As the projects developed, the composition of the team usually changed and included more operational users especially at the implementation stage. Some of the members were only able to be part-time and this could lead to problems for the project, for example the part-time telecommunications consultant at the beginning of the Travel Company project.

How far were top management involved in the introduction of the network systems?

Initially it is vital to involve top management users in macro-planning so that the overall organizational and business perspective can be ensured, rather than the technical perspective dominating the project. This involvement should continue throughout the project and represent a 'driving force' championing the network. Barki and Hartwick (1989) see that the influence of the top management sponsor is vital in imposing a normative influence over those users who have low involvement and neutral attitudes and this process was clearly significant in the case of Tom Farmer and Kwik-Fit. Doll and Torkzadeh (1988) found that the most important factors in ensuring the success of computer systems were the establishment of Executive Steering Committees, the development of overall development plans and mutually agreed development priorities between top management and the IS department. The systems are even more likely to be a success if top management also develop a linked implementation plan for the whole organization. As Leonard-Barton and Kraus (1985) say, the key to success is to identify needs at a high level and to define a solution at end-user level.

The support of top management was intermittent at the Ambulance Service, the Travel Company and the libraries. Some senior managers were content to play a more withdrawn sponsoring role like the Travel Company's General Manager, but the projects were more easily managed when the project had a active champion like the DGM at ScotRail and Tom Farmer at Kwik-Fit.

Investigation: were operational users involved in the investigation phase?

Meador and Rosenfeld (1986) write that more errors are introduced into a new computer system at the initial requirements analysis stage than at any other, and that they are more costly errors to repair and have greater impact on eventual system effectiveness. They assert that time spent on front-end analysis saves much time in the long run by cutting down on implementation problems and user resistance. They advocate a process starting with structured interviews with users, then decision analysis, data analysis, technical analysis and finally management orientation. Although the process is time consuming and labour intensive they feel the results, in terms of systems effectiveness, justify the methodology. It also leads to a higher level of user involvement with the system and 'ownership'. Cognitive mapping is one method of investigating the problems involved in complex computer systems described by Montazemi and Conrath (1986) and by Eden (1992) in a special issue of the *Journal of Management Studies*. The technique can be useful where the analyst has not been able to acquire a full set of information from the users who are operating in an ill-structured, uncertain decision-making environment. This method could not be used comprehensively in a nationwide organization such as those we are considering here, but a scientifically selected sample of a typical user population could be used with the idea of giving a wide range of users the perception that they were involved in the development of the system and then using them as opinion leaders. Kwik-Fit involved operational users at an early stage of investigating possible systems to introduce into the depots, whereas the Travel Company involved one operational user in the initial investigation process. ScotRail and the libraries made limited attempts to involve operational users at this preliminary stage which was dominated by senior managers.

Analysis: what was the dominant model of user/analyst interaction in the case organizations?

Salaway (1987) writes that an honest and realistic relationship between the analyst and the user is the key to successful computer systems. Errors are built into the design as a result of faulty interactions from a very early stage. She identifies two models of user/analyst behaviour.

Model one has four governing variables;

● achieving goals;
● maximizing wins/minimizing losses;
● minimizing the expression of negative feelings;
● rationality.

The aims of the people using this interaction model were control over their own tasks and protection of their own position. Model two had three governing variables:

● valid information;
● free and informed choice;
● internal commitment.

Model one is the most common model of user/analyst behaviours and is inherently error-prone as the participants advocate their own ideas, do not seek new information to challenge their own ideas, and do not challenge existing norms. This leads to poor quality information which in turn forms an inadequate basis for system design. Model two, in contrast, aims to eliminate sources of error by generating valid information, identifying, seeking out and exploring sources of conflict, and generating and testing information. The main characteristic of Model two is 'inquiry', as opposed to Model one's 'advocacy' and defensiveness. User/analyst interactions using Model one will lead to error-prone systems due to lack of relevant information, whereas Model two interactions should produce more accurate and useful information where both participants learn from the process. The quality of user/analyst interaction could be improved by training in communications skills for both analyst and user and would leave the user feeling that they had been genuinely involved.

Cooper and Swanson (1979) also identify the user/analyst interaction as being the critical phase of system development. They suggest that the use of personality and behaviour profiling may aid mutual understanding between the two participants. They advocate a greater emphasis on search and intelligence before analysis and design and final selection or choice, with continual iterations and feedback at each stage to amend initial assessments.

From the evidence in the cases it would seem that the dominant model of user/analyst interaction was Model one and that misunderstandings between the technical and business staff at this stage were built into the system when it was designed. The Ambulance Service and the Travel Company changed to Model two later in the projects, following a learning process with users. Kwik-Fit managed to use Model two throughout.

Design and development

What are the particular problems posed by the design and development of computer network systems and did the case organizations use any innovative techniques to overcome them?

Rockart and Crescenzi (1984) describe a series of methods used to involve top level management at South-Western Ohio Steel in the introduction of a large-scale computer system. The requirements analysis stage started with the definition of critical success factors by interviewing all key managers. The first stage engaged management's attention and ensured that the system would meet the most critical business needs, providing a clear definition of both the business and IS needs. Martin (1982) also advocates the benefits of using managerial critical success factors when designing computer systems and convincing managers that their concerns are central to the design and development process.

The second phase at South-Western Ohio Steel involved using a 'focusing workshop' to discuss the critical success factors identified and to narrow the number down to the most critical and a manageable number. Third a 'decision scenarios workshop' was held demonstrating three proposed prototypes to show management how systems could assist the decision-making process and further develop their understanding of the technical system. The next phase was the building of a prototype so that management could see results quickly with minimum costs. The prototype noticeably increased management enthusiasm about the system's potential. Much has been written about this method of design and development which uses prototype systems for the users to experiment with and modify (Henderson and Schilling, 1985; Jansen, 1985; Kraushaar, 1985). Prototyping is useful in addressing the users' inability to specify their information needs and can be a useful mechanism in supporting user-analyst learning. There is no tightly written specification for the system: the analyst has a preliminary discussion with the user and quickly produces a conceptual model of a possible system for the user to explore, evaluate and modify. Rockart and Crescenzi (1984) conclude that the process resulted in the users having a feeling of control rather than just token involvement and support, but we found limited evidence of similar techniques being used in the case organizations. Kwik-Fit used a similar system when the consultants from the USA came over and visited the Kwik-Fit depots demonstrating the new system. Although extending this process to all the staff in a nationwide organization could be extremely time-consuming and complicated, an adaptation designed for top management and cascaded down through key staff at all levels could be useful in engaging their support for the introduction of computer network systems, whilst leaving the control of the project in the hands of the technical staff.

An innovative approach called 'the Chief Developer Team' is described by Kozar and Mahlum (1987). Here most of the team members are not trained systems personnel but knowledgeable members of the user group who are tutored by technical staff in techniques to enable them to define and document the existing system and its deficiencies. The building of the new physical system is delayed as long as possible, as the emphasis is on recognizing the problem or opportunity rather than actually solving the problem. The team builds models of the existing system and the new requirements with the help of an outside consultant or Chief Developer. After the initial phase, the Chief Developer or consultant is phased out and a systems professional phased into the team to turn the specification into a technical system. The IS department becomes the facilitator of systems rather than the developer but still retains ultimate control. It is interesting that this is almost exactly the way ScotRail designed and developed their network except for the absence of the external consultant. The Travel Company's initial pilot and Kwik-Fit's Edinburgh pilot worked in a similar way. The approach was successful in the case described by Kozar and Mahlum (1987) because the users had a committed role in the development and also produced accurate and relevant requirements specification before starting the technical development. This led to a real feeling of system 'ownership', but was still directed by the initial intervention of the Chief Developer. This method could be used for the development of network systems providing that care was taken in making the selection of the original team of users representative of all levels and areas within the organization. Another complication could be, as in the case of ScotRail, in persuading the users to take part in this process when they felt that the main aim of the exercise was to divest them of their jobs.

El Sawy (1985) describes a method of development that involves the users through a process of what he calls 'cultural infusion'. A core group is formed from those users who are most enthusiastic about the system, who both need it most and will benefit most from it and can be used as opinion leaders. A support person is appointed to lead the group: they are the opinion leader or champion of the particular system. This core group is then educated thoroughly in the system and then used to persuade other users. The computer services department then cuts itself off from the development group and leaves its diffusion to the users. The support person is the key to the diffusion to the rest of the organization. This rather subversive approach could be successful in the introduction of networks, as the training of the rest of the users is in the hands of non-technical staff. However the method is crucially dependent on the quality of the support person chosen and their political skills. Several of the case organizations had tried methods similar to this: ScotRail used their long-serving Manager of Management Services to spread enthusiasm for the system, the Cooperative tried to find an enthusiast in each library, Kwik-Fit relied on enthusiasm filtering down from the top and linking reactions to the computer system to loyalty to Tom Farmer and the Company. The Travel Company and the Ambulance Service had not identified an opinion leader to spread knowledge and enthusiasm about the system, and this may be one reason why they initially faced more difficulty than some of the other organizations. Later on in the project the Travel Company used the branch managers as opinion leaders by training them at headquarters and then making them responsible for training their own staff.

Implementation

Were there particular problems during the implementation of computer network systems and how did the change agents overcome them?

If the users have not been given a sense of ownership of the project during the development stages, resistance problems will manifest themselves during implementation.

One consequence of the most commonly used development methodologies is the separation of the design stage from the implementation stage. Top management and systems designers tend to generally concentrate on the strategic, creative analysis and development stages and may almost ignore the implementation stage which is regarded by many as tactical and routine and safely left to lower levels of technical management and operational users. In other words they concentrate on the Content and Control agendas and ignore the Process agenda until the implementation phase, by which time it may be too late to avoid resistance and disruption. This separation leads to problems with user-acceptance as they feel that the system has been designed with little reference to their needs and then left them with the responsibility of solving the operational problems of the new system. As Quinn writes (1980: 85):

> executives and their companies generally have fallen into the trap of thinking about strategy formulation and implementation as separate sequential processes. They rely on the awesome rationality of their formally derived strategies and the inherent power of their positions to cause their organizations to respond. When this does not occur, they become bewildered, if not frustrated and angry.

Ironically implementation is probably the most important part of the development cycle and the one that is most likely to determine system success or failure. Users' attitudes to the system are determined by their initial response to the system if they have not been involved in the preliminary stages. This was illustrated by the initial response of some of the Travel Company branches to the new system. Leonard-Barton and Kraus (1985) see the implementation period as a time when there is a shift of 'ownership' of the system from the technicians to the users. Baronas and Louis (1988) see it as a period of transition during which the control, autonomy and skill-base of the users is threatened and they may actually passively resist its implementation, e.g. the reaction of some staff to ScotRail's early 1980s networks. Without open opposition they can delay or display only token support, exploit the technical staff's ignorance of organizational politics and the business side of the system, well demonstrated by some of the early reactions to the Travel Company system. This is what Keen (1981) describes as 'counterimplementation'. It was noticeable in both the Travel Company and the Ambulance Service that there were different reactions from different branches depending on a range of factors, for example personal characteristics of the individuals concerned and geographical differences.

It is effective to allow users perceived control (Baronas and Louis, 1988) by giving them some limited power over the timing of implementation. This can be difficult when implementing networks as they are large scale and inevitably imposed from the centre. Often, the users know little about the system or its purpose before it is introduced at their particular site, as clearly demonstrated from the cases. As a result they feel limited commitment and ownership of the system because they have had restricted involvement in the development of the system and its rationale. At this point 'back-stage' methods may become essential.

BACKSTAGE ACTIVITY

What evidence was there that 'backstage' manipulative techniques were used to ensure the success of network systems?

The literature on participative management 'ethically the correct procedure' (Child, 1984) consistently advises that manipulation and threats as project management techniques are counterproductive. Nevertheless in large complex projects it may be necessary to resort to them due to lack of time, resources and expertise, as well as the scale and complexity of the project. It is also necessary to confront the political realities of managing complex projects in Quadrant 4. Keen's solution to this paradox is a political approach, a 'countercounterimplementation' strategy which establishes who can 'foul it up', coopts likely opposition early on, provides clear incentives and benefits from the new system, creates a 'bandwagon' and so on, a 'backstage' political strategy that few technical staff have the skills to operate. This strategy depends heavily on the presence of a 'fixer' with prestige, visibility and legitimacy, for example Alex Lynch of ScotRail and Tom Farmer of Kwik-Fit, and based on negotiation, mobilizing coalitions. As he says: 'Getting things done, whether Down and Out or Up and In requires the careful building of coalitions based on complex negotiations. The larger the scope of the project and the more strategic the goals, the truer this will be.' (Keen, 1981: 27). Alex Lynch concentrated on leading from the front and exercising strong normative political pressure on sometimes reluctant Area managers to push the project through, using large implementation meetings to pressure the less enthusiastic managers to cooperate. Tom Farmer assumed, accurately, that he had the full support of his managers. The Travel Company set up the Users' Forum to exert peer pressure on more resistant branch managers. The Ambulance Service did not use manipulative political techniques to get support for the radio system from the depots, which may have been one factor delaying its successful implementation.

It is widely recognized (Burns, 1961; Keen, 1981; Kanter, 1983; Pettigrew, 1985; Morgan, 1986; Argyris, 1988; Morley, 1990) that the role of the change agent is inherently manipulative and political, and that while the 'frontstage' activities of technical and strategic logic and user-participation strategies are important to provide organizational credibility at all levels, the 'backstage' activity is key to success or failure.

Introducing any organizational change is essentially a political process.

Political skills: negotiating, interpersonal, internal marketing and selling skills are just as important as technical skills. As Kanter (1983: 226) puts it 'skill at managing organizational relationships is vital'. Much has been written about the choice of 'opinion leaders' (Kanter, 1983), how to deal with 'hedgers' (Leonard-Barton and Krauss, 1985), and how to mobilize support and neutralize opposition. Kanter (1983) also writes at length about the tactics to be used: pre-selling, trade-offs, making cheerleaders, securing 'blessings' from top management, 'selling rather than telling' and so on. Doll and Torkzadeh (1988) among others, write about the importance of top management support for any change, to apply normative pressure to 'hedgers' and to those with low self esteem who may find change most threatening. These political strategies are even more likely to be employed when introducing networks, as the scale of change greatly increases the likelihood of internal political problems. Keen suggests a counter strategy which was largely adopted by Alex Lynch (DGM) the 'fixer' for the implementation process for ScotRail: Establish clear direction and objectives; establish simple phased programming; adopt a fixer/facilitator/negotiator role; seek and respond to resistance; rely on face to face communications; create a prior 'felt need'; build personal credibility; coopt support early on; and exploit a crisis'.

Kanter also suggests a strategy with familiar features: Wait them out; wear them down; appeal to higher authority; invite them in; send emissaries; display support; and warn them off.

Argyris (1988) suggests a strategy of 'mixed messages', as for example telling the travel company's branch staff 'you will have more local autonomy' at the same time as issuing the directive 'we need a strategic perspective'. This strategy was also used by ScotRail, the libraries and Kwik-Fit and is an approach particularly relevant to nationwide organizational network systems.

If backstage techniques are to be successfully employed it is important that the change agent has access to the backstage politics of the organization. A change agent who has little insight into internal power politics will be unable to operate this type of strategy successfully. Alex Lynch of ScotRail had worked within ScotRail for many years and apart from being senior he also understood the internal workings of ScotRail intimately. The chief librarian in the large university library had exceptional political skills and insight despite being fairly new in the post. In contrast, the Travel Company and the Ambulance Service did not have a fixer with this type of skill.

SUMMARY AND CONCLUSIONS

Managing the Process agenda is central to success in large-scale complex Quadrant 4 network projects, when change agent vulnerability is high. Used together, the 'front-stage' and 'back-stage' methods can be highly effective. Used alone, 'frontstage' or 'backstage' methods may fail. The organizations in the cases varied in their use of the two types of approach. The change agents within ScotRail were able to concentrate on the political 'backstage' activities as the technical/content side of the project had been delegated firmly to the technical departments. The Travel Company concentrated heavily on the content and control agendas. Kwik-Fit worked hard on all three agendas and both 'backstage' and 'frontstage' activities, but relied heavily on the charisma of Tom Farmer who swept the company forward by sheer strength of personality. The Ambulance Service concentrated on content, control agendas and neglected the political, process agenda and 'backstage' activity. The Library Cooperative concentrated on content and control, but they did not have easy access to the political/cultural/social agendas of their member libraries. They needed to adopt someone within the library to be change agent, who had good knowledge of the political situation within the library and good interpersonal skills to manage the 'backstage' and the process agenda; with commitment to the change project even if they did not have strong technical abilities.

The introduction of computer networks offers organizations the prospect of increased efficiency, effectiveness and competitiveness. Despite the problems related to their scale and complexity, the pay-off in improved service, productivity and ability to seize new opportunities is perceived by all organizations in the sample to be fully worthwhile. Equally, the implications of a partially functioning or underperforming network system are correspondingly dramatic for the future of the organization, as can be seen in the case of the Travel Company during the first 18 months of the implementation process. The development methods used for the older generation of stand-alone computer systems have been found inadequate even for these more limited applications, but are still largely in use today. They have led to unsatisfactory systems in the past primarily due to their concentration on the technical aspects of the system to the exclusion of human, organizational and political factors. The risks of an unsatisfactory network system are too high. The Process agenda and both 'frontstage' and 'backstage' change management techniques are needed to make sure that the full potential of networks is exploited for the benefit of the whole organization.

9

CHANGES TO STRUCTURE, CONTROL AND WORK ORGANIZATION

There is considerable evidence about the effects of stand-alone computer systems on the human aspects of organizations. Has the use of networked computer systems continued previously observed patterns, or is something different happening? Have computers linked in networks had different effects on the human aspects of organizations? The cases presented earlier provide empirical evidence on four questions about the human implications of such systems for the people who use them, and for the broader system of social relations which make up the organization.

1 What do they mean for the design of individual tasks, and for the way groups of staff work together?
2 How do they change the tasks of managers and the balance between central and local decision-making?
3 What, if anything, happens to the allocation of tasks between departments?
4 What are the effects of computer networks which create links between organizations?

In presenting and interpreting this evidence we try to distinguish those outcomes which are inherent in the technology itself, and those which reflect the choices of managers and other players in the project. Many studies of stand-alone computer systems concluded that organizational changes were not determined by the technology itself, but by the choices which managers made when planning and implementing the change (Wilkinson, 1983; Buchanan and Boddy, 1986; Long, 1987). Though working from the same non-determinist perspective, McLoughlin and Clark (1994) qualify this emphasis on management choice by arguing that technology can have an independent effect on the work tasks which have to be accomplished, as a result of the fundamental architecture and technology of the engineering system. While acknowledging the influence of social forces on the innovation process, they argue that at some point the features (the technology and/or the architecture) of the engineering system become substantially fixed – and that 'these technical influences subsequently become one factor shaping... the design space available to organizational actors, within which choice and negotiation over organizational outcomes may be made' (p. 133).

COMPUTER NETWORKS AND THE DESIGN OF TASKS

Studies during the 1980s of the links between stand-alone computer technologies and the design of work showed the malleability of such systems, in that technically similar systems were found to be associated with markedly different working arrangements (Robey, 1981; Wilkinson, 1983; Buchanan and Boddy, 1983; Sorge *et al.*, 1983). While the precise link between such working arrangements and performance was sometimes ambiguous, a common conclusion was that expensive, sophisticated equipment and systems worked best when expensive, skilled and committed people were in charge. Drawing on ideas drawn from the quality of working life debates of the 1970s, it was argued that most people sought intrinsic satisfaction from their work, and this implied designing the new jobs so that they met certain psychological requirements of work (McLoughlin and Clark, 1994; Walton and Susman, 1987). Failure to do so would result in a deskilled, uncommitted and inflexible workforce which would not be competitive.

It was therefore argued that the potential benefits of computer systems would be fully realized only when technical and work design issues were dealt with in an integrated fashion, so as to make the most of both the equipment and the people working it. The more the organization was operating in uncertain and demanding markets, the more important it was that staff acted with commitment and skill. For example, Boddy and Buchanan (1986) recommended that work should be designed in a way which complemented rather than replaced the skills of those who would be using the new system. In practice this was rarely done systematically, with a variety of other organizational considerations often blocking that approach (Symon and Clegg, 1991).

Networked systems raise the same issues of work and organization in a more acute form, as the networks themselves link different parts of the organization more closely together, by the timely movement of data and information between different members of staff. These also raise new issues in the area of work design, such as where tasks are to be carried out, the scope for variation in tasks between different locations, and the implications where people who are physically distant need to work interdependently.

McLouglin and Clark (1994) concluded that stand-alone computing technologies had four fundamental consequences for the tasks required:

1 The elimination or reduction of manual tasks and skills.

2 The generation of more complex tasks, involving more mental, problem-solving and interpretative activities.

3 The continuing need for some tacit skills associated with the previous technology.

4 A different (typically more passive) relationship between the user and the technology compared to that existing in previous systems.

How far does a similar pattern emerge from our studies of networked systems?

Do computer networks eliminate or reduce manual tasks and skills?

The systems introduced all required transaction data to be entered manually at some stage, usually during the transaction itself, and this often replaced the use of paper and pencil. Subsequent manipulation and distribution was done electronically, with little manual intervention. Companies were thus able to reduce the number of clerical staff, or to grow the business with the same number. The location of those remaining manual tasks typically moved from the centre to the branches. This broad trend was to some extent offset by changing circumstances requiring more administrative data.

Mcloughlin and Clark's (1994) studies showed that introduction, for example, of electronic telephone exchanges had greatly reduced the demand for certain types of manual skills, and similarly that the use of computer-aided drafting equipment eliminated some traditional drafting skills. There was less need for action-centred, hands on physical performance of tasks. Similar conclusions were drawn by Buchanan and Boddy (1983), Wilkinson (1983) and many others. However Buchanan and Boddy also concluded that there was little if any direct effect on employment arising from the introduction of the stand-alone computer systems which they examined.

In the present study, a major objective of three of the companies in introducing computer networks was to reduce or at least contain the amount of time which staff spent on manual administration and paperwork. At the travel agent, each booking taken by a clerk for a package holiday generated a mass of administration to ensure that the booking was properly recorded and accounted for. The paperwork was previously completed at the branch, either by the sales staff when they had time (including overtime) or by separate clerical staff. It was then sent to Head Office by post, where other clerical staff checked the information and keyed it into the computer.

This process was cumbersome and costly, and led to errors, misunderstandings, and stress and conflict between the staff in the branches and those in Head Office, and distracted the sales staff from their primary tasks. Sales staff now keyed in the administrative data during the transaction, and this data was then passed automatically to the mainframe at Head Office. It was then no longer necessary to employ staff there to check and enter the administrative data; previously about forty staff had done this work, but by 1993 there were none. Most left or were redeployed to other work at Head Office or in the branches. This enabled the company to handle much more business with the same staff: while the branch network grew from 275 in 1989 to over 400 in 1993, there was no increase in the number of staff at Head Office.

At ScotRail the computer networks were used to support management efforts to reduce the number of administrative staff, especially at Regional Headquarters and in the area offices. Before the change there were ten area offices, each of which had, in the mid-1980s, installed computer networks, based on personal computers linked by a Novell file server. They performed a range of administrative tasks for the area, such as compiling crew rosters and calculating wages; they were also able to enter data directly into BR mainframe systems. Their introduction had enabled substantial reductions in staff, as they eliminated the need for many manual administrative tasks.

The next stage in reorganization was intended to ensure that decisions were taken at the lowest rational point, reducing the need for many intermediate jobs, which had existed mainly to pass information from one level to the next. The number of areas was reduced from ten to five to bring further savings, and the whole change was supported by rearranging the existing computer networks and building new communication links. The redesigned organization led to a loss of some 200 posts at Regional Headquarters.

At Kwik-Fit, as at the travel agent, each transaction created an administrative load, to ensure accurate restocking, accurate financial information and to provide management information. The computer network overcame this by using an EPOS system to capture all the transaction data, and a communication link to transfer it automatically to the mainframe at Head Office overnight.

The system had a clear effect on the work of depot managers and their staff, who no longer had to spend time on manual, paper-based administrative tasks. This form-filling work had previously been a major chore, and taking it away allowed them to concentrate on running the depot and dealing with customers. All staff in the depot, but especially the manager, spent time at the terminal. These were an integral part of the job in the depots, being used by all staff to enquire about stock availability or prices, or to prepare invoices and receipts.

Since transaction data was now entered at the point of sale, Head Office staff were no longer required to check and key in the data. This enabled Head Office staff numbers to be kept very low, although the company grew rapidly. The ratio of administrative staff to depots had fallen dramatically – a much bigger business was being run with no increase in the number of purely administrative staff at Head Office. However, more people were employed on activities which grew with the business – such as property management and training.

In the other cases eliminating manual tasks was not a major objective, but there was still evidence of it happening. For example, the creation by the Library Cooperative of an integrated library system allowed libraries to eliminate timeconsuming manual loan systems, and to reduce the number of professional cataloguers. At General Insurance the use of PMS enabled claims to be assessed and processed through the system, thus eliminating much paper-based administration.

At the Ambulance Service, the planners no longer physically sorted cards representing patients into groups of tasks for the drivers to deal with and then adjusted the loads as the day went by (the process known in one control room as 'hot seat planning'). The computer dealt with many aspects of this but, although it enabled the administrative load in existing tasks to be reduced other changes introduced at the same time increased the amount of manual administration. Management reacted to the introduction of service level agreements and a more competitive environment by requiring more management information about performance: so planning assistants had to spend more time entering data into the management information system than they had before, and also spent time handling and analysing performance data required by management which the system could not yet produce automatically.

The Millennium Management Information System was intended to gather and distribute information about performance and expenditure, so as to support local managers in operating the service cost effectively. No significant manual tasks were replaced, though keyboard and data entry skills were a bigger part of the job. There was no evidence yet that the system in itself was adding to the complexity of clerical tasks – in many cases it was creating data entry tasks which had not been performed before. Some of these tasks were performed by administrative staff, but others became part of the work of Planning Assistants and district ambulance officer, adding to the variety of their work, and, in the view of some managers, distracting them from their primary roles.

Do computer networks generate more complex tasks for staff

Staff dealing with customers were now more likely to have to key data into a computer terminal during the transaction in addition to previous tasks, adding an extra complexity to the job. This task was sometimes seen as distracting staff from, or even conflicting with, what they saw as their primary task. In other cases the ability of the systems to hold and present data to staff as required reduced the complexity of their work.

McLouglin and Clark (1994) found that in both the cases mentioned earlier, the loss of manual tasks had been balanced by a need for more abstract mental tasks – such as visualizing what the three dimensional images represented in reality. They termed these, following Zuboff (1988), the 'intellective skills', as they comprised more mental than physical activity.

At the Travel Company, the branch accounting system was designed to capture all administrative data at the time of booking. Management decided not to have a separate clerical function in the branches, so data entry was done by sales staff. They used the existing computerized, and complex, reservation system linked to an airline or a tour operator to make the reservation – that process was not affected by the change. Once the reservation was confirmed, they entered directly onto the screen the details of the reservation, details of those travelling, the payment arrangements, and so on, in the presence of the client.

This system had changed the work of the branch staff. They saw themselves primarily as sales people, whose main job was dealing with customers. Administrative work had had to be done, but could be left until later, or was done by someone else. Now they had to complete all the administrative tasks relating to the present customers before they started dealing with the next one. In the past, some of these tasks would have been done by the same staff later in the day; some by a clerk in the branch; and some (checking and data entry) by staff in a distant Head Office. It could take up to 15 minutes to enter all the details required from the customer. This was unacceptable, as it delayed staff and customer, and potential customers may leave if a queue built up.

At Kwik-Fit too, data had to be entered while the customer was present, by depot staff. However, the details were relatively simple, and many messages were pre-coded, so the time required was insignificant. The increase in complexity was slight, and terminals had come to be seen as an integral part of the work in the depots.

At the libraries adopting the Cooperative's system, the task was slightly more complex than before as it now involved understanding and using the computer system. Junior staff felt their job had become more interesting, and that their skill and status had been enhanced. The system freed professional staff to spend more time dealing with requests from the public, rather than handling paper. Since these requests could be dealt with faster they had increased in number, and had become a more important part of the librarians' job.

In the ambulance service, the APTC computer used the data to propose an appropriate grouping of patients to be collected, and thus eliminated the need for the planning officer to use the original forms to plan the routes. However the officers had to complete and confirm the grouping, using their traditional geographic knowledge: the computer would support them in this traditionally complex task, which had become more complex as a result of wider organizational changes. They would themselves work on the computer as required, to deal with a change or other request. In this case, the computer network reduced task complexity for the planning officers, and increased it for the planning assistants, who now had to key data into the system while taking it off the telephone, adding to the variety of work.

On the A & E side, details about resource status in relation to incidents were held by the computer, automatically updated and presented to the controller: this had previously been kept in their head or on paper slips, and the complexity of their job was thereby reduced. However it was also increased by the larger geographical area now handled from each control room. The control assistants had previously only recorded information from the telephone before passing this to the Control Officer. Management had decided that the assistants should now work on all stages of the process: they now entered data into the system, and could allocate and despatch vehicles. This significantly raised the complexity and responsibility of their job, though the Control Officer retained overall responsibility. The Control Officers themselves found the job less stressful than it had been before.

Are some tacit skills associated with previous technology still required by staff?

In all cases they were, as network requirements were added to the existing core activities.

McLouglin and Clark (1994) concluded that while manual skills had been substantially replaced by intellective skills, the tacit knowledge about the processes being carried out was still required – especially in being able to visualise the consequences of actions taken. This was similar to the conclusions reached in Buchanan and Boddy's (1983) study of computerization in a biscuit-making plant.

At the Ambulance Service, a deliberate decision had been taken to retain human skills even though much of the geographical knowledge was now held within the system. Clearly some manual tasks were eliminated, and there was less dependence on geographical knowledge, although keyboard skills of a defined standard were required. The task had been very complex and stressful when only the manual systems were available and had become more so as control rooms were closed. However, geographical knowledge and awareness of the situation was still needed by the control staff, as they were responsible for making the final allocation decision; they could over-rule the computer to take account of, for example, a sudden blockage to a road, or an unfolding major incident.

Staff in other cases continued all their normal sales and customers service activities and supplemented these with computer work. For example, staff in the travel agent developed the skill of maintaining a dialogue with the customer as they entered the data. By maintaining eye-contact and showing the customer the screen, they could check that the data was being entered correctly, and reduce the scope for error and confusion later.

At the libraries, the on-line cataloguing system changed the role of librarians. Being able to draw down a standard entry for a new acquisition led to a deskilling of cataloguing work, with some staff feeling that their professional skills had been taken over by the system, and senior staff were less able to fill in temporarily for absent colleagues. To overcome this, one library deliberately trained senior staff to ensure they could use the new system as well as their junior colleagues. More generally many other library skills were unaffected, and more time could be spent with the public.

Do computer networks change the relationship between the user and the computer?

Typically staff have a closer link with the networked computer, as they interact directly with it, and see it as an integral part of their work.

For example at the Travel Company, sales staff now spent no time completing forms, less time responding to queries from Head Office, and more time working on the screen. Whereas previously their relationship with the company's internal computer system had been indirect (passing paper for keying), it was now direct and active. They spent more time with the customer, though the extra time was spent on administration rather than selling. The transaction was completed in its entirety during the face-to-face contact with the customer, rather than being fragmented between different times, people and places.

At Kwik-Fit, the Ambulance Service and at General Insurance a similar pattern was observed, of staff providing an immediate link between the customer and the wider systems of the company, by entering or retrieving data during the transaction. However, views of this were also affected by the perceived quality of the system: at General Insurance, for example, aspects of management information systems were seen by middle managers as unhelpful, and as obstructing their effective working.

Do computer networks reduce autonomy by imposing greater discipline and uniformity?

A clear theme in many of the cases was that computer networks led to greater uniformity between locations, and less autonomy in the way tasks were performed.

Studies of stand-alone computer systems in manufacturing by Blumberg and Gerwin (1984) and Adler (1991) indicate that workers experienced a significant loss of autonomy as FMS systems were introduced, while Millman and Hartwick (1987) report that the use by staff of mainframe computers and PCs required them to work more accurately and consistently.

At both the Travel Company and at Kwik-Fit it was seen as essential that staff in the branches went through a precise closing down procedure at the end of the day, to enable communication over the network to take place. Indeed management at the travel agent clearly saw the system as a way of imposing discipline and standardization on widely dispersed branches. Staff had previously developed relatively independent ways of working with the manual system, and had also regarded administration as a secondary activity to their primary sales job. The branch automation programme was a way of unifying the company which had grown rapidly by acquisition and opening its own new branches. The system demanded that transactions were entered accurately – the IT director pointed out that a paper form

left so much autonomy with the person filling it in

– whether a box was completed or not, for example. The new system did not permit that, as everything had to be completed before the clerk could move on to the next stage of the transaction. It became less important for the branch manager to ensure policies at this level were followed, as this was built into the system.

At Kwik-Fit, the information entered would directly affect operating processes, such as stock ordering, so accuracy was important – for example, to enter exactly the right description of the tyre being fitted, not something near it. Care was taken to ensure that staff understood this.

The system tightly limited the scope of depot staff to offer a discount or special deal to a customer, as this would be spotted at Head Office the next day, and would need to be justified. Ensuring conformity to the company guidelines was a major benefit which managers at Kwik-Fit saw in their system. The established company procedures had been built into the design of the terminals in the depots, and the overnight feedback to Head Office very quickly showed up any deviation from standard practice. It reinforced the procedures and removed a lot of the complexity usually associated with size from the running of the business, as all transactions had to conform. It focused staff attention on doing things the company way, and tightly constrained the way tasks were performed.

There was some evidence that staff in the libraries lost autonomy or freedom of action. With the introduction of the on-line catalogue, for example, one large metropolitan library was able to introduce a standard unified catalogue for the whole service, in place of the manual system, which had allowed each branch library to have their own. However, another library claimed that it had retained a variety of systems, and therefore had experienced little loss of autonomy.

There was still variation in local practice in the way in which the APTC system had been implemented in the Ambulance Service, so that autonomy was little affected. There was an interest at Head Office in gradually bringing procedures into line, so as to be seen to be providing a consistent national service. This was probably being achieved more by the concentration of work in a smaller number of controls than through any technological means. On the A & E side, however, the work of the controllers was subject to tighter scrutiny by local control managers. Details of every incident were automatically recorded on the computer, and all the actions taken by staff dealing with the incident could be reviewed to ensure that correct procedures were followed.

In summary, computer networks have had more visible effects than stand-alone systems in reducing the number or proportion of manual staff employed, and have generally led to those tasks being carried out away from the centre, usually at the point of the transaction with the customer. Task complexity was increased in some cases, especially where the use of the network system was in addition to traditional tasks of dealing with customers. Networks often led to a reduction in the autonomy which staff had over how they carried out their work, although feedback was likely to be more immediate and accurate.

DO COMPUTER NETWORKS AFFECT THE ROLES OF MANAGERS?

Computer networks enable changes in management roles, as well as in those of their staff. They can alter the roles directly, and also by leading to changes in the decisions to be dealt with at each level of the hierarchy. Some early predictions were that computers would lead to more centralized organizations, and the decline of the middle manager:

> We believe that information technology will...make centralisation easier. By permitting more information to be organised more simply and processed more rapidly, it will extend the thinking range of individuals. It will allow the top level of management intelligently to categorize, digest and act on a wider range of problems. Moreover by quantifying more information it will extend top management's control over the decision processes of subordinates (Leavitt and Whisler, 1958: 43).

Others argued that the technology would in practice be used to provide more information to those at lower levels, enabling their decisions to be better informed, and their position enhanced:

> It seems hardly conceivable that the social forces which are present today...could permit the separation of society into two classes – one, an elite corps of thinkers (top managers, technologists or some combination of the two), and the second, all other human beings. If, during the next decade or two, we do not see a continued trend in the direction of business decentralization, we must look for the

failure, not in any unalterable laws of technological advance, but in the decisions of businessmen (Burlinghame, 1961: 126).

In practice the evidence has been mixed and, as with the design of jobs, studies of stand-alone systems show a wide variety of responses. Boddy and Buchanan (1986) quote a variety of cases, some where centralization had clearly occurred, but others where this did not appear to have been either the intention or the result of the installation. In contrast, Markus (1983) reports a case where centralization of financial control was very clearly the driving force behind the introduction of a new system – with predictable responses from those lower down in the organization. A review by Robey (1983) led him to conclude that, on balance, computer systems led to greater centralization, as only minor decisions were in practice decentralized, while the major ones were more likely to be taken at the centre. Where structure did change, it usually took the form of sustaining and reinforcing existing structures.

Computer networks heighten these possibilities for change in managerial work and in hierarchical structures. Their technically inherent ability to transmit data rapidly over wide areas makes it possible to feed the centre with much more data than hitherto, permitting greater central control; or alternatively, to provide more information to the periphery, enabling managers there to act with fuller information in the light of local conditions.

While the nature of the technology is likely to affect information roles directly, managers are not just information passers. They also perform interpersonal and decisional roles, which are less amenable to computerization. This perspective was also used by Pinsonneault and Kraemer (1993), who predicted that the effect of networks on the three management roles would be mediated by the centralization of decision-making.

Are managers' roles changing for wider reasons?

In five of the cases, wider business pressures were putting new and tougher demands for performance on managers.

Dopson and Stewart (1993) conducted a European-wide review of IT and managers, in the course of which they identified the extent to which wider business pressures are putting more demands on the managers formal role, independently of the introduction of IT systems. They note, for example, that many managers are having to take responsibility for a wider range of tasks, are more accountable for results, and face a stronger emphasis on performance.

At the Travel Company, for example, branch managers had clear targets to meet in terms of the profit which their office earned, and competitive pressure and changes in ownership made it more important that these targets were met. In the Ambulance Service, major changes in the roles of managers had preceded the introduction of the computer network. The Divisional Directors and their managers were under great pressure to meet performance targets for the service, and faced the prospect of competitive tendering and more demanding customers in the hospital – who were themselves under pressure to meet quality targets. Managers at all levels were therefore expected to monitor the performance of their service, and to keep costs, especially staff costs, within budget. The pressures were increasing as the Service moved towards independent Trust Status.

At General Insurance, wider company policy was to make branches more like autonomous profit centres, with managers being less concerned with administration, and more with sales and profitability. At Kwik-Fit this had always been at the core of the manager's job, who was seen as running their own small business, while at ScotRail the primary thrust of the organizational changes was to put more responsibility onto area managers in preparation for privatization. So these cases are representative of wider trends, which also imply that the introduction of a computer network may in some respects act as a moderating variable, reinforcing or diminishing changes initiated by more fundamental changes in the business environment. They may be affecting, but not causing, the changes observed.

How do the informational roles of managers change?

Senior managers used the systems to obtain more rapid and accurate information about the state of the business; middle managers generally were not getting the information which they felt would be most useful for them. In some cases the information handling role of junior managers had been eliminated. Where the system automatically transmitted changes in company policy to staff, the managers' dissemination role was reduced; similarly the automatic transmission of routine data to the centre enabled more time to be given to the spokesperson role, such as in dealing with customers.

Foster and Flynn (1984) found that the use of an information management system enabled top managers to by-pass established communication channels and to gain direct access to middle management data, leading to a centralizing of decision authority. This was supported by Malone *et al.* (1987). Conversely, Wildavsky (1983) pointed out that IT overwhelms managers with unordered data that needs further processing to be of value. Middle managers are able to uncover relevant details, analyse decisions in greater depth, and so use the information to make a difference to what they do.

At the Travel Company, senior managers at Head Office now had overnight information on each branch's performance the previous day. This not only helped operational control, but supported much closer analysis of business trends. The company was aiming for a system which gave managers at each level the information they needed. However, by 1994, Divisional Directors did not have rapid access to the central data. They still relied on the traditional system whereby branch managers telephoned the Divisional Office and repeated the information to a clerk, who entered it onto a PC spreadsheet. This 'home-made' system provided the Divisional Directors with their weekly reports on branch performance, about 5 weeks before they would receive the official version from Head Office.

Since the branch accounting system automatically transmitted all transaction data directly to Head Office, the roles which branch managers and staff previously performed in transmitting that information were beginning to be bypassed, as anticipated by Malone *et al.* (1987). However, as we have seen, they still needed to provide area managers with weekly sales information as the central system was not yet able to do this quickly enough. At Kwik-Fit, an unexpected benefit was the information the system now gave to senior managers about the performance of branches and products. They began to use the information to model alternative pricing and marketing strategies, and generally to understand better how the business worked.

The depot managers had previously spent much of their time dealing with administrative information, and passing this to Head Office. The MAT terminals transmitted all that information directly, completely eliminating the depot manager's role in preparing and sending routine information. Conversely, routine operating information from Head Office to the branch (price changes, or instructions about an aspect of policy) was passed automatically to all branches simultaneously, reducing the scope for error and inconsistency. It also meant that they were under more sustained pressure for performance, as information on this was visible and rapidly available.

At General Insurance, senior managers were able to gather information on branch performance, allowing them and the branch managers to look in more detail at the business, and to evaluate alternative directions more systematically. However, branch managers and their staff considered too much of their time was spent entering data for the central system: and they varied in their views about the quality of the information which they received in return.

By 1994 the Management Information System in the Ambulance Service was providing more comprehensive information about costs in each region, division and station, and this was regarded as useful by senior management at Headquarters, conscious of the competitive conditions in which they were now operating.

In the past local managers had performed a relatively slight informational role, concentrating mainly on ensuring day-to-day operations, with little need to be concerned about costs or performance. This had now changed dramatically, and the Millennium system was intended to support them in their new role. It took information about activity from the various operating systems, related that to centrally prepared information about costs, and passed summarized performance data back to the line managers.

However, local managers took the view that the information they obtained was neither reliable or timely. They found the system hard to use, and time-consuming to extract the summary data which they needed. The system had originally been developed as a financial management system, based around a mainframe computer, which had been extended into a network environment. The information needs and time-scales of line managers in a potentially commercial environment were different from the original users', and the data available did not support the line managers' current needs.

At General Insurance, the PMS system gave both Head Office and Branch Managers more information, with which to manage the business and decide the most profitable lines of activity.

Do managers now have more time for interpersonal roles?

In two of the cases the systems undoubtedly released managers from administrative tasks, to spend more time with staff and customers: this trend was not evident in the other cases.

At Kwik-Fit, removing the administrative burden allowed depot managers to spend more time on the interpersonal roles, especially in managing their staff and dealing with customers – seen by the company as a major benefit of the system. Area managers had always been expected to provide a very direct and personal form of leadership for the depot managers, as a way of maintaining high levels of commitment from the staff in the depots. So although information about depot performance was available at Head Office, senior managers insisted that personal contact with the depots was maintained, and deliberately shaped the system to ensure that area managers had to visit their depots frequently to keep in touch.

A major objective of the change at General Insurance had been to enable managers to get away from the office to make contact with clients, and several comments from Branch Managers indicated this was happening: though practice varies between branches. It had also improved relations between managers, as discussions were based more on fact then hunch.

At the Travel Company, the system had reduced the amount of time which the branch managers spent in liaison with Head Office: this had mainly been to sort out difficulties created by the manual administration system, and was largely eliminated by the automated system. Apart from that, they were still managing the staff in their branch on a day-to-day basis, and continued previous patterns of contact with their area and Divisional managers. One motive for the wider changes at the Ambulance Service had been to make managers more visible, so as to act as figurehead and liaison for their local service: but wider changes had re-inforced their internal administrative role.

Do computers affect the decisional roles of managers?

The answers varied. At two companies the autonomy of managers in the branches was more curtailed, and their decisions were subject to closer scrutiny by senior managers. At a further two the networks were introduced to support a move to greater local autonomy – and in one this was successful, and in the other not. In a final case the networked system supported both a devolution of some decisions to area managers, and a centralization of other decisions to Board Level.

Malone (1987) and Foster and Flynn (1984) predict a removal of decisions from middle management to senior management: Wildavsky (1983) implied that to use the information in practice would require action by middle managers, whose decision roles would therefore be strengthened, a view supported by Dawson and McLoughlin's (1986) study of a computerized freight system, in which a new middle management role was created to use the information now available. Smith (1988) shows that some EPOS systems have led to more centralized management decisions, while in others they have supported decentralization.

At the Travel Company, there had been some loss of independence at branch level, since branch activity was now subject to closer monitoring from the centre, for example by reviewing a daily transactions report from each branch. However, it was also expected that the decisions of branch and area managers would be better informed, on the basis of better information. For example they were being encouraged to look at business results each month and make decision on staffing etc. in the light of the likely effect on profitability at the branch. It was also beginning to be used to assess the effects of discounts and special offers, so basing decisions on more systematic analysis, though this was limited by the very limited on-line access which was presently available.

Prior to the introduction of the MAT system at Kwik-Fit, depot managers had had considerable decision-making autonomy. Information about activity in the depots took weeks to reach Head Office, so that depot managers decided what stocks to hold, what suppliers to use and what discounts to offer. Area managers had found it hard to manage that situation, especially as the company grew rapidly, with many new depots coming in. Staff at Head Office found it hard to run the administration, and senior management was losing track of business performance.

At the time of its introduction, the MAT system unambiguously increased the control exercised by Head Office managers over those in the depots. By transferring information overnight from each depot it permitted closer monitoring of depot staff, and showed problems clearly and quickly. Since information on their performance was readily available to the depot managers, they were also able to discuss trends and problems with their area managers on a common, factual basis. All decisions on pricing, stocks etc. moved to Head Office. Top management began to see new aspects of the business which they had not previously been aware of: with lower management increasingly constrained as to the way they ran their depot.

However, in 1993 the company introduced a significant change by creating geographical divisions, each with about seventy-five depots, operating almost as autonomous business units. Management introduced the change in order to be more responsive to the market. While the computer network had provided information to Head Office about depot activity, managers at the centre had found it hard to act on that information as the company grew – they lacked both local knowledge and direct authority over the depots to implement their decisions. This is an example of the point made by Wildavsky (1983), that managers need to be able to interpret the new data available if they are to make good use of it. Divisional general managers were therefore appointed, with direct profit responsibility for the branches in the Division. They were also given greater autonomy over decisions about, for example, purchasing, staffing, and depot investment. All information about depot performance collected each day at Head Office was now processed and sent on immediately to the Divisional Office. Senior managers hoped that with these more clearly drawn lines of responsibility the divisional managers would make better use of the information which the system provided about the state of the business and the performance of the depots. In other words, middle management's decisional role was strengthened, and the flow of information to them was increased to improve the performance of the business. In the continuing tension between the pressure for corporate control and local responsiveness, the company has moved from a centralized to a divisional structure – but with information still flowing through the centre.

At ScotRail a central part of the Omega strategy was to make local managers more directly accountable for achieving results with the available resources, and more decision-making responsibilities were being devolved from the region to the areas, especially over finance and personnel matters. The underlying idea was to push control and decision-making down the region to the lowest rational level. This clearly enhanced the decisional roles of the Managers in the new larger areas. This was facilitated by the computer network, but was driven by other factors. As outlined in the case study, the organizational changes came first, and were supported by the computer networks.

In addition, these allowed information to flow directly from the Area to BR Headquarters computer systems, by-passing regional managers. Their decision-making power was undermined by decisions to remove some issues from Regional control altogether, and deal with them at Board level. Freedom to access and amend data at regional level was also limited, further implying a shift of influence from that level, to the areas or to the Board.

At the Ambulance Service, the Millennium system was intended to support local managers in running their areas: but most found the system too slow and cumbersome to be of much practical use in their day-to-day decisions. The information needs and time-scales of line managers in a potentially commercial environment were different from the original users, and the data available did not support the line managers' current needs. Consequently they were not using the system as much as they would have expected to, and it was not yet having a major impact on the decisions they made in managing the day-to-day decisions of the service – such as whether to meet a staff shortage by authorizing overtime, or permitting service standards to fall.

At General Insurance, the PMS system enabled decisions on new lines of business, or on branch management, to be made on better information. Senior management felt more confident in their strategic decisions, and branch managers more confident in managing their clients. However they too, like managers in the ambulance service, were limited by the lack of good quality, timely and on-line information – which was what they needed to meet the new demands of their jobs.

As managers become subject to greater pressures for performance, how have computer networks affected their roles? The have had significant effects on managers' information roles, with the gathering and processing aspects of that for many junior managers being almost eliminated. Middle managers, facing tougher pressures, were not always getting the information which their decisional role demanded, reflecting system development priorities being set elsewhere in the organization. A clear effect in many of the cases was that managers were able to spend more time on interpersonal aspects of the role, such as dealing with customers or staff.

DO COMPUTER NETWORKS AFFECT DEPARTMENTAL OR FUNCTIONAL BOUNDARIES?

Earlier empirical studies, mainly of stand-alone systems, have shown that structures have changed less than the technologies. While many systems made significant structural changes possible, and perhaps depended on them for really effective use, the organizational changes have often not been made (Robey, 1983; Voss, 1988; Symon and Clegg, 1991).

For example Robey's study (1983) of eight organizations which had introduced a variety of computerized information systems concluded that these were often introduced without structural change, especially in those cases where the purpose was to improve administrative processing. They noted changes in the numbers of staff in existing departments, but no examples of departments being merged or realigned. A similar conclusion was drawn by Sorge et al. (1983) following their careful comparative study of twelve UK and German companies which had introduced computer numerically controlled machine tools. They reported that they had observed

> solutions to CNC applications which are organizationally simple, and (those which are) complex; some emphasise functional differentiation, and others integration of functions within positions or departments (p. 147).

Boddy and Buchanan (1986) also reviewed the relationship between computer systems and organization structure. They too identified situations where the new technology had been fitted into existing departmental and functional structures, but also reported cases where significant organizational changes had been made. Computer technology had both led to the elimination of old functions, and to the introduction of new ones. In some cases these functional changes had been accommodated without any overt changes in the broad structural arrangements of the company, while in other cases substantial organizational changes had been made.

In their study of networked systems, Rockart and Short (1989) refer to the 'wiring together' of units within a firm, and of firms to each other. They point out that computer networks make it possible for information to flow to one location and for greater control to be exercised over geographical separate units, once they are logically and physically wired to Head Office. The same process also allows design, engineering and manufacturing functions to become more closely intertwined in the design of new products; and for companies to become closely attached to customers through devices such as terminal based order systems. All this may take place with or without formal changes in structure. They identified five ways in which computer networks enable companies to manage their functional or geographical sub-units:

1 Integration across the value-added chain – managing the effort of adjacent functions, through, for example, the network's ability to move information electronically between them.
2 Integration within functions – managing the effort of multiple units within the same function, by, for example, better information flow or common database.
3 IT enabled team support – through e-mail or computer-to-computer links to support widely dispersed members.
4 Planning and control – using the network to speed up the annual planning and controlling processes of the business, including the possibility of enabling more managers to be part of that process through on-line exchange of information.
5 Integration between organizations.

What were the effects on the value chain?

Four of the cases included examples of networks being used to pass information across steps to the value chain either to take out costs, or to add value.

Rockart and Short (1989) found that network systems often lead to the collapse of the multi-stage value-added chain into a smaller number of segments: product development, product delivery, and customer service. They found networks being used to integrate activities within these stages more closely.

At Kwik-Fit a major benefit of the MAT system was the tighter integration achieved between the separate functions within the value chain. When a customer in a depot enquired about the price and availability of a particular tyre, the staff used the MAT terminal to generate a quotation on screen, which could then be printed and given to the customer. If this was accepted and the work done, the transaction was updated with payment details etc., and used locally to update stock and other records for the depot. All such transaction details were then sent automatically to Head Office that night, where the data was used not only to provide management information, but to arrange distribution of parts to replace stocks used, and to place new orders on suppliers. This backward movement through the value chain was then reversed: as suppliers delivered the parts, invoice and delivery information were automatically matched, and stock records up-dated, ready for the next customer query.

It was also used to add value to the chain itself in the case of Fleet customers. They could specify their requirements in advance, so that if one of their vehicles was taken to a depot, the type or quality of part fitted was in accordance with the Fleet company's wishes. All invoice and accounting details were then presented electronically to the Fleet customer in an agreed format, which fitted their accounting procedures.

At the Ambulance Service the networked systems were used to reduce costs or add value at certain stages in the value chain, though this was not a concept the service used. For example, the command and control system automatically transmitted instructions about an incident from the computer in the control room to an electronic display in the vehicle, eliminating the need for (occasionally disrupted) voice contact. Information from the same screen was then automatically archived for later processing into management information within the service, and as the basis for measuring the quality of service delivered.

The information was also used to add value to the service provided to hospitals, the main customers of the service. For example, it became much easier to provide them with information about who was ordering ambulance services, and for what categories of patients. The hospitals valued such information in controlling their costs. Improved planning systems also allowed patients to be delivered closer to specified appointment times.

At the Travel Company, the early stages in the value chains between the travel agent and the tour operator were already linked by computer networks. The branch automation system continued the link back into the company's own administration. By linking the retail offices to the mainframe computer the task of entering data at Head Office from paper generated at the branches was eliminated, which took significant direct and indirect costs out of that link in the value chain.

Do networks facilitate integration within functions?

In four of the six cases this clearly happened, though there was also a case of functional disintegration, arising from incompatible computer systems.

Rockart and Short (1989) quote several examples where computer systems have been used to improve working relations within a function – such as oil trading, foreign exchange dealing and maintenance. The common link, they argue, is the recognition that no unit in a function is completely independent, and that networks offer a way of improving the way they work together.

The MAT system clearly enhanced integration within functions at Kwik-Fit. For example, a depot which was unable to meet a customer request from its own stock could phone Head Office, or a nearby depot who, given the power of the system, could readily say whether the part was available. Accounting functions, such as the reconciliation of orders to suppliers, deliveries, and invoices from suppliers were all done automatically within the system, and those functions had become more tightly integrated within Head Office. The branch network also became more integrated, as performance measures and systems were common between them all.

At the Ambulance Service there were significant effects on integration within the control function. Once requests for PTS transport had been keyed in from the telephone, the proposed schedule was adjusted by the planning officer and a final list printed off for the driver. When the runs were complete, the information was then transmitted electronically to Headquarters, where it was used for statistical and management information purposes.

On A & E work the system integrated the sub-functions of taking messages and allocating vehicles: and the control assistants' tasks, were now scarcely distinguishable from those of the control officer, except that the latter retained overall responsibility. However, because the A & E and PTS used fundamentally different computer systems, the two activities were *less* integrated, as staff no longer moved between them.

At the Travel Company, the activities within each retail outlet became more integrated, as the back-office administration connected with a reservation was now done by the clerk who dealt with the reservation, using the same machine. The previously separate administrative function within the branches was eliminated. It also helped integrate the branches as a whole, ensuring they followed standard company procedures, using standard data definitions, in a way that had not been possible with manual systems. Management also felt the branch accounting system had made it easier to integrate widely dispersed branches, and especially new acquisitions, as the computer systems incorporated company policies. Towards the end of the study, the company reached an agreed merger with a large travel business based on the Continent, and it was decided that all the branches owned by the other partner would come onto the system, which would again assist functional integration.

Do networks support teamwork?

The effects on team work were limited, except in the sense that the information on performance available through the system enabled existing management teams (at all levels) to work on the basis of up-to-date and accurate information, rather than hunch and guesswork.

Jones and Scott (1987) found that the use of FMS systems had contrasting effects on team formation, reflecting differences in management policy: Millman and Hartwick (1987) report that managers found their relations with fellow workers after the computerization were either unchanged, or had improved.

Within the A & E service the network system led to several developments in teamwork. Instead of working on relatively distinct parts of the task, assistants and officers now did all tasks on the new system, though the officer retained final responsibility. Second, the use of digital radios rather than voice to pass messages from the control room to ambulance crews, and vice versa, diminished direct human contact. Management also realized that the crews may not fully appreciate the significance of some tasks the crews were now required to do, or how they affected the work of the control staff. Crews were therefore encouraged to visit the control room to see the system working, and a working party was set up between control staff and crews to meet from time to time to discuss the operation of the system. As mentioned in the previous section, the acquisition of radically different computer systems led to the creation of two distinct teams in each control room, most of whose members, at the time of the study, could only work on one system, although senior staff were trained on both.

At General Insurance, Branch managers claimed that they and their staff worked more as a team following the introduction of PMS, and relations with other branches had also improved. At the Travel Company, relations with Head Office were said to have improved, because data flowed more quickly and there was much less scope for disagreement and conflict over the provision or interpretation of information.

How significant are their effects on planning and control?

The ability to use network systems for this purpose was not always envisaged at the start of the project, but was discovered in three of the cases on the way through. The ability to achieve this result varied considerably, and required additional organizational changes to be effective.

At Kwik-Fit the effects on business planning and control were significant. The system provided accurate information on current performance which was routinely compared against targets on a weekly and monthly basis. It was also used to model the possible effects of price or other changes, and to monitor the effects if they were introduced. However, to use the information required further organizational changes. Similar uses of the information from the computer network were being made at the Travel Company and at General Insurance.

The MIS system was intended to support the planning and control of the Ambulance Service, in the more difficult environment it now faced. Experience of this was mixed. Information about the volumes and types of work done was now being collected for the first time, and was regarded as an essential tool in planning the pattern of services which the hospitals were likely to seek. However, the features of the system referred to earlier ensured that middle managers were reluctant to use it, and it was having little effect on the way divisions were managed.

In conclusion, it appears that, in contrast with the experience with stand-alone systems, the ability of networked systems to move information across stages in the value chains is facilitating greater functional integration, and several companies discovered unexpected possibilities for planning and control in the course of the changes. The effects on team-working in these cases were so far limited, but beginning to appear.

WHAT ARE THE EFFECTS OF COMPUTER NETWORKS THAT CREATE LINKS BETWEEN ORGANIZATIONS?

The final theme concerns the effects of interorganizational systems – computer networks which transmit information across organizational boundaries. These are a natural extension of the use of networks to link geographically separate parts of the same organization, though their use depends not only on the creation of industry-wide technical standards, but equally importantly on the willingness of enough players in an industry to take part. Major choices between collaboration and competition are raised in creating an industry-wide network. Once available, the different players face choices about whether or not they use the system – and in some cases there is no real choice: companies agree to use the system for their transactions with particular customers, or they don't get the business.

Interorganizational networks are not new. The first stage of the American Airlines' Saber project was implemented in 1961, as the carrier sought to build tighter links with independent sales agents (Copeland and McKenney, 1988) and the potential competitive advantages have long been recognized (Kaufman, 1966; Cash and Konsynski, 1985). More radically, interorganizational computer systems are seen as having the ability to change the nature of the relationships between firms. Short and Venkatraman (1992) refer to this as the process of redefining the business network, as firms move from being suppliers of defined goods and services to engaging in what they call a 'value-adding partnership', supported by networked computer systems. However, Benjamin *et al.* (1990) note that the scope for obtaining sustained competitive advantage from such systems is elusive.

Do interorganizational networks change the location and experience of work?

There were examples in the cases of the location of work being changed, though no significant effects on the nature of the work seemed to follow from being linked to another organization.

Networks have the effect of transferring the performance of tasks from one organization to another. The physical activity, and the cost of entering and validating the data is passed to another body – from the supplier to the customer (or vice versa), from the principal to the agent, perhaps from the firm to the private individual. For example Copeland and McKenney (1988) show how certain routine manual tasks were transferred from the airlines own offices to that of the sales agents as the reservations systems were introduced. However after a review of eighteen applications of EDI to order processing, Benjamin *et al.* (1990) concluded that there had been little change in the work of staff in either the buyer or the supplier organizations:

> Along with few staff reductions, there was very little change in the tasks performed by those using the systems (p. 36)

partly, they believed, as a result of deliberate management policy to ensure easy acceptance of the system. One exception was that in one case, where orders were now placed electronically, there was less need for staff to have good telephone skills, and more need for them to be able to review the information entered onto their computer system by the customer.

One example of an interorganizational link in the present study was that established in the Ambulance Service between one control room and a major hospital. This meant that for those orders, the recording task was now carried out in the hospital by their staff, rather than by Ambulance Service staff. At Kwik-Fit, links had been established in both directions, principally to the company's suppliers and to their major Fleet customers. Orders for parts were sent electronically to suppliers by EDI for a growing proportion of their purchases – about 70 per cent at the time of the study. In return, most delivery notes and invoices were sent electronically by the supplier to the company. Again the initial order entry task had moved to the customer. On the Fleet business, details of all transactions, together with invoices and other management information were sent automatically from Kwik-Fit's computer to the customer – and again payments were received electronically. This implied that many of the accounting activities which would otherwise have been done by the Fleet customer were now performed by the supplier's staff and systems – with no remarkable consequences for the skills or work of those involved.

The Travel Company's systems had for several years been linked to industry-wide reservation systems which gave access to the tour operators and airlines own reservation systems. These enabled available holidays to be scanned in the travel agents office: once a choice was made by the customer, the reservation was made electronically over the system.

Libraries using the Head Office also found that cataloguing work moved from their own staff to those engaged at the Cooperative's network, and so reduced the number of cataloguers employed by the libraries themselves.

How do networks change relations between organizations?

Several of the cases indicate changes in the nature of the relationship between the case study firm and other enterprises, but these changes were gradual and evolutionary, rather than sudden and radical.

Cash and Konsynski (1985) predicted radical change:

> Interorganizational systems will radically change the balance of power
> in buyer-supplier relations, provide entry and exit barriers, and...
> shift the competitive position of (firms)

Benjamin *et al.* (1990) studying eighteen applications of EDI, have commented on the limited nature of the organizational change taking place between firms using it for order-processing. But taking a longer term perspective, Short and Venkatraman (1992), based on their study of the

Baxter Healthcare system for ordering, tracking and managing hospital supplies show that major interorganizational changes took place over the 30-year evolution of the system.

Kwik-Fit had originally developed the links to its Fleet customers through the BACS system to improve the efficiency of invoicing and to help customers control their costs. They were gradually extending the services provided, and were being more closely integrated with the management of the customers vehicle stock – for example by following customer-prescribed routines when a vehicle from that customer was presented for repair.

The Ambulance Service had limited electronic links with the hospitals at the time of the study, but was expecting to be able to provide progressively more detailed information to the hospitals about the quality and costs of services provided – and to be able to discuss with them alternative ways of providing the service at an acceptable cost. In this way the service hoped to become more closely tied to their customers, and so protect their competitive position. The Library Cooperative clearly involved a radical change in relationship, in the sense that activities previously done by each library were now performed by the cooperative. The Travel Company found that enhanced internal systems, complementing the established link to the tour operators, automatically provided information about sales and commissions. This had been complex and expensive to calculate, and a source of dispute. The position of the Travel Company relative to their suppliers was said to have been strengthened by this innovation.

Our conclusion is that contrary to expectations, the effects of interorganizational systems have been more limited than expected. The challenges involved in making significant changes in this area are obviously considerable, and little progress had yet been made at the time of the study by these organizations.

CONCLUSIONS

This review of the links between networked computer systems shows both similarities and contrasts with earlier studies of stand-alone systems. One of the clearest effects is the reduction they have caused in the number of manual tasks to be carried out, as much of the rekeying and manual processing and retrieval of data disappears. Unlike the earlier experience with stand-alone systems, this has had visible effects on the employment opportunities available in the companies studied. Another common effect has been that staff are now expected to work in more predictable and consistent patterns, basing their actions closely on the requirements and routines of the screen. In general, the introduction of networks has reduced the number of hands-on, action-based tasks: immediacy is in some ways being replaced by distance.

There was clear evidence of the networks enabling staff to gain new and deeper levels of understanding about their work operations – the 'informating' process referred to by Zuboff (1988). This in turn meant that staff had scope for developing higher level intellective skills, in place of some of the manual, action-centred skills which were displaced.

The performance of staff and managers was made more visible as the networks were installed. It became much easier for supervisors or managers to know whether staff were following established operating procedures, so that any deviation could very rapidly be drawn to their attention and corrected. Managers too were subject to closer scrutiny – daily or weekly performance figures compared to budget could often be available to senior managers overnight – again prompting rapid feedback and expectations about corrective action. However, it was also clear in at least three of the cases that while the hardware could have provided middle managers with more useful data for their needs, the software which had been installed prevented this. Whether consciously or not, system development priorities had not been directed at meeting the information needs of middle managers.

The emphasis in most cases was on transmitting performance information to the centre – which then raised the question of whether the information could be effectively used by managers remote from the action. This mirrored the debate which Dawson and McLoughlin (1986) reported in BR when installing a computerized freight management system. Aware of the impending information overload at the centre, management made a structural change by introducing the new grade of area freight assistant, specifically to enable computer-generated data to be used closer to the action. A similar process of structural adjustment to make good use of new information was evident in at least two of our cases.

Cross-functional integration was beginning to happen, as information was moved between stages in the value chain, and as some previously separate functions became more closely integrated. The use of the systems for more detailed planning of activities was a benefit which companies were discovering as the systems came into use – and was bringing significant and unexpected benefits.

Finally, it was evident that the nature of computer networks meant that their design and shape continued long after what has traditionally been regarded as the 'design' or even the 'implementation' stage. The systems continued to grow and change as new hardware or software was added, or as the location of terminals in the network was changed in response to user requests or business developments – in other words the social shaping of the technology was a continuing rather than a discrete process. So too were the working and organizational arrangements around the system. Managements' approach to these matters was not fully formed at the outset of the project, but emerged during it in the light of experience, learning, and new conditions – again similar to McLoughlin and Clark's (1994) account of the BR freight project, in which

> a sub-strategy concerned with changing management organization emerged during the process of change, and...was focussed on improving the overall control and performance of the freight operation (p.189).

The long-term nature of computer network projects makes them particularly open to incremental changes in the organizational arrangements that are created. The 'dimensioning' of both the technology and the architecture of the system can continue to be adapted to suit new requirements – although as our cases show, some forms of underlying technology and architecture were easier to modify than others. This potential for further adaptation in work and organizational arrangements is perhaps the major distinction between stand-alone and networked computer systems.

10
CONCLUSIONS

This brief concluding chapter examines how managements in the organizations studied made use of the possibilities in the development of networked computer systems. What aspects of organizational performance did they seek to improve? How did they support those objectives with changes in organization and structure? What issues do widely-dispersed networks raise for those managing the process of implementation? And more generally, what can the study of these major projects, aimed at implementing the information technology aspect of strategy, tell us about the strategy process as a whole?

WHAT BENEFITS WERE EXPECTED, AND WHAT WERE ACHIEVED?

Studies of stand-alone computer systems have shown the wide range of business objectives to which they may contribute. A distinction is commonly made (Boddy and Buchanan, 198; Porter and Millar, 1985) between the use of computer systems to achieve operational goals, and their use for strategic goals. The former refers to situations where the emphasis is on using the technology to improve the performance of existing operations. The technology is seen as a way to cut costs, save staff, give management more control. The focus is on internal processes, and towards achieving relatively predictable and measurable increases in efficiency.

Strategic applications, in contrast, are characterised as being those where the uses of computer technology have been more radical, often being directed towards the provision of goods or services which were not possible with earlier equipment. The technology is seen as a way to do new things, give staff new information, or to enter new markets. The focus is more likely to be external, and towards achieving benefits that are less predictable, and much harder to quantify in advance – 'innovation at an acceptable price' was how one person described her senior managers' view of their move to a networked system.

These approaches are not necessarily incompatible. Operating improvements are often essential to survival, and the experience gained gives the confidence to move on to more innovative applications. The risk is mainly that of lost opportunity, if operating improvements are pursued without sufficient thought being given to more radical uses which may be inherent, but not yet realized, within the technology.

Keen (1985) makes a similar approach to the implications of networked computer systems when he distinguishes three ways in which they can contribute to performance:

1 Running the business better: e.g. by managing widely distributed inventories better, so that service can be improved, and/or stock levels reduced; by improving internal communications; or by improving links with suppliers.
2 Getting an edge in an existing market: e.g. by using networks to redefine the nature of the service provided to customers – for example by putting a terminal in the customer's office to make it easier for them to do business; or by differentiating a standard product by adding value or making it easier to use.
3 Repositioning the business: e.g. by using technology to move beyond the existing boundaries of the business, to add new services to existing ones, or to make use of an existing telecommunications infrastructure to make new services available.

Rockart and Short (1989) reviewed several cases in which companies had used electronic networks to coordinate their activities and to develop new service strategies. They report, for example, the benefits one business obtained from being able, through a centrally coordinated electronic service system, to monitor maintenance work across the country, and to allocate resources accordingly. The company found that the system was also able to provide design staff with direct access to fault data, which could then be used to modify products to enhance their reliability.

Others (e.g. Cash and Konsynski, 1985) have studied the use of networked computer systems to move data between organizations. An example is that of tour operators who arrange for information about their holiday packages to be provided on the terminals of independent travel agents (Palmer, 1988). The travel agent dealing with a customer reviews the availability of particular options, and makes reservations, directly through the terminal, in communication with the tour operator's central system.

Johnston and Vitale (1988) propose that the growing popularity of such systems lies in the belief that they can contribute directly to important sources of competitive advantage. These advantages lie in the ability of networks to enhance companies' comparative efficiency, or their bargaining power. The former include improving the efficiency of their internal operations, or of their links to other organizations, as already discussed. The latter include the use of networks to raise switching costs (once a customer has taken on a suppliers network, the cost of taking the business away is increased); and to provide a unique product or service feature. All the parties must be able to see enough potential benefits so as to have an incentive to join such a network.

Whatever the expected benefits, how likely are they to be achieved? A study by Voss (1988) of fourteen organizations which had introduced (stand-alone) Advanced Manufacturing Technologies highlighted the distinction between 'technical success' and 'business success'. The former refers to situations where the technology is installed, running, teething troubles overcome, and with little down-time. The latter is achieved when the system is contributing significantly to the competitive position of the business, by improving performance on variables which are valued by customers – such as Flexibility, lead-times, quality etc.

Discussion with managers in the plants concerned led Voss to conclude that while all were able to report technical success, the proportion able to report business success was much lower, mainly due to the more complex organizational changes that were needed.

A similar note of caution with regard to networks has been introduced by Benjamin *et al.* (1990). They reviewed many examples of interorganizational computer systems, and concluded that gaining sustained competitive advantage from EDI systems was rare:

the prospects of hitting the jackpot with an EDI system are still slim (p- 35).

Only one of eight systems studied had brought a sustained competitive position – mainly because others rapidly introduced similar systems. The main reason for investing in EDI was defensive – it had simply become a cost of doing business in the sector concerned.

In summary, studies of computer networks have shown that, as with earlier systems, they can be used in ways that have the potential to provide significant support to the broader competitive position of a business. This support may be given by one or more of these four approaches:

1 As a way of gaining a competitive edge, by being the first to adopt a particular system in an industry. This is likely to be most pronounced in sectors where there is a significant information content in either the product or in the value chain (Porter and Millar 1985) – and where high volumes of transactions have to be handled within or between organizations. This also occurs where products have a limited life, and perhaps a high value – this will encourage investment in systems that will improve operating decisions (such as travel or hotel reservations).

2 As a way of supporting broader business strategies, such as a desire to operate over a wider geographical area, perhaps on a global scale, while at the same time being able to react quickly to local needs and opportunities. This enables a company to get the advantages of both integration and flexibility. One suggestion is that only by having rapid and timely data flows are big companies able to operate on a world scale – and to protect themselves from others operating in that way. Another incentive could be a desire to reduce layers of management and generally increase responsiveness, and a sense that this is made more possible by the availability of networked systems.

3 As a way of staying in business, or defending an established position. It may be necessary to respond to the use of networks by established competitors, or by new ones entering an industry, perhaps because of changes in regulatory policy. Similar pressure may come from more demanding customers who perhaps require the investment as a condition of trade. This may be an example of the Freeman argument, that companies in certain types of industry, where network systems become the normal method of operation don't have much choice but to invest. This could also arise within an organization, where a local management group has no choice but to invest in an organizationally compatible system, if its place in the corporation is to remain secure.

4 As a way of surviving on the technology treadmill. Investment in further networks may simply be an inevitable consequence of earlier decisions. Having taken certain decisions to go down a particular technological route, and established a trajectory of innovation, it may become very hard for management to avoid enhancing and developing the system to maintain the position.

In the present study, a highly relevant feature in relation to benefits achieved and expected was that in all cases the projects were lengthy activities, extending over many years. The initial decision to invest set off a long process during which the aims and the design of the project evolved in ways that were not predicted at the start. For example, Kwik-Fit originally focused on the pressing need to solve an administrative overload, as their manual system tried to cope with the growing volume of paper generated by the growing business. Very soon after the system became operational, it became clear to management that the data about branch operations which the system generated gave a new and unexpected insight into the business. This in turn enabled management to monitor and control branch performance much more closely.

Enhancements continued to be made to the system which enabled new services to be offered and new markets entered. Changes were made not only in technology, but also in the structure, when a divisional structure was introduced, at least in part to enable better use to be made of the management information generated by the system. By 1995 the company was significantly larger and more diverse than it had been when the initial investment was made. Much of this was attributed to the unforeseen flexibility provided by the system, which itself had evolved radically since its inception.

The other cases illustrate similar tendencies, particularly the response to outside forces. For example, at ScotRail and the Ambulance Service effective internal systems enabled flexible responses to privatization plans which were imposed on them – and which in themselves had led to significant changes in both the originally planned IT and organizational strategies. The distinctive feature of long term projects to implement computer networks is the scope they offer to discover new targets on the way through.

DID MANAGERS DEFINE OR DISCOVER THE AGENDA?

A common theme of early studies has been that those implementing major IT projects should have a broad rather than a narrow agenda of change. Thus Buchanan and Boddy (1983), Long (1987), Voss (1988) and Symon and Clegg (1991) concluded that the success or otherwise of the systems they studied could be traced to the extent to which management attended to organizational as well as technological implications in the change proposed.

Was the technology implemented as originally intended?

The starting point in five of the six cases was clearly technological, in the sense that much time and effort was devoted to the analysis of technical options and possibilities. For example, management at Kwik-Fit made careful analyses of what was available, before deciding to develop a unique system, based on an established package. That was duly implemented in

1982, but was continually enhanced in the years which followed. Some of these were adaptations to the software, as management at headquarters discovered the value of the data the system could generate, and asked for more. A major change occurred in the hardware when it was decided to replace the original ICL mainframe with one supplied by DEC – in response not only to growth but to management's view at the time that the organization would take on a more decentralized character. The architecture of the system also evolved – as when, in response to Divisionalization in 1993, significant additional terminals and equipment were placed in divisional offices, which had previously had only limited facilities, reflecting their previously limited role.

Each of the other cases reflect a similar evolution of their computer networks over the years following initial installation. Sometimes, as in the Ambulance Service, this was in response to clear changes in the business environment, which made it necessary to add new information management facilities, which had not previously been needed. Or, as in Kwik-Fit, it was because an opportunity to provide a new service was spotted which could add value to the transaction, as well as improving internal efficiency (such as providing an automated credit card processing facility through the depot terminals). In others, as in the Library Cooperative or General Insurance, changes reflected technological developments which enabled existing installed systems to be upgraded – but with the effect that the systems in use at the end of our study were significantly different from those which management had had in mind when they began the project.

Did the organizations change as originally intended?

It is fair to say that in five of the six cases the project was conceived and initially set up as a technological innovation, without much attention being given to organizational issues. However as each of the projects progressed, other factors were put on the agenda, as it was realized that the new system opened up possibilities – for changes in work, reporting relationships, organization structures, and in the kind of information which could be provided – which had not been envisaged at the beginning. For example, the Travel Company found it necessary to consider, and then to redesign, branch working arrangements; and the amount of data provided to Divisional Directors was still a matter of debate several years after the system went live. At the Ambulance Service the Command and Control system opened up the possibility of changing the roles of control assistants and control officers – and this change was introduced as well as the technology.

Although ScotRail was an exception in that management there designed the organizational changes before considering the technical implications, the common point still stands that the agenda to be handled in implementing major computer networks was in all cases found to be wider than originally envisaged (see also Voss, 1988). Decisions had to be taken in respect of each of those agenda items (see Boddy and Buchanan (1992) for a fuller account of the content, process and control agendas). And it was from the accumulation of those actions, few of which were planned when the project began, that produced the 'engineering system' (McLouglin and Clark, 1994) in operation at the conclusion of our study.

How do these observations relate to our understanding of the strategic planning process? While traditionally presented as an orderly, rational activity in which systematic analysis of options were carefully weighed to produce a long-term plan, much recent work sees strategy formation as being in reality much more evolutionary and tentative in nature. For example, Mintzberg and Waters (1985) distinguish between deliberate – realized as intended – and emergent strategies – realized despite, or in the absence of, intentions.

They argue that a perfectly deliberate strategy has to fulfill three conditions. First, precise and well-articulated intentions; second, the intentions being common to virtually all actors in the organization; third, collective intentions must be realized exactly as intended. The environment to enable this would have to be completely predictable. This is at one end of the continuum. At the other extreme is the perfectly emergent strategy, in which there is consistency in the actions taken over time – but without these actions being guided by earlier intention.

The process we have observed in these organizations implementing computer networks – made up of a stream of actions from which patterns emerged – is remarkably similar to Mintzberg and Waters' views on strategy formation, especially their concept of strategy as an emerging, rather than as planned, process.

In particular, it seems to correspond to what they regard as the most realistic perspective on strategy formation – namely an 'umbrella' approach to strategy. This describes the situation in which managers 'set general guidelines for behaviour – define the boundaries – and then let other actors manoeuvre within them' (Mintzberg and Waters, 1985: 263). When the environment is complex, perhaps uncontrollable and unpredictable, the pattern of actions cannot be set in one central place, at one time. Only the boundaries of action can be set there, with strategies being allowed to emerge within those boundaries, as the project unfolds in stages, and as the world outside is seen to impose new requirements – and as issues are discovered which need to be on the agenda.

The cases also show how the scope for choice in each of these areas of action was bounded – but the width of those boundaries varied. For example, the scope for choice in technological matters was often constrained by features of the technology itself, or by decisions already made by other parties. Conversely, considerable choice was often available with regard to the organizational items on the agenda – how the staff would interact with the system, how work would be organised around it, or how quickly it would come into full operation.

WHAT EFFECTS DID REALIZED BENEFITS HAVE ON EMERGING STRATEGIES?

What were the main organizational effects?

As the agenda gradually broadened, shaping the elements of the emergent strategy, a significant area was the changes which were made in the organizations' patterns of structure and control. Chapter 9 demonstrated that computer networks, intentionally or not, produced significant changes in organizations – though not always in line with original intentions. For example, in the Ambulance Service the computerization projects were part of a wider set of changes to improve the performance and image of the service. This had begun with moves to centralize controls, make managers more accountable for their budgets, and release local officers from routine tasks so that they could be more visible. As the project progressed, the environment changed. Competitive tendering and service level agreements increased the pressure on the service to set and meet competitive standards of performance. It became much more important for the service to manage resources effectively – so the Management Information System came to play a more prominent part in the project, especially as it offered the prospect of enabling managers to monitor and control current operating decisions much more closely.

Similar patterns could be seen in several of the other cases. Many routine manual tasks were removed and the location of the remaining tasks typically moved from the centre to the branches. There was also strong evidence that computer networks have led to greater unifgrmity between locations and less autonomy in the way tasks were performed. The role of managers sometimes changed, particularly in eliminating the information handling role of middle and junior level managers. In many cases the autonomy of managers at lower levels was curtailed, with their decisions subject to closer scrutiny by senior managers. There were however exceptions to this in that some of the networks were introduced to support a move to local autonomy. However our overall conclusion was that networks were being used to increase the degree of internal discipline, consistency and control within the organization.

Did greater internal control support external performance?

If the pattern of greater consistency and control which emerged from the stream of actions made during the implementation process is an accurate interpretation of events, it raises the question of how this relates to the benefits which companies expected and achieved from their networked systems. Part of the conventional wisdom in organization theory is that organizations in volatile and uncertain business environments need to develop adaptable and flexible internal structures. This is usually taken to imply the adoption of policies which enhance the autonomy and discretion available to staff, so that they are better able to act responsibly and rapidly as business circumstances change.

Is there a contradiction here, between the business environments which the organizations were facing, and the fact that their computer networks appear to be producing more controlled and consistent ways of working? Not necessarily. What seems to have happened is that by enabling tighter internal procedures on some aspects of the organizations' processes, computer networks have enabled them to respond more effectively to external opportunities. They were often introduced initially to rationalize procedures, and to remove the administrative burden of the existing business reflecting a traditional management interest in effective control, especially in widely dispersed organizations which were increasingly hard to monitor by traditional paper-based methods. This operating perspective towards networks was generally achieved, though with different degrees of success.

In addition, however, it was discovered that this greater discipline and control opened up the possibility of responding more quickly to new opportunities. Networks removed the complexity of size and scale, and enabled the business to act as a more coherent whole, in which all the parts could be relied on to follow a particular lead or practice. So while aiming to use networks to create a tightly coupled internal system, they also found that this enabled them to respond to changes in technology, or in the business that arose during the development and enhancement of the originally intended network. For example, while the Ambulance Service patient transport systems were intended to improve operating efficiency in the scheduling of vehicles, it was found that a by-product of the system was enhanced management information which was of value to their customers, and which was expected to help the service fend off potential competitors who lacked the systems to offer that additional service benefit. Kwik-Fit is another clear example of this, and the Travel Company and General Insurance were likewise using the discipline and consistency provided by the systems to see and respond to external changes, opportunities and threats.

Our cases show examples or tendencies in the direction of both deliberate and emergent strategies, rather than extreme forms of either, but seem to support Mintzberg and Waters' contention that emergent strategies are more common, and that this represents a more realistic perspective on the strategy process. The organizations in our study all developed deliberate strategies to use computer networks to impose internal discipline and control, which then enabled emergent strategies to evolve in response to external opportunities. Their broader strategies for the business as a whole were thus able to be more responsive to the outside world, corresponding to the notion of an emergent strategy. Although perhaps a paradox, it does appear that network systems which create a more tightly coupled business also enable it to follow a more responsive and flexible external strategy.

WHAT DOES AN EMERGENT STRATEGY IMPLY FOR THE PROCESS OF CHANGE?

How much scope did managers have to shape 'the stream of actions'?

It appears then that the computer networks created by the case study organizations emerged in a series of steps, each dealing with some aspect of technology, organization, or the process of change itself. Sometimes these were dealt with in conjunction with each other, sometimes simultaneously, more often in sequence – but at each step, those involved faced some kind of choice. How significant were the choices that were realistically available?

A conclusion of many earlier studies of computer systems was that technology opened up a range of choices, which could be exercised by those able to influence the course of the change (Walton, 1982; Sorge *et al.*, 1983; Boddy and Buchanan, 1986; Long, 1987). The choices made were expected to reflect the preferences and relative power of those with a role in the change, and their view of the context in which the organization was operating. This context refers not only to technical matters, but also to such things as the volatility and uncertainty of the business environment (Boddy and Buchanan, 1986). Organizational strategies and designs, according to this view, are not determined by the technology alone, but reflect to a relatively high degree the choices made by those responsible for implementing the system.

This 'managerial choice' view of the process of innovation has been challenged by those who argue that larger forces within the economic environment will in practice severely limit the scope for autonomous action (Freeman and Soete, 1986). They acknowledge that some choices exist in how technological possibilities shape the direction and form of an organization. Details of policy, work design, or department structures can take several different forms and still produce acceptable economic results. But the fundamental decisions, such as whether or not to adopt a particular major technological advance, where critical control features are located, or the pace at which the change is to be brought in, are largely determined by events beyond the influence of managers in a particular company. Freeman argues that these broader economic and technical forces significantly limit the discretion of individual managers. If they want to be in a particular kind of business, it is inevitable that sooner or later they will be obliged to adopt the technologies which make up the essential toolkit of serious players in that sector.

Our cases show that in some of these issues, the choices open to management were indeed very narrow – if the broader hardware and software decisions had been taken elsewhere, or had, as in the Ambulance Service and in the libraries, been determined outside the organization, local managers had very little scope for choice in those matters. Similarly they were sometimes constrained by wider policies about the organizational changes which they are able to make – such as agreements on grading or the allocation of staff to new jobs, as in ScotRail, or in very tight central control over working practices, as in Kwik-Fit.

In other areas of the change agenda the scope for choice was considerable – especially in terms of local working arrangements, or in the speed at which the change was introduced. The Ambulance Service and General Insurance illustrate wide differences in practice being instituted in the branches, at least in the early phases of the projects.

Even when choice theoretically exists, it cannot be assumed that managers will make use of that option. For example, in the Travel Company the need for Divisional Directors was questioned at one point, as the branch automation system promised to take over many of the information monitoring and transmission roles which they had previously undertaken. For a variety of reasons, not least the potential opposition from the people concerned, senior managers chose not to make this possible organizational change. Symon and Clegg (1991) and McLoughlin and Clark (1994:

191–3) also give examples of available choices not being exercised, reflecting wider political considerations.

How does an emergent strategy appear to those inside the organization?

Although those implementing the computer networks were usually doing so in an iterative and piecemeal fashion, in response to unexpected technical and business developments, it did not always look like that to those on the receiving end. To staff the changes often looked as if they were imposed, particularly if they worked at a significant distance from the centre of the organization. Staff (and indeed their managers) in the distant branches of General Insurance and of the Travel Company, and in one of the control rooms of the Ambulance Service, had little contact with system development staff, and perhaps little with those managers initiating the network.

In part this reflected the widely dispersed nature of the organizations, which the technology was intended to help manage. Inevitably some are going to be in closer contact with decisions than others, and this needs to be acknowledged in the planning process. In part also the strategy itself had sometimes been imposed on the organization as a whole by impersonal external factors such as the requirement to have a particular type of system to remain in that business – or when a software package was imposed on a subsidiary by a parent organization. The Ambulance Service had little choice over the use of the Millennium software, however unsuitable, as that was the system used by its sponsoring organization, and the Travel Company had little choice but to use the package provided by the tour operators to link it into their systems. Some kinds of technology were simply required of the organization as a fact of life of doing business.

But the issue of perceived imposition also reflects a problem arising directly from the emergent quality of the information technology strategy itself. If the changes had involved the implementation of a perfectly planned strategy, effective communication mechanisms would have been able to cope. But the more the technological and organizational agendas were created during the project – the more emergent the strategy became – the more difficult it was to keep all concerned up to date. It became more likely that some would feel that the changes were being imposed, with predictable effects on their attitudes.

So the nature of the organizations, and the emergent process by which computer networks are created means that implementing a common system across many sites implies paying particular attention to the management of the processes. For example, it became particularly important to communicate the reasons for change, and to ensure that extra care was taken to identify what does *not* need to be imposed (by leaving scope for local adaptation wherever possible).

Differences in the amount of discretion over items within the content agenda may also have implications for the processes used to implement change. For example, if the boundaries of discretion are narrow (for example over the choice of communication system), people are likely to feel those features have been imposed. To avoid that, process needs to include heavy upward communication in the design phase and/or heavy downward communication to ensure people know and understand why those actions have been taken. For example, the perception that many managers in the Ambulance Service had that too much staff time was spent on administrative tasks may suggest that they had not yet fully appreciated, or accepted, external changes and senior managements response to them. This could be contrasted with the very intensive consultation exercise which Kwik-Fit carried out, albeit only with selected managers, before designing their initial system.

Alternatively, if the boundaries are set wide, so that wide variations in practice occur, the process needs to include heavy lateral and upward communication after the event, to share experience and learning across sites. Partly this can happen through managers further up the hierarchy sharing information, but could also include the practice, which was beginning to happen in the Ambulance Service, of those in charge of particular control rooms sharing experience in a structured way about their respective experiences of a new system.

Another approach to managing strategy formation suggested by Mintzberg and Waters in their discussion of the 'umbrella' strategy is that it might best be managed by controlling the process – by, in particular, making sure the right people are on the project team. They can then be left to make the decisions on the details of the content, so that an effective plan emerges from the process rather than from being unrealistically planned in advance. They argue that this would be a more robust approach to managing an emergent strategy than one stressing central control. However, even in an emergent strategy, planning needs to be done by such teams, and senior management needs to create monitoring and control mechanisms to ensure that the emerging network strategy is still in line with the simultaneously emerging business strategy (Boddy and Buchanan, 1992).

All of which implies that, as Chapter 9 argued, realizing the potential benefits of computer networks will depend on those implementing the system having a deft touch in the way they go about it, and in doing the things which would help ensure that the emergent strategy is also an effective one.

DID THE ORGANIZATIONS LEARN FROM THEIR EXPERIENCE OF IMPLEMENTING COMPUTER NETWORKS?

Did the development of emergent strategies indicate a strategic learning process?

Mintzberg and Waters (1985) wrote that 'the fundamental difference between deliberate and emergent strategy is that whereas the former focuses on direction and control – getting desired things done – the latter opens up this notion of 'strategic learning'. Defining strategy as intended and conceiving it as deliberate, as has traditionally been done, effectively precludes the notion of strategic learning.'

Emergent strategy itself implies learning what works – taking one action at a time in a search for that viable pattern. Emergent strategy means not chaos but unintended order. Such behaviour is especially important when an environment is too unstable or complex to fully comprehend, as it is when considering the impact of computer networks on organizations. Strategy, according to Mintzberg and Waters, 'walks on two feet, one deliberate, the other emergent...managing requires a light touch – to direct in order to realise intentions while at the same time responding to an unfolding pattern of action'. The case organizations showed contrasting abilities to learn from experience and adapt strategy accordingly. Burgoyne (1992) proposed a set of characteristics common to learning organizations. One characteristic was interorganizational learning. This characteristic was clearly identified in the Kwik-Fit case study where considerable time and effort was put into the initial selection and design of the system. A wide search was made to find a company to design and deliver a purpose-built system, precisely suited to the established needs of the business. The vision was in seeing a solution, in a completely different setting, and adapting the underlying concept to their business. Ideas were actively sought from a completely different industry, and a resource identified which could be adapted.

In contrast, the search processes in ScotRail were constrained by technical choices made by the BR Board and common to the whole railway network. The Ambulance Service had little choice and the search for a system went no further than the parent organization. The Millennium system had been acquired for financial management and it was then introduced into the Ambulance Service despite the fact that it had not been designed to meet the needs of line management for current operational information. The libraries had to accept the basic technical system supplied by the Cooperative if they wished to be a member of the Cooperative, even though they could customize the system to a limited extent.

Another characteristic identified by Burgoyne was whether the organization had a learning approach to IT strategy. Again Kwik-Fit demonstrated a willingness to test ideas and experiment and then either drop or continue the innovation in response to preliminary results. Having quickly found that the original EPOS system exceeded expectations, Kwik-Fit then initiated many further developments and enhancements. This followed partly from the fact that Tom Farmer knew the business intimately, which ensured a close relationship between his thinking about the future strategic needs of the business and the targets set for the IT department. In other case organizations there were barriers to the flow of ideas between those in charge of business strategy and the IT department. This was clearly seen in the Ambulance Service where there was little evidence of a learning strategy for developing Millennium, with a block between action and policy. ScotRail's IT group had no access to the strategic planning process at either national or local level. The IT personnel in the Travel Company were not extensively involved in the strategic thinking of senior management.

Burgoyne also stresses the importance of participative policy making. Kwik-Fit made strenuous efforts to find out the views of the depot staff on the system with the system designers spending some weeks in the depots, making sure that they were intimately familiar with the way the business worked, and this principle was maintained throughout the project. This characteristic was not as visible in the other case organizations, although there were signs of changes of approach later on in their respective projects. The Travel Company started with limited participation in the steering group which substantially increased when the User's Forum was introduced. The Ambulance Service began to increase participation by encouraging control room managers to compare experiences of the APTC at their regular meetings.

In summary, the level of learning evident in the case organizations varied greatly with Kwik-Fit showing a great ability to learn and adapt strategy accordingly. Other organizations had less freedom of manoeuvre and demonstrated much lower levels of learning. For example, both the Ambulance Service and ScotRail were constrained by decisions made centrally by their parent organizations. The libraries' ability to learn was constrained by the necessity to be a member of the Cooperative and to accept the Cooperative's systems.

In what ways did the case organizations learn from the research process?

Our view is that long-term organizational research is the only way to obtain a realistic picture about what is really going on in organizations. 'Snap shot' research produces a partial, misleading picture of what is always a complex continually changing situation. That situation is made up not only of events, but also the attitudes and political actions of individuals – which are particularly complex in the case of computer network systems. We recognize not only the importance of trying to attempt a holistic approach in terms of both time (history/present/future) and space (horizontal and vertical cross sections of the organization), but also that the longitudinal research process in the context of large network systems has met with some problems in both deciding the right time to stop researching and write up, and with providing the organizations concerned with useful feedback.

Realistically, we were working within a set research period, the period funded by the Leverhulme grant, and this meant that both money and time were limited, making longitudinal commitment to organizations difficult. As a result it was also difficult to keep up with the rapid pace of change in the organizations concerned. Despite our best intentions, the research remains essentially a series of snap-shots in space and in time. If we had been able to devote more time to the research process it would have been more of a learning process for the organizations concerned. As it was, feedback to them was at a comparative early stage of the project, and did not include many of the adjustments and adaptations that the organizations made later on. One of the most useful learning experiences that the research provided for the organizations concerned, was that many of the interviewees used the interviews as a way of expressing opinions about the organization and the impact of the technology. Interviewees also used interviewers as liaison persons between them and management. They felt this was a safe strategy because we guaranteed confidentiality. Some of the organizations found it useful to use the research to find out their employees' views and often adjusted their strategy as a result.

Ideally, to improve both the outcome of the research and the learning outcomes of the organizations we would engage in a more systematic selection of contacts with the organization, rather than relying heavily on opportunistic contacts to supply access into the organization which meant they could take the opportunity to act as gatekeeper as they so chose. We would also prefer to organize closer engagement with the company, being able to spend longer periods in the organization, becoming embedded and not so noticeable, reducing the 'hawthorn effect'. We would also prefer wider vertical and horizontal cross sections for the interviewing sample and to structure into the research proposal the opportunity to follow up at regular intervals, over a period of years, once the main research period has been completed. However, we have to acknowledge that this is the ideal, and that in current circumstances, research methodology will have to be designed within the realms of realistic levels of research funding.

ORGANIZATIONS IN THE NETWORK AGE VERSUS ORGANIZATIONS IN THE COMPUTER AGE

In concluding an earlier work (Buchanan and Boddy, 1983) one of the authors ventured some conclusions about the likely shape of organizations as they were increasingly affected by the ever-widening use of mainly stand-alone computer systems. It may be constructive to conclude this book by drawing some comparisons with the earlier work.

One of the themes in the earlier work was the emphasis on managerial choice in shaping the effects of computer systems. In contrast to some prevailing views which stressed the deterministic nature of technology, the case studies in that research showed the wide areas of choice which were available during the implementation process, particularly concerning the uses to which the technology would be put, the kinds of systems to be installed, and how work was organized in relation to the technology. The present study provides a rather different emphasis, and suggests that the scope for management choice in relation to computer networks is more limited. From an external perspective, many organizations had little choice but to adopt the use of network systems if they were to remain in their particular business. For example, the major players in the travel industry were now basing their business around the use of sophisticated networks, implying that any organization wishing to operate in that industry needed to conform. Internally, the nature of network systems meant that many aspects needed to be compatible with each other, implying a high degree of central initiation and design. This limited the choice available to many players lower in the organization or more distant from the centre.

A second major theme in the earlier work was the relationship between computer systems and the design of work. The evidence was very clear that a wide variety of work designs were being chosen in relation to very similar technological systems. The conclusion was drawn that work design was not influenced by the technology in use, but by the choices which managers made reflecting their wider political and organizational interests. In particular, the suggestion was made that technology opened up the possibility of redesigning work in relation to computer systems, which would enhance the autonomy and discretion of staff. Again, our conclusions from the present study are different. A common theme has been the use of networked computer systems to ensure that staff operate within tighter guidelines controlling how they do their work, and make it possible for senior management to monitor much more closely the daily or weekly operations of geographically remote groups of staff, significantly diminishing the autonomy and discretion not only of operators, but of junior and middle managers.

A third theme was the relationship of computer technology and employment. On the basis of the studies of stand-alone systems (which in no organization studied had led to redundancies), it was concluded that the introduction of computer systems had not had any significant effect on employment and that the relationship between computing and information technologies thus appears to be a tenuous one' (Buchanan and Boddy, 1983: 258). The picture which emerges from our study of network systems is quite different. Although directly related redundancies were rare, it was clear in all six cases, that the use of network systems reduced job opportunities through, for example administrative data being entered at the point of the original transaction, which could then be automatically processed and distributed throughout the organization for management purposes with little further human intervention. In these cases, significant growth in the business had taken place with little if any growth in the number of administrative staff. This is consistent with reports from many other organizations with slower growth, which have made significant redundancies, attributing these in part to the wider use of computer networks.

The economic pressures on organizations of all kinds is leading to constant efforts to reduce staff overheads, aided by the availability of ever more sophisticated technology. There is growing evidence, including the detailed information from the cases in this study, that this is affecting employment opportunities on a potentially dramatic scale.

BIBLIOGRAPHY

Adler, Paul S. (1991) 'Workers and Flexible Manufacturing Systems: Three Installations Compared', *Journal of Organizational Behavior* 12, 447–60.

Argyris, C. (1970) 'Resistance to Rational Management Systems', *Innovation*, 10, 28–35.

Argyris, C. (1988) 'Review Essay: First and Second Order Errors in Managing Strategic Change: the Role of Organizational Defensive Routines', in A.M. Pettigrew (ed.), *The Management of Strategic Change*, Oxford: Blackwell, 342–51.

Barki, H. and Hartwick, J. (1989) 'Rethinking the concept of User Involvement', *MIS Quarterly*, March, 53–63.

Baronas, A. M. K. and Louis, M. R (1988) 'Restoring a sense of Control during Implementation: How User Involvement leads to System Acceptance', *MIS Quarterly*, March, 111–23.

Benjamin, R I., de Long, D. W. and Scott Morton, M. S. (1990) 'Electronic Data Interchange: How much Competitive Advantage?', *Long Range Planning*, 23(1) 29–40.

Bernstein, A. (1985) 'It's 1985. Do you know what your Information Management Policy is?', *Business Computer Systems*, March, 70–6.

Blackler, F. and Brown, C. (1986) 'Alternative Models to guide the Design and Introduction of new Information Technologies into Work Organizations', *Journal of Occupational Psychology*, 59, 287–314.

Blumberg, M. and Gerwin, D. (1984) 'Coping with Advanced Manufacturing Technology, *Journal of Occupational Behaviour*, 5, 113–30.

Boddy, D. and Buchanan, D. A. (1986) *Managing New Technology*, Oxford: Blackwell.

Boddy, D. and Buchanan, D. A. (1992) *Take the Lead: Interpersonal skills for Project Managers*, Hemel Hempstead: Prentice Hall.

Bourgeois, L. and Brodwin, D. (1984) 'Strategic Implementation: Five Approaches to an elusive Phenomenon', *Strategic Management Journal*, 5, 241–64.

Buchanan, D. A. and Boddy, D. (1983) *Organizations in the Computer Age*, Aldershot: Gower.

Burlinghame, J. F. (1961) 'Information Technology and Decentralization', *Harvard Business Review*, 39(6) Nov–Dec.

Burns, T. (1961) 'Micropolitics: Mechanisms of Institutional Change', *Administrative Science Quarterly*, 5, 257–81.

BIBLIOGRAPHY

Cash, J. I. and Konsynski, B. R (1985) 'Information Systems redraw Competitive Boundaries', *Harvard Business Review*, **63**, 134–42.

Checkland, P. (1990) *Soft Systems Methodology in Action*, Chichester: Wiley.

Child, J. (1984) *Organization: A Guide to Problems and Practice*, London: Harper and Row.

Child, J. 'New Technology and Developments in Management Organization', *Omega*, **12**(3) 21 1–23.

Coch, I. and French, J. R P. (1948) 'Overcoming Resistance to Change', *Human Relations*, **1**, 512–32.

Collins, F. and Mann, G. J. (1988)'Change-related Behaviour and Information Systems', *Omega*, **16**(5) 369–81.

Cooper, R. B. and Swanson, E. B. (1979) 'Management Information Requirements Assessment: The State of the Art', *Database*, Fall **11**, Part 2, 5–16.

Copeland, D. G. and McKenney, J. R. (1988) 'Airline Reservation Systems: lessons from history', *MIS Quarterly*, **12**(3) 353–70.

Curley, K. F. and Gremilion, L. L. (1983) 'The Champion in DSS Implementation', *Information and Management*, **6**, 203–9.

Dawson, P. M. B. and McLoughlin, I. P. (1986) 'Computer Technology and the Redefinition of Supervision', *Journal of Management Studies*, **23**(1).

Dearden, J. (1987) 'The Withering Away of the IS Organization', *Sloan Management Review*, Summer, 87–91.

Dickinson, R M. (1984) 'Telecom Management: an Emerging Art', *Datamation*, March, 120–30.

Doll, W. J. (1985) 'Avenues for Top Management Involvement in successful MIS Development', *MIS Quarterly*, March, 17–35.

Doll, W. J. and Torkzadeh, G. (1988) 'The Measurement of End-User Computing Satisfaction', *MIS Quarterly*, June, 259–73.

Dopson, S. and Stewart, R. (1993) 'Information Technology, Organization, Restructuring and the Future of Middle Management', *New Technology, Work and Employment*, **8**(1) 10–20.

Eason, K. D. (1977) 'Human Relationships and User Involvement in Systems Design', *Computer Management*, May, 10–12.

Eason, K. D. (1982) 'The Process of Introducing Information Technology', *Behaviour and Information Technology*, **1**(2) 197–213.

Eason, K. D. (1988) *Information Technology and Organizational Change*, London: Taylor and Francis.

Eason, K. D. (1989) 'Designing Systems to match Organizational Reality', in *People and Computers, Proceedings of the HCI '89 Conference*, Nottingham, BCS/ Cambridge University Press, 57–69.

Eden, C. (1992) 'On the Nature of Cognitive Maps', *Journal of Management Studies*.

El Sawy, O. (1985) 'Implementation by Cultural Infusions: An Approach for Managing the Introduction of Information Technologies', *MIS Quarterly*, June, 131–40.

Foster, L. W. and Flynn, D. M. (1984) 'Management Information Technology: Its effects on Organizational Form and Function', *MIS Quarterly*, **8**(4) 229–36.

Franz, C. R and Robey, D. (1986) 'Organizational Context, User Involvement and the Usefulness of Information Systems', *Decision Sciences*, **17**, 329–59.

Freeman, C. and Soete, L. L. G. (eds) (1986) *Technological Change and Full Employment*, Oxford: Blackwell.

Gibson, C. F. (1981) 'Managing Organizational Change to achieve full Systems Results', *Proceedings of the 13th Annual Conference of the Society for Management Information Systems*, 75–94.

Grindley, K. (1992) 'Information Systems Issues facing Senior Executives: the Culture gap', *Journal of Strategic Information Systems*, 1(3) 134–41.

Gunson, N. and Boddy, D. (1989) 'Computer Network Systems: Managerial Problems and Opportunities', *Journal of General Management*, 15(2) 41–56.

Gunton, T. (1990) *Inside Information Technology: a Practical Guide to Management Issues*, New York: Prentice Hall.

Hall, W. and McGuley, R. (1987) 'Planning and Managing a Corporate Network Utility', *MIS Quarterly*, 437–49.

Hamilton, S. (1988) 'The Complex Art of Saying No', *Computing*, 13 October, 30–1.

Handy, C. (1994) *The Empty Raincoat*, London: Hutchinson.

Hayes, R. S. and Garvin, D. A. (1985) 'Managing as if Tomorrow mattered', in Rhodes, E. and Wield, D. (eds), *Implementing New Technologies*, Oxford: Blackwell, 264–73.

Henderson, J. C. and Schilling, D. A. (1985) 'Design and Implementation of Decision Support Systems in the Public sector', *MIS Quarterly*, June, 148–69.

Hirscheim, R A. (1985) 'User Experience Work and Assessment of Participative Systems Design', *MIS Quarterly*, Dec 295–303.

Holland, C. and Lockett, G. (1992) 'IT Strategy in Retailing: Organizational Change and Future Direction', *Journal of Strategic Information Systems*, 1(3) 134–41.

Ives, B and Jarvenpaa, S. L. (1991), 'Implications of Global Information Technology: Key Issues for Management', *MIS Quarterly*, Mar, 33–49.

Ives, B. and Olson, M.H. (1984) 'User Involvement and MIS Success: A Review of Research', *Management Science*, 30(5) 586–603.

Ives, B., Olson, M. and Baroudi, J. J. (1983) 'The Measurement of User Information Satisfaction', *Communications of the ACM*, 785–95.

Jansen, M. A. (1985) 'Prototyping for Systems Development: A Critical Appraisal', *MIS Quarterly*, Dec, 305–15.

Johnson, G. (1990) 'Managing Strategic Change: the Role of Symbolic Action', *British Journal of Management*, 1(4) 183–200.

Johnston, H. R. and Vitale, M. R. (1988) 'Creating Competitive Advantage with Inter-organizational Information Systems', *MIS Quarterly*, June, 153–65.

Jones, B. and Scott, P. (1987) 'Flexible Manufacturing Systems in Britain and the USA', *New Technology, Work and Employment*, 2(1) 27–36.

Kanter, R M. (1983) *The Change Masters: Corporate Entrepreneurs at Work*, London: George Allen & Unwin.

Kantrow, A. (1980) 'The Strategy-Technology Connection', *Harvard Business Review*, 58(4) 6–21.

Kaplan, R. S. (1986) 'Must CIM be Justified by Faith Alone?', *Harvard Business Review*, 64(2) Mar–Apr, 87–95.

Kaufman, F. (1966) 'Data Systems that cross Company Boundaries', *Harvard Business Review*, 44(1) Jan–Feb, 141–50.

Kearney, A. T. (1990) *Barriers to the Successful Application of Information Technology*, London: Dept of Trade and Industry and CIMA.

Keen, P. G. W. (1981) 'Information Systems and Organizational Change', *Communications of the ACM*, 24(1) Jan, 24–33.

Keen, P. G. W. (1985) 'Computers and Managerial Choice', *Organization Dynamics*, 14, Autumn, 35–49.

Kotter, J. P. and Schlesinger, L. A. (1979) 'Choosing Strategies for Change', *Harvard Business Review*, 57(2) 106–14.

Kozar, K. A. and Mahlum, J. M. (1987) 'A User-generated Information System: An Innovative Development Approach', *MIS Quarterly*, June, 163–74.

Kraushaar, J. M. (1985) 'A Prototyping Method for Applications Development by End Users and Information Systems Specialists', *MIS Quarterly*, Sept, 189–97.

Lawler, E. E. (1986) *High Involvement Management: Participative Strategies for improving Organizational Performance*, San Francisco: Jossey Bass.

Leavitt, H. J. and Whisler, T. M. (1958) 'Management in the 1980's', *Harvard Business Review*, 36(6) Nov–Dec.

Leonard-Barton, D. and Kraus, W. A. (1985) 'Implementing New Technology', *Harvard Business Review*, 63(6) Nov–Dec, 102–10.

Lewin, K. (1951) *Field theory in Social Science*, New York: Harper and Row.

Long, R. J. (1987) *New Office Information Technology*, Beckenham: Croom Helm.

McLoughlin, I. and Clark, J. (1994) *Technological Change at Work*, Milton Keynes: Open University Press.

Maidique, M. A. (1980) 'Entrepreneurs, Champions and Technological Innovations', *Sloan Management Review*, 21(2) Winter, 59–75.

Maish, A. M. (1979) 'A User's Behaviour Towards his MIS', *MIS Quarterly*, Mar, 3, Part 1, 39–52.

Malone, T. W., Yates, J. and Benjamin, R. I. (1987) 'Electronic Markets and Electronic Hierarchies', *Communications of the ACM*, 30(6) 484–97.

Markus, M. L. (1983) 'Power, Politics and MIS Implementation', *Communications of the ACM*, 26(6) June, 431–44.

Markus, M. L. and Robey, D. (1983) 'The Organizational Validity of Management Information Systems', *Human Relations*, 36(3) 203–26.

Martin, E. W. (1982) 'Critical Success Factors of MIS/DP Executives', *MIS Quarterly*, June, 6(2) 1–9.

Martin, N. and Hough, D. (1992) 'The Open Systems Revolution', *Logistics Information Management*, 5(3) 19–23.

Meador, C. L. and Rosenfeld, W. L. (1986) 'Decision Support Planning and Analysis: The Problems of Getting Large-scale DSS started', *MIS Quarterly*, June, 159–77.

Miles, R. (1990) 'A Stitch in Time', *Computing*, 2 Oct, 18–19.

Millman, Z. and Hartwick, J. (1987) 'The Impact of Automated Office Systems on Middle Managers and their Work', *MIS Quarterly*, 11(4) 479–90.

Mintzberg, H. (1994) *The Rise and Fall of Strategic Planning*, New York: Prentice Hall.

Mintzberg, H. and Waters, J. A. (1985) 'Of Strategies, Deliberate and Emergent', *Strategic Management Journal*, 6, 257–72.

Montazemi, A. R. and Conrath, D. W. (1986) 'The use of Cognitive Mapping for Information Requirements Analysis', *MIS Quarterly*, Mar, 45–55.

Morgan, G. (1986) *Images of Organization*, London: Sage.

Morley, L. (1990) 'Expense Account', *Computing,* 2 May, 18–19.

Mumford, E. (1981) 'Participative System Design: Structure and Method', Systems, Objectives, *Solutions,* 1(1) 5–19.

Mumford, E., Land, F. and Hawgood, J. (1978) 'A Participative Approach to the Design of Computer Systems', *Impact of Science on Society,* 28(3) 235–53.

Myers, I. B. and McGulley, M. (1985) *Manual and Guide to the Development and Use of the Myers Briggs Type Indicator,* Palo Alto, CA: Consulting Psychologists Press.

Necco, C. R., Gordon, C. L. and Tsai, N. W. (1987) 'Systems Analysis and Design: Current Practices', *MIS Quarterly,* Dec, 461–75.

Newman, M. and Rosenberg, D. (1985) 'Systems Analysis and the Politics of Organizational Control', *Omega,* 13(5) 393–406.

Olson, M. H. and Ives, B. (1980) 'Measuring User Involvement in Information Systems Development', *Proceedings of First International Conference on Information Systems,* 130–43.

Olson, M. H. and Ives, B. (1981) 'User Involvement in Systems Design: An Empirical test of Alternative Approaches', *Information and Management,* (4), 183–95.

Palmer, C. (1988) 'Using IT for Competitive Advantage at Thomson Holidays', *Long Range Planning,* 21(6) 26–9.

Pettigrew, A. M. (1985) *The Awakening Giant: Continuity and Change in ICI,* Oxford: Blackwell.

Pinsonneault, A. and Kraemer, K. L. (1993) 'The Impact of Information Technology on Middle Managers', *MIS Quarterly,* 17(3) 271–92.

Porter, M. E. and Millar, V. E. (1985) 'How Information gives you Competitive Advantage', *Harvard Business Review,* Jul–Aug, 149–60.

Quinn, J. B. (1980) *Strategies for Change: Logical incrementalism,* Homewood, Ill: Richard D. Irwin.

Ring, T. (1989) 'When it's not Enough to be Technically Brilliant', *Computing,* 14 Sept, 28–9.

Robey, D. (1981) 'Computer Information Systems and Organization Structure', *Communications of the ACM,* 24(10) 679–87.

Robey, D. (1983) 'Information Systems and Organizational Change: a Comparative Case Study', *Systems, Objectives, Solutions* 3, North Holland: Elsevier Science.

Rockart, J. F. (1982) 'The Changing Role of the Information Systems Executive', *Sloan Management Review,* 24(2) Fall, 3–13.

Rockart, J. F. and Crescenzi, A. D. (1984) 'Engaging Top Management in Information Technology, *Sloan Management Review,* Summer, 3–16.

Rockart, J. F. and Short, J. E. (1989) 'IT in the 1990's: Managing Organizational Interdependence', *Sloan Management Review,* Winter, 30(2) 7–17.

Salaway, G. (1987) 'An Organizational Approach to Information Systems Development', *MIS Quarterly,* June, 245–64.

Schon, D. A. (1963) 'Champions for Radical New Inventions', *Harvard Business Review,* 41(2) Mar–Apr, 77–86.

Short, J. E. and Venkatraman, N. (1992) 'Beyond Business Process Redesign: Redefining Baxter's Business Network', *Sloan Management Review,* Fall, 7–21.

Sorge, A. (1983) *Micro-electronics and Manpower in Manufacturing,* Aldershot: Gower Publishing.

Smith, S. L. (1988) 'How Much Change in Store? The Impact of New Technologies on Managers and Staffs in Retail Distribution', in Knights, D. and Wilmott, H. (eds) *New Technology and the Labour Process*, London: Macmillan.

Swanson, E. B. (1982) 'Measuring User Attitudes in MIS Research: A Review', *Omega*, 10(2) 157–65.

Symon, G. and Clegg, C. W. (1991) 'A Study of the Implementation of CADCAM', *Journal of Occupational Psychology*, 64, Part 4, 273–90.

Tait, P. and Vessey, I. (1988) 'The Effect of User Involvement on Systems Success: A contingency approach', *MIS Quarterly*, Mar, 12, 91–108.

Vitale, M. R. (1986) 'The Growing Risks of Information Systems Success', *MIS Quarterly*, Dec, 327–34.

Voss, C. (1988) 'Success and Failure in Advanced Manufacturing Technology', *International Journal of Technology Management*, 3(3) 285–97.

Walon, R. E. (1982) 'Social Choice in the Development of Advanced Information Technology', *Technology in Society*, 4, 345–51.

Walton, R. E. and Susman, G. I. (1987) 'People Policies for the New Machines', *Harvard Business Review*, Mar–Apr, 98–106.

Whipp, R., Rosenfeld, R. and Pettigrew, A. (1988) 'Understanding Strategic Change Processes: some Preliminary British Findings', in Pettigrew, A. (ed.), *The Management of Strategic Change*, Oxford: Blackwell, 14–55.

White, K. B. and Leifer, R. (1986) 'Information Systems Development Success: Perspectives from Project team Participants', *MIS Quarterly*, Sept, 215–23.

Wildavsky, A. (1983) 'Information as an Organizational Problem', *Journal of Management Studies*, 20(1) 290.

Wilkinson, B. (1983) *The Shopfloor Politics of New Technology*, London: Heineman Educational.

Yadav, S. B. (1983) 'Determining an Organization's Information Requirements: A State of the Art Survey', *Database*, Spring, 15(3) 3–20.

Zuboff, S. (1988) *In the Age of the Smart Machine*, New York: Heinemann.

INDEX

Printed and bound by CPI Group (UK) Ltd, Croydon, CR0 4YY
08/05/2025
01864380-0001